The Texas Right

D1565359

NUMBER THIRTY-NINE
Elma Dill Russell Spencer Series in the West and Southwest
Andrés Tijerina, General Editor

A partial list of titles in the series
may be found at the back of the book.

THE
TEXAS

RIGHT

The Radical Roots of Lone Star Conservatism

Edited by David O'Donald Cullen & Kyle G. Wilkison

TEXAS A&M UNIVERSITY PRESS | COLLEGE STATION

First edition

Manufactured in the
United States of America
This paper meets the requirements of ANSI/NISO Z39.48–1992
(Permanence of Paper).
Binding materials have been
chosen for durability.
∞

LIBRARY OF CONGRESS CATALOGING-IN-PUBLICATION DATA

The Texas Right : the radical roots of Lone Star conservatism / edited by
David O'Donald Cullen and Kyle G. Wilkison. — 1st ed.
p. cm. — (Elma Dill Russell Spencer series in the West and Southwest ; v. 39)
Includes bibliographical references and index.
ISBN 978-1-62349-028-7 (cloth : alk. paper) —
ISBN 978-1-62349-029-4 (pbk. : alk. paper) —
ISBN 978-1-62349-111-6 (e-book)
1. Radicalism—Texas—History. 2. Conservatism—Texas—History.
3. Right-wing extremists—Texas—History. 4. Religious right—Texas—History.
5. Tea Party movement—Texas—History. 6. Social movements—Texas—
History. 7. Texas—Politics and government—1865–1950. 8. Texas—Politics
and government—1951– I. Cullen, David O'Donald, 1951–
II. Wilkison, Kyle Grant, 1960– III. Series: Elma Dill Russell
Spencer series in the West and Southwest ; no. 39.
HN79.T43R383 2014
303.48'4—dc23
2013022038

To Mary Lenn Dixon

Contents

Acknowledgments vii

From "Turn Texas Loose" to the Tea Party: Origins of the Texas Right
David O'Donald Cullen 1

Texan by Color: The Racialization of the Lone Star State
Michael Phillips 10

"The Evils of Socialism": The Religious Right in Early Twentieth-Century Texas
Kyle G. Wilkison 34

"He, Being Dead, Yet Speaketh": J. Frank Norris and the Texas Religious Right at Midcentury
Samuel K. Tullock 51

The Far Right in Texas Politics during the Roosevelt Era
Keith Volanto 68

Establishing the Texas Far Right, 1940–1960
George N. Green 87

The Paranoid Style and Its Limits: The Power, Influence, and Failure of the Postwar Texas Far Right
Sean P. Cunningham 101

Focus on the Family: Twentieth-Century Conservative Texas Women and the Lone Star Right
Nancy E. Baker 119

Texas Traditions and the Right: Continuity and Change
Michael Lind 155

About the Contributors 173

Index 175

Acknowledgments

This work grew out of an East Texas Historical Association meeting roundtable discussion of a collection of essays titled *The Texas Left: The Radical Roots of Lone Star Liberalism.* In conversations about the influence of radical movements in shaping post–World War II liberalism in the state of Texas, a question arose if similar influences explained contemporary conservatism. This is a beginning toward an answer to that question. Just as recent monographs have moved the origins of the civil rights movement to well before the 1954 *Brown* decision, in recent years historians have made similar arguments about contemporary conservatism: that an understanding of the Reagan era must include movements, organizations, and individuals that long preceded the 1980s.

We have been fortunate that a group of historians working in this field joined us for this project. Their efforts reflect a generation's worth of archival research and reflection that build upon the work of many scholars representing a variety of topics. Scholars of every ilk, most especially historians, cannot do their work without the invaluable help of librarians and archivists; on behalf of our contributors, we thank all those whose everyday, unassuming dedication to their craft made this volume possible. We also must thank Texas A&M University Press's anonymous reviewers for their comments and suggestions. Many more thanks are due to Thom Lemmons and all the outstanding staff at the Press for their dedication to the discipline of history. We are indebted to copyeditor Lona Dearmont and indexer Sherrye Young for their careful work on this book.

Lastly, we owe more than we can repay to Mary Lenn Dixon, editor-in-chief at Texas A&M University Press, whose support and confidence made this project possible. Her long and fruitful commitment to publishing new scholarship has forever changed and enriched the practice of Texas history.

The Texas Right

From "Turn Texas Loose" to the Tea Party

Origins of the Texas Right

DAVID O'DONALD CULLEN

The triumph of the Texas Right in the late twentieth century can be tracked by Republican Party electoral victories. In 1979 William Clements became the first Republican governor of Texas since Reconstruction. In 1994 the *Texas Observer* proclaimed the death of the "yellow-dog Democrat." In 1995 George W. Bush began the first of two terms as governor. In 2004 the Republican Party captured every statewide office, and Rick Perry was in the fourth year of what would become a record for consecutive terms held by one person in the governor's office. By 2010 the state's Republican Party had become the model for other states hoping to defeat Democrats, control the scope and direction of federal authority, shrink state governments, and reduce taxes. The state's voters had reversed a century-long partisan voting pattern put best by the iconic Texas writer O. Henry: "We have only two or three laws, such as against murdering witnesses and being caught stealing horses, and voting the Republican ticket."[1]

A number of observers have sought to explain the ascendancy and dominance of conservatism as represented by the state's GOP. Two works long a part of the historical canon of the state, George N. Green's *The Establishment in Texas Politics* and Chandler Davidson's *Race and Class in Texas Politics*, have been joined by a number of scholarly works appearing over the last decade and a half. But a persuasive synthesis has yet to appear that explains what informed, influenced, and shaped the Texas Right. Of course, to be successful, such an analysis would eschew the parochial and attempt to place Texas within the national context. Certainly, understanding the transformation of the Texas Republican Party of the 1860s (the sometimes radical agent for progressive, government-enforced social change) to the twenty-first-century Texas Republican Party (which explicitly rejects the former), requires knowing the twentieth-century story of the American—not just Texan—political landscape.[2]

Nevertheless, the Texas details do remain crucial, and the historical Texas political landscape rewards its viewers with some of the starkest and most riveting scenery there is. The traditional narrative of Texas conservatism emphasizes the following political groups: Jeffersonian Democrats of 1936, the Texas Regular Movement of 1944, the Dixiecrat Party of 1948, the Shivercrats of the 1950s, state members of the John Birch Society, and Reagan Democrats. These political groups, however, can only be understood in light of the underlying historical impulses that produced their formation.

For example, in 2010 some members of the Texas Tea Party and the state's Republican Party called for secession and, if need be, a revolution. They argued that the federal government interfered in the private and economic lives of Texans. Although not endorsing secession, Governor Rick Perry did publicly sympathize with these sentiments and suggested in his book *Fed Up!: Our Fight to Save America from Washington* that Texans were victims of oppression. While threats of secession may have been extreme, even by Texas standards, the politics behind them were not new. Besides the obvious connection to Texas and the South's original secession movement, the latest iteration conformed to a continuing pattern within Texas conservatism of seeing the federal government as the enemy. In 1892 would-be gubernatorial candidate George Clark unsuccessfully ran against reformer James S. Hogg for the Democratic Party nomination, calling for personal and corporate liberty and admonishing the federal government to "turn Texas loose" from regulation. Clark, a corporate attorney and old-guard Redeemer, was a reactionary conservative who expressed views held by many Texans regardless of partisan affiliation. Through him, the antiregulation, probusiness origins of the contemporary Texas Right can be traced back to the critique of the modern American government that began among reactionary conservatives within the state's Democratic Party. These radicals and reactionaries informed, influenced, and eventually established the agenda that, beginning in the 1970s, Texas Republicans would embrace as their own program to save the Lone Star State. In fact, Texas politics foreshadowed the political transformation of the new Republican Solid South. The roots of class warfare, racial prejudice, and gender bias expressed themselves well before Republican reaction to the Great Society programs or the civil rights movement of the 1960s. Before the call for voter identification laws there were the poll tax and the "white primary"; before W. A. Criswell there were W. F. Lemmons and J. Frank Norris; before the War on Terror there was the War on Socialism; before the Christian Coalition there were the Christian Americans; and before the Tea Party there was the Texas-sponsored Southern Committee to Uphold the Constitution.[3]

What was the cause of the Right's discontent? Earlier explanations for the origins of right-wing sentiments revolved around the concept of status anxiety and cultural alienation. In *The Radical Right*, originally published in 1955, essays by Daniel Bell, Seymour Martin Lipset, Talcott Parsons, and Richard Hofstadter suggested that one could only understand the supporters of Joe McCarthy and the John Birch Society by examining the conflict over social status and cultural norms in the post–World War II United States. In "The Intellectuals and the Discontented Classes," David Riesman and Nathan Glazer argued that the Lone Star State exemplified this anxiety: "Texas demonstrates in extreme form the great shift in the character of American politics and political thinking since the Second World War." McCarthy supporters and Birchers perceived themselves as victims of a society that rejected their values and argued that the country was being betrayed from within, especially by entrenched Washington politicians and academic intellectuals who looked down upon them. These authors argued that the forces that shaped the attitudes of the Right were unique to the circumstances of 1950s America. The suggestion that status anxiety best explained the discontent of the Right was controversial when published because it ignored class as an explanatory factor. Another criticism of that collection of essays, however, is the absence of any discussion of historical factors that might explain more efficiently the appearance of a well-organized body of discontented Americans. John Lukacs presents a simpler argument for the existence of the Radical Right. In *Democracy and Populism: Fear and Hatred*, Lukacs argues that "one of the fundamental differences between extremes of Right and Left is this: in most instances hatred moves the former and fear the latter." Like the writers of the essays in *The Radical Right*, however, Lukacs is responding to right-wing personalities and organizations from 1950 forward, largely ignoring historical precedents.[4]

Although both books agree that what distinguishes the Radical Right from moderate conservatives is a conspiratorial worldview held by the reactionary conservatives, neither provide a more encompassing thesis. As the essays in this book suggest, right-wing Texans have been reactive—responding to perceived threats and challenges that create a suspicion of the democratic process and emphasizing liberty over equality and economic individualism over community interests. In addition, the state's Radical Right have what is more an attitude than a coherent conservative ideology, and they are often at odds with conservatives outside the state. For example, M. E. Bradford, professor of literature at Southern Methodist University, hoped to be appointed by President Reagan to head the National Endowment for the Humanities but lost the position to William Bennett. Bradford, who worked for George Wallace's 1968 presidential campaign, considered this a betrayal by the Republican Party. He and fellow right-wingers started referring to themselves as "paleoconservatives," arguing that they were upholders of the tenets of conservatism who were betrayed by the electorally pragmatic Republican Party.[5]

In post–World War II America the Radical Right became closely associated in the popular imagination with two specific regions, Southern California and Texas. The nation discovered the Texas Right when articles appeared in *Life* magazine in 1950 and in the *Reporter's Notebook, Fortune*, and the *Nation* in 1954. In 1962 the *Nation* noted that "virtually every Radical Right movement of the postwar era has been propped up by Texas oil millionaires." These publications suggested that Texas was an important player in shaping the modern Radical Right, especially providing money and organizational skills. Additionally, it is now clear that the Texas Radical Right foreshadowed the emergence of the Tea Party phenomenon in 2009. In fact, some argue that Texas influenced the nation's extreme right-wing shift that characterized American politics beginning in the 1990s. In 2004 the authors of *The Right Nation: Conservative Power in America* concluded that "Texas is America's America or at least conservative America's America."[6]

One shared characteristic of the contemporary and historical Radical Right is the belief in eliminationism: a politics and culture that avoids public debate with opponents, argues that the political process cannot be relied upon to solve urgent problems, and instead pursues the outright elimination of the opposing side through suppression, removal, or extermination.[7] The first three chapters in this collection of original essays profile the attempt to eliminate those who threatened the economic elite of the state between the 1870s and the 1930s. These essays also push the historical origins of the Texas Radical Right to well before the appearance of President

Franklin Roosevelt's New Deal programs of the 1930s. Michael Phillips examines the motivation and policies of right-wing Texans to control the state's freed slave population following the Civil War, control the immigrants arriving from Mexico and eastern Europe beginning in the early 1900s, and the response by the wealthy to the threat posed by the Alliance Movement and the Populist Party in the 1880s and the 1890s. Among the measures proposed to control those perceived as threats to white Anglo-Saxon Protestants was the use of lynching, sterilization laws, and vigilante groups like the Ku Klux Klan. Kyle Wilkison explores the first religious Right in Texas by chronicling the Texas pulpit's support for the economic and social status quo in the early twentieth century. The growing electoral support for the Texas Socialist Party between 1900 and 1914 claimed the attention of the denominational press, who argued that Socialists were godless anarchists intent on destroying traditional values such as white supremacy in the Lone Star State, ignoring the deeply religious nature of much of the Texas socialist movement. Elsewhere Wilkison has shown how the Texas elite used the poll tax and white primary laws to control the political process and eliminate the Socialist vote. By the end of World War I, however, the elite turned to another method, declaring that Texas Socialists were not only un-American but worked in cooperation with the new enemy, communism. Both the national and state governments arrested socialists and suppressed their publications, in the process destroying the party.[8] Sam Tullock provides a biographical approach to understanding the development of contemporary right-wing megachurch ministers by examining the career of J. Frank Norris. Simultaneously pastoring large congregations in Fort Worth and Detroit, Norris demonstrated a successful combination of religious and political sensationalism that made him a fixture on the Texas and national Right. Thus, well before Roosevelt's New Deal, Johnson's War on Poverty, or the civil rights movement, there existed in Texas reactionary groups willing to use extreme measures to protect themselves from the organizing abilities of the poor and the disenfranchised.

The next three chapters demonstrate the political response to this threat. Keith Volanto examines the right-wing response to Franklin Roosevelt's policies during the Great Depression. Although most Texans supported Roosevelt, a growing number of the state's economic elite turned against the president and attempted to limit his power, especially following the passage of the National Labor Relations Act of 1935. Among the critics of Roosevelt were oil baron Hugh Roy Cullen, John Kirby, owner of three hundred thousand acres of East Texas pinelands, and Vance Muse, a publicist for Kirby Lumber Company. Kirby and Muse founded the Southern Committee to Uphold the Constitution, the Southern version of the American Liberty League. Muse was the driving force behind the state's "right to work" law. Cullen attempted to deny Texas votes for Roosevelt through the Jeffersonian Democrats. The organization argued that Roosevelt and the national Democratic Party were cooperating with known communists. George Green focuses on the Texas elites' response to labor union activity among Texas workers. Linking union efforts to communism was the method used by political and economic leaders in Houston, Dallas, and West Texas to neutralize organized labor's inroads into the Lone Star State. During his meteoric rise, Texas embraced Joe McCarthy more than any other Southern state. The Red Scare influenced Texas politics throughout the 1950s. Sean Cunningham examines the result of the Red Scare in Texas, arguing that the state's Republican Party, almost nonexistent between 1900 and the 1950s, prospered in the 1950s and 1960s by identifying with such anticommunist movements as the John Birch Society, financed in large measure by Texas oil money. By the 1970s a redefinition of the state's political culture replaced partisan political loyalties. The Texas Right successfully used cultural issues to identify Republicans as the true representatives of the values and beliefs of conservative Americans. According to Cunningham, this strategy produced a "cowboy conservatism" that emphasized rugged individualism, supported a libertarian free market, endorsed a Christian code of conduct, and claimed a confidence in the inevitable progress of human nature. Ronald Reagan's appearance in Dallas at the 1984 Republican national convention ostensibly confirmed that the values upheld by the Texas Right were exactly what the country needed to recover from the liberalism of the 1960s and 1970s. Nancy Baker tells the story of conservative Texas women and their relationship and undervalued importance to the Texas Right by identifying the major figures and organizations and their methods to achieve political success. She concentrates on what motivated nonpolitical figures to take political action and the results of those actions for Texas politicians. Finally, Michael Lind provides a summation of the state's politics that emphasizes both continuity and change among right-wing Texans. His essay confronts the problem of definition, with a discussion of what was meant by "liberal" and "conservative" in the nineteenth versus twentieth centuries. Finally, Lind rejects the status anxiety theory to explain reactionary right-wing activity in terms of ethnocultural or political culture theory.

By identifying the origins of the Texas Right in the era before the anti–New Deal reaction, this collection continues a historiographic pattern that has characterized newer studies of the civil rights movement, American involvement in Vietnam, and second-wave feminism. Additionally, by placing the Texas Right into historical context, it is clear that economic and political motives provide a useful understanding of the driving force of the Radical Right whether in 1912 or 2012. Today's Tea Party is but an echo of similar concerns expressed over one hundred years ago.[9]

Notes

1. Charles Deaton, "The Republican Upset!" *Texas Government Newsletter* 6 (November 13, 1978): 1–2; James Cullen, "Sick Yellow Dog," *Texas Observer*, November 25, 1994, 7–10, 21; O. Henry, "Law and Order," in *Sixes and Sevens* (1923; repr., Charleston: Nabu Press, 2010), 151.

2. George N. Green, *The Establishment in Texas Politics: The Primitive Years, 1938–1957* (Westport, CT: Greenwood Press, 1979); and Chandler Davidson, *Race and Class in Texas Politics* (Princeton, NJ: Princeton University Press, 1990). There are two monographs that provide a history of the Texas Republican Party. One is a standard institutional profile and the second looks at the party through the career of John Tower: Roger M. Olien, *From Token to Triumph: The Texas Republican Party since 1920* (Dallas: Southern Methodist University Press, 1982); and John R. Knaggs, *Two-Party Texas: The John Tower Era, 1961–1984* (Austin: Eakin Press, 1986). For works that provide a history of the party before 1920, see Alwyn Barr, *Reconstruction to Reform: Texas Politics, 1876–1906* (Austin: University of Texas Press, 1971); and Carl Moneyhon, *Republicanism in Reconstruction Texas* (Austin: University of Texas Press, 1980). For an examination of the development of the modern-day Republican Party, see Ricky F. Dobbs, *Yellow Dogs and Republicans: Allan Shivers and Texas Two-Party Politics* (College Station: Texas A&M University Press, 2005); and Sean P. Cunningham, *Cowboy Conservatism: Texas and the Rise of the Modern Right* (Lexington: University Press of Kentucky, 2010). Gregory L. Schneider's *The Conservative Century: From Reaction to Revolution* (Lanham, MD: Rowan & Littlefield, 2009) is one of the few works that also argues that the Radical Right's influence upon the Republican Party dates from the 1890s, not in response to the New Deal programs of the 1930s.

3. Rick Perry, *Fed Up!: Our Fight to Save America from Washington* (New York: Little, Brown, 2010); "What's All That Secession Ruckus in Texas?" *Time*, April 18, 2009, http://www.Time.com (accessed July 27, 2011). For the career of George Clark, see Barr, *Reconstruction to Reform*, 90–92 ; Walter L. Buenger, *The Path to a Modern South: Northeast Texas between Reconstruction and the Great Depression* (College Station: Texas A&M University Press, 2001), 31–34; and Gregg Cantrell, *Feeding the Wolf: John B. Rayner and the Politics*

of Race, 1850–1918 (Wheeling, IL: Harlan Davidson,2001), 36–38, 41. The Clark quote is cited in Buenger, *Path to the South,* 13.

4. David Riesman and Nathan Glazer, "The Intellectuals and the Discontented Classes" in *The Radical Right,* ed. Daniel Bell (New York: Transaction Press, 2001), 105. The first edition appeared in 1955 under the title *The New American Right* in response to Joe McCarthy. A second edition, published in 1963 and renamed *The Radical Right,* was in response to the John Birch Society and Southern reaction to the civil rights movement. The third edition (cited above) resulted from the heated political dialogue of the 1990s and the bombing of the federal building in Oklahoma City in 1994. Both the 1963 and 2001 editions contain the essays from the 1955 book. John Lukacs, *Democracy and Populism: Fear and Hatred* (New Haven, CT: Yale University Press, 2005), 203. For discussions of status anxiety theory as it relates to Texas, see George N. Green, "Some Aspects of the Far Right in Texas Politics," in *Essays on Recent Southern Politics,* ed. Harold M. Hollingsworth (Austin: University of Texas Press, 1970), XX–XX; Alan C. Elms, "Psychological Factors in Right-Wing Extremism," in *The American Right Wing: Readings in Political Behavior,* ed. Robert A. Schoenberger (New York: 1969), 158; and Alan C. Elms, "Those Little Old Ladies in Tennis Shoes Are No Nuttier Than Anyone Else, It Turns Out: Pathology and Politics," *Psychology Today* 1 (1970): 27–31, 58–59. For a personal story of growing up in Dallas when the nation labeled the city a haven for right-wingers, see Lawrence Wright, *In the New World: Growing Up with America, 1960–1984* (New York: Alfred A. Knopf, 1988). For a reassessment of status anxiety theory, see Kendrick Oliver, "Post-Industrial Society and the Psychology of the American Far Right, 1950–74," *Journal of Contemporary History* 34 (1999): 601–18. For an examination of the Far Right rhetoric in 1950s Texas, see Heather Hendershot, *What's Fair on the Air? Cold War Right-Wing Broadcasting and the Public Interest* (Chicago: University of Chicago Press, 2011).

5. Patrick Allitt, *The Conservatives: Ideas and Personalities throughout American History* (New Haven, CT: Yale University Press, 2010), 245–48. For an examination of Bradford's ideology, see Fred Arthur Bailey, "M.E. Bradford, the Reagan Right, and the Resurgence of Confederate Nationalism" in *Painting Dixie Red: When, Where, Why, and How the South Became Republican,* ed. Glenn Feldman (Gainesville: University Press of Florida, 2011), In the introduction, Feldman concludes that "this is a tale of continuity" regarding the emergence of the contemporary Radical Right in the South. Further, he argues that a "politics of emotion" and a "status quo" society best explain the reactionary politics of the region.

6. Unsigned editorial, *Nation,* March 22, 1954; Charles J. V. Murphy, "Texas Business and McCarthy" *Fortune Magazine* 49 (May 1954): 100–101, 208; unsigned editorial, "The Conservative Revival," *Life,* May 15, 1950, 38–39. See also Bryan Burrough, *The Big Rich: The Rise and Fall of the Greatest Texas Oil Fortunes* (New York: Penguin Press, 2009), especially chapters 7 through 12. The quote about Texas oil money funding radical right-wing groups is cited by Burrough, *Big Rich,* 126; Bob Moser, "Texas's Wild Tea Party" *Nation,* May 30, 2011, 19–20; John Micklethwait and Adrian Wooldridge, *The Right Nation: Conservative Power in America* (New York: Penguin Press, 2004), 134. Also see Michael Lind, *Made in*

Texas: George W. Bush and the Southern Takeover of American Politics (New York: New American Books, 2003); Gilbert Garcia, *Reagan's Comeback: Four Weeks in Texas That Changed American Politics Forever* (San Antonio: Trinity University Press, 2012); Gail Collins, *As Texas Goes . . . How the Lone Star State Hijacked the American Agenda* (New York: Livewright Publishing, 2012). Darren Dochuk argues that beginning in the 1930s Texas immigrants brought with them a "Texas Religion" to Southern California that greatly influenced the political climate, especially in Orange County. See his *From Bible Belt to the Sun Belt: Plain-Folk Religion, Grassroots Politics, and the Rise of Evangelical Conservatism* (New York: W. W. Norton, 2011).

7. David Neiwert, *The Eliminationists: How Hate Talk Radicalized the American Right* (Sausalito, CA: Polipoint Press, 2011).

8. Kyle G. Wilkison, *Yeomen, Sharecroppers, and Socialists: Plain Folk Protest in Texas, 1870–1914* (College Station: Texas A&M University Press, 2008), 162–206.

9. By pushing the origins of the Texas Radical Right to well before the New Deal era, this essay collection answers a call by Kim Phillips-Fein to reconsider the historical beginnings of right-wing conservatism. See her "Conservatism: A State of the Field," *Journal of American History* 98 (December 2011): 723–43; especially pp. 737–89. For a concise overview of the emergence of post–World War II conservatism see her, *Invisible Hands: The Making of the Conservative Movement from the New Deal to Reagan* (New York: W. W. Norton, 2009).

Texan by Color

The Racialization of the Lone Star State

MICHAEL PHILLIPS

The bitterest political conflict occupying Texans for much of the period from the 1880s through the 1930s did not concern urbanization, unions, Prohibition, the post–World War I Red Scare, or the New Deal. A real battle—resulting in thousands of often harrowing deaths and injuries—raged over racial identity, over who could be considered real Texans, and over who would politically exist or suffer civic invisibility. African Americans were lynched in gruesome public spectacles, and the Texas Rangers engaged in a virtual pogrom against Mexicans and Mexican Americans in South Texas that may have claimed as many as five thousand lives.[1] Often, black-white or black-brown relations did not constitute the central front of this conflagration. Much of the struggle took place within what is today broadly considered the white community.

After the Civil War, Texas elites feared that poor and working-class blacks and whites might find common cause in changing an emerging capitalist economy that benefited few. By the early 1920s the early Texas Right justified the gap between rich and poor Anglos by attributing economic inequality within the white population to biological differences. Whites, elites claimed, were superior to blacks. Some within the ruling caste, however, were more white than others. Alleged racial inequality within the "white" community was presented as a justification for disenfranchisement. By the 1920s, members of the revived Ku Klux Klan argued that democracy was an innately Anglo-Saxon trait and that voting rights placed in the wrong hands—those of blacks, immigrants, and poor (and therefore lesser) whites—would result not in freedom but anarchy. Inconsistently constructed on random criteria such as pigmentation, hair texture, or culture and geographic origin, race has at times been a synonym for nationality, language, religion, and even class. The number of accepted racial categories expanded or contracted in Texas between the 1880s and 1930s, based not on empirical data but on economic and political convenience.

In Texas, the idea of race became a means by which Anglo elites stifled class conflict and attempted to co-opt the working class into accepting domination by the wealthy.[2] A particular racial identity—whiteness—became the currency by which one could purchase at least symbolic membership in the ruling caste. Fluid and flexible, the concept of race could be manipulated, based on the needs of the ruling class, to marginalize and disempower radicals.

Creating a race hierarchy in which one gained membership in an elite caste and avoided enslavement simply based on skin color admirably served the self-interests of the wealthy and powerful before the Civil War. Millions of whites in the antebellum South lived lives of desperate poverty and had little or no political influence, yet they could claim a superior status to the black-skinned "property" that often toiled endlessly beside them. During the period between the founding of the Texas Republic in 1836 and the end of the Civil War in 1865, the state had a tiny "Mexican" population. Therefore, the racial universe consisted largely of two shades: black and white. According to the 1861 state secession convention, African American Texans "were rightfully held and regarded as an inferior and dependent race" fit only for slavery. The secession declaration did not address the status of Mexicans in the Confederate state of Texas but did declare that all whites were "entitled to equal civil and political rights."[3]

With the abolition of slavery in 1865, however, racial politics became infinitely more complex. The post–Civil War Thirteenth, Fourteenth, and Fifteenth Amendments to the US Constitution abolished slavery and granted citizenship rights, including the right to vote, to African American men. The caste privilege enjoyed by otherwise powerless poor whites had disappeared, and hence they had lost their assumed vested interest in the existing power structure. Elite whites feared the resentments of the white underclass and began to strip them of even the symbolic wages of whiteness. Such poor whites, without money and with diminished political power, would be seen by elites as needing new incentives to remain loyal to a system of nascent capitalism, built on a brutally unequal distribution of wealth. Former Texas congressman and Confederate postmaster John H. Reagan, even as he languished in a Union prison after the war, wrote an "open letter to the people of Texas" in which he proposed changes in state laws that would have inevitably stripped some whites of voting rights.

Reagan realized that the North would not accept a new state constitution that denied suffrage only to African Americans. Reagan proposed "fixing an intellectual and moral, and, if thought advisable, a property test, for the admission of all persons to the exercise of the elective franchise, without reference to race or color."[4] It would be a mistake to assume that this rhetoric was merely a cynical dodge to get around the wording of the Fifteenth Amendment to the US Constitution, ratified in 1870, which prohibited a state from denying voting rights "on account of race, color, or previous condition of servitude." Four years before the Fifteenth Amendment, Reagan was already privately proposing restrictions on white suffrage. In a letter to Texas governor J. W. Throckmorton, he wrote that any intelligence test required of potential voters that "would only affect the negroes, and would allow whites of a less degree of intelligence . . . to vote, would do no good towards securing the great ends we desire to attain."[5]

Anglo elites viewed these lesser whites with greater apprehension because of the failed biracial Populist political crusade of the 1880s and 1890s. After the Civil War, Texas farmers became even more reliant on cotton cultivation for their livelihoods. Overproduction aggravated by the rapidly spreading system of sharecropping and foreign competition combined to devastate the state's farmers. These hardships radicalized farmers and led to the formation of the People's or "Populist" Party in the early 1890s. The Populists called for a vast expansion of the nation's money supply, government ownership of railroad and telegraph lines and for Austin and Washington to provide direct credit to farmers.[6]

Embracing ideas smacking of socialism, the Populists also presented the spectacle of struggling white and black farmers working together for a common objective. This class-based political movement threatened to revolutionize Texas politics forever. The state's Democrats accused the Populists of undermining white supremacy.[7] Democrats used the terrorism that proved effective in crushing the state's Republican Party in the 1860s and 1870s. During Election Day in 1896, forty Democrats in Robertson County held rifles while surrounding the courthouse to block entrance by black voters. The county judge later wrote, "I went down to the polls and took my six-shooter. I stayed there until the polls closed. Not a Negro voted."[8]

In the early twentieth century, future governor Pat Neff set out to eliminate the ill effects of uninformed voters, black or white, on Texas government. Neff and another important Texas House member from the period, Thomas B. Love, considered themselves progressives. Yet the genealogies of modern-day political ideologies are tangled. White progressives in the first decades of the twentieth century took what today would be considered liberal positions, advocating, for instance, a major expansion in the size and scope of the national and state governments. However, particularly in the South, progressives, like their most reactionary peers, supported white supremacy and segregation, and their rhetoric influenced the modern right's efforts to restrict voting, from voter identification laws up to suggestions of repealing the Fourteenth Amendment.[9]

In his first race for the state House of Representatives in 1898, Neff called for an "educational qualification" or "property qualification" requirement for voters. He endorsed the poll taxes adopted by other Southern states. The poll tax, he said, "has proven to be a good law and seems to me should be enacted into the laws of Texas."[10] He failed twice to pass a poll tax in his first legislation session, but Neff succeeded in 1901, when his poll tax amendment passed both the House and Senate and won voter approval by a two-to-one margin in 1902.[11] The new tax proved a serious barrier to the poorest Texans, white and black, who wanted to vote. Neff and his allies seemingly believed that not only should no black Texan be allowed to vote, but that some whites were similarly lacking in the cultural and biological inheritance needed for good citizenship.[12]

Neff strongly supported not just the poll tax and the whites-only primary but also Prohibition. Viewing African Americans as congenitally self-indulgent, he partially blamed black voters for the failure of a Prohibition amendment. (Voters turned down Prohibition amendments to the Texas Constitution in referendums in 1908 and 1911.) Disenfranchising African Americans, Neff and his allies argued, greatly improved the chances of Prohibition becoming law.[13] Neff made much the same argument about a group of suspect whites. According to Neff, he mainly wanted to restrict voting by Germans, not African Americans and Mexican Americans, because of the former group's opposition to Prohibition. When asked about the English-only provision of the new voting laws, Neff denied that his target was Spanish-speaking Mexicans. "That was to stop the Germans down at Fredericksburg. . . . A lot of them couldn't speak English . . . so they couldn't vote. . . . [T]hey were all wet voters, those Germans down at Fredericksburg."[14]

Texas' Anglo elites, however, continued to focus on elimination of black voters. Since the collapse of the state Republican Party in the 1870s and the Populists in the 1890s, the Democrats held a virtual monopoly on elective office. The state legislature in 1923 prohibited African Americans from voting in Democratic primaries. By the 1920s only Democrats had a plausible chance of winning general elections, so this measure essentially disenfranchised African Americans. In 1927 El Paso dentist Lawrence A. Nixon, provided legal assistance by the state's NAACP, won a unanimous decision in the *Nixon v. Herndon* decision, in which the US Supreme Court ruled that the 1923 law denied African Americans their Fourteenth Amendment rights. In response, the legislature passed a new law that did not require, but still allowed, political parties to deny blacks the right to vote in primaries. In 1932 the Supreme Court overturned this new legislative dodge in *Nixon v. Condon*. Finally, the legislature passed a bill permitting the Democratic Party to declare itself a "voluntary organization" with the right to freely choose its membership and qualifications without reference to state law. The Supreme Court upheld this approach in the 1935 *Grovey v. Townsend* case, and the Democratic Party successfully barred African Americans voters from its primaries until 1944, when the court reversed itself in the *Smith v. Allwright* decision that finally killed the white primary.[15]

Yet the threat posed by black voters was soon amply supplemented by the rising tide of Mexicans, Jews, and other eastern and southern European immigrants entering Texas in the late nineteenth and early twentieth centuries. Until 1900, new arrivals to Texas overwhelmingly came from other Southern states. Mexican and European immigrants increased markedly in the first two decades of the twentieth century. The percentage of foreign-born Texans increased both in raw numbers and in terms of the percentage of the total Texas population between 1880 and 1920. The state's total population grew from almost 1.6 million in 1880 to about 4.7 million in those forty years. The number of foreign-born within the state grew from 114,616 to 362,832 in those four decades. The number of foreign-born residents particularly increased after the turn of the century. In a period of rapid overall population growth, the percentage of the foreign-born in Texas increased from 5.9 percent in 1900 to 7.8 percent in 1920.

Mexican immigration, particularly in the decade of revolution and political and economic chaos south of the border from 1910 to 1920, had the biggest impact. About one hundred thousand Mexicans crossed into Texas in that decade. By 1930 the Mexican population in the state numbered seven hundred thousand, about 12 percent of the total population. (They had equaled about 6.5 percent of the population in 1850.) Anglos felt the impact of immigration more deeply in cities and in South Texas. For instance, in the Rio Grande Valley, the Mexican population climbed from 80 percent of the population to 92 percent.[16]

Not all the new Texans inspired the same reception. Assimilation to Anglo norms, and acceptance of Jim Crowism and rule by wealthy Anglos, allowed some European immigrants to achieve conditional whiteness. By the 1890s Texas Jews embraced the thoroughly westernized Reform movement of Judaism.[17] At Dallas's Congregation Emanu-El, Reform Jews followed Southern Protestant patterns of religious practice. The temple was built like a church, with services mostly in English. Congregants often used the title "minister" to refer to the clergy rather than "rabbi." Texas Jews rarely spoke Hebrew, and consequently, their religious gatherings strongly resembled Protestant gatherings.[18]

Mexicans and Mexican Americans who arrived in Texas after 1900 had a harder time winning even tentative acceptance as white, because many had darker skin than their Anglo compatriots, and because they were largely descended from Native Americans (regarded as racially inferior by Anglos) and from the Spanish, seen as the most backward of the European "races" by those of northern European descent. "Those Mexicans who could not look and act the part of Europeans were accorded a subordinate status," historian James Diego Vigil wrote. "Generally speaking, *gente de razon* [upper income and lighter-skinned "men of reason," as Mexican elites had designated themselves in opposition to the "unthinking" *indio* and *mestizo*] had a somewhat easier time because of their Latin background. It was the poorer, darker individuals unassimilated to the European model who suffered the worst abuse."[19]

In an attempt to earn whiteness, upper-class Tejanos in the 1830s and 1840s often sided with Anglos in their efforts to marginalize darker-skinned Mexicans of lower income. "To protect their interests . . . many of the *gente de razon* joined Anglos in oppressing the resistance acts of the Mexican masses," James Vigil observes. By the last decades of the nineteenth century, this strategy had failed. The *gente* "too lost out in the end, becoming bankrupt and poverty-stricken in some instances. . . . [D]espite the division between the two groups . . . Anglo-Americans regard them as one—as Mexican—except for ceremonial occasions when elements of the native-born become 'Spanish.'"[20] In the early twentieth century, Mexicans and their descendants in Texas were seen as nonwhites by most of the Anglo population.

The higher economic status and the important position as retail merchants enjoyed by some Jewish families (the department store–owning Marcuses and Sangers in Dallas and the grocery store–operating Weingartens in Houston) allowed them to prove their usefulness to the Jim Crow regime and to climb the racial ladder. Many Jewish merchants faithfully enforced Jim Crow laws, not allowing black customers to try on clothes, sit at the lunch counters, or share the same restrooms as white customers.[21] Light-skinned and seen as intelligent and amenable to white racism, several upper-class Jews achieved partial acceptance into the ruling class. As one Jewish leader, Stanley Marcus, put it, a Dallas Jew could be heard if he possessed "muscle," meaning that he was an executive in an important business that could advance the city elites' political and economic agenda.[22]

Acceptance of Jews as fully white, however, vanished when working-class Jews organized unions. In 1935, when about one hundred Dallas women dressmakers decided to unionize, the International Ladies' Garment Workers Union (ILGWU) dispatched Meyer Perlstein from New York to organize union locals. About one-third of the ILGWU membership in Dallas was Jewish, as was their most prominent spokesman. Even though Perlstein had achieved US citizenship twenty years earlier, in headlines the *Dallas Morning News* described him as a "Russian-born Jew." This label aimed at painting the ILGWU organizer and his union as foreign, Bolshevik, and nonwhite in the eyes of the public.[23]

White newspapers accorded wealthy Jews like the Sanger and Marcus families a respect never accorded African American or Mexican American merchants. Wealthy Jews never faced residential segregation nor were excluded from whites-only primaries. But independent of class status, they never achieved full acceptance as part of the white race. If Jews were allowed into political life, middle-class and upper-class members of the community still were not able to join Houston's elite River Oaks Country Club. Public school children in districts like Dallas were taught that Jews constituted an "Asiatic" race. As late as 1942, Jews were included as a distinct racial group along with "Anglo-Saxon," "South European," "Mexican," "Negro," and "Asiatic" on the ID cards issued by the City of Dallas's Department of Public Health. Rabbi David Lefkowitz of Dallas's Temple Emanu-El fought to abolish the department's "Hebrew" racial classification. "The use of the word 'Hebrew,' under any circumstances, except as the designation of the original language of the Bible, is incorrect," Lefkowitz wrote. "The designation 'Jewish' is a proper one for religion. . . . You are not, of course, seeking to determine the religion of those to whom you distribute the identification cards, otherwise you would put down Episcopalian, Baptist, Catholic, Methodists, etc. In this group, the word Jewish could well be included, but not in the former."[24]

Occupying a position lower than Jews in the Texas racial hierarchy, Tejano organizations like the League of United Latin American Citizens (LULAC), founded in 1929 in Corpus Christi, Texas, sought to achieve whiteness by "Americanizing" the Mexican population in Texas through English-language courses, public service to the wider civic community, and by keeping their distance from African Americans. Some LULAC chapters expressed their white identity by erecting a color line between the membership and blacks. One LULAC council expelled a member for marrying a "Negress," and members socially shunned the interracial couple. A member of the council bitterly complained that "[a]n American mob would lynch him. But we are not given the same opportunity to form a mob and come clean."[25] A Dallas labor leader, Pancho Medrano, said Mexican American leaders did not want to associate themselves with the black civil rights struggle. "[W]e tried to get the Mexican Americans to start moving," he recalled. "Everywhere, wherever we went . . . we tried . . . to stir them to demonstrate or to picket or demand; and nearly all the leadership, especially LULAC's or the American GI Forum . . . would always say, 'No.' . . . Especially the LULAC's; they say, 'We have more pride or education than that. You leave this to the Negroes. They are the ones who do all this—the burning and marching and all that violence. We don't want to do anything with that.'"[26]

Whether Jewish, Mexican, or Italian, many of these Texas immigrants were not seen by Anglo elites as capable of full assimilation. As Jews and Mexicans moved up and down the hierarchy it became clear that whiteness gained could be whiteness lost. A sure way to lose whiteness was to support the African American civil rights struggle. The immigrant community feared a loss of status, especially when they considered the extreme poverty and disease mortality rates suffered by Texans of African descent. Marginal whites had a powerful incentive to support antiblack segregation.

Designating schools, businesses, jobs, hospitals, and even restrooms as whites only, elites convinced even the poorest whites that they were part of a racial aristocracy. Slavery was gone, but a new set of legal disabilities afflicted the nonwhite in Texas. It is not surprising that as they often became as poor and politically powerless as their African American neighbors, that marginal whites sought to reassert their racial supremacy through terrorism. Race riots raged in 1908 in Beaumont, while similar outbreaks struck the African American communities in Sherman, Port Arthur, Houston, and other cities in the early twentieth century.[27] From 1882 until 1930, Texas lynch mobs murdered at least 492 Texans, including 143 whites and 349 blacks, the third most lynchings of any state in the nation. (This NAACP estimate of Texas lynchings might be low according to recent scholars such as Cynthia Skove Nevels and William Carrigan. Not only did more blacks probably die from mob violence than the NAACP statistics indicate, but that number also excludes as many as five thousand Mexicans murdered by Anglos in South Texas after the 1910 Mexican Revolution.) These killings provided gruesome public spectacles of white power. In May 1916 a mob of fifteen thousand burned to death a black youth, Jesse Washington, while children stood in attendance.[28]

In addition to being systematically disenfranchised and violently hunted by enraged whites, blacks suffered de jure and Mexicans de facto segregation in education, housing, and travel. If conservatism can be defined as the belief in preserving existing power relations, and the right can be defined as those who use even radical means to achieve that objective, then the ideology of white supremacy and the policy of segregation admirably served the needs of the right to maintain wealth and power in the hands of a small Anglo elite. Segregation, largely arising in the 1880s at the same time as the Populist revolt, represented a radical break from the Southern norm that prevailed from antebellum times to the end of Reconstruction, when African Americans and poor whites often lived and worked near each other. In the aftermath of populism's collapse in the 1890s, segregation became the radical means by which the right played divide and conquer. No longer sharing living space, barbershops, movie theater seats, or emergency rooms with African Americans, poor and working-class whites increasingly defined themselves less as part of the working class, which included blacks, and more as part of an elite racial caste.

In 1891 the Texas Legislature passed a law that mandated railway and streetcar segregation.[29] In Houston, the lack of a zoning law prevented the implementation of strictly enforced Jim Crow housing, but the haphazard pattern of urban development did disperse black and white working-class voters, diminishing the political potency of these groups even before the implementation of a new charter instituting at-large city elections in

1904.[30] In Dallas, a 1907 amendment to the city charter provided for segregation in schools and public amusement sites. In 1916 Dallas became the first city in Texas to allow racial housing segregation by law. The measure created three categories of neighborhoods—white, black, and open. The Texas Supreme Court overturned the ordinance in 1917, but in 1921 the Dallas city council passed a replacement ordinance, allowing residents of a neighborhood to request that their block be designated as white, black, or open.[31] Physical separation produced alienation between poor Anglos and impoverished African Americans. The message of white supremacy was visually reinforced through Jim Crow as cities like Dallas, Austin, Waco, San Antonio, and others crammed their black populations into tiny neighborhoods where residents suffered willful neglect. Texas cities failed to supply African American and Mexican American neighborhoods regular sanitation disposal, indoor plumbing, reliable ambulance, police and fire department services, or enforcement of city building and safety codes. Jim Crow neighborhoods became disease vectors, the crammed housing conditions making epidemics more likely.[32] Poor whites, who often lived in similar conditions,[33] used intimidation and violence to make sure that African Americans and Mexican Americans did not move into their neighborhoods.

Blackness came to be associated with disease, dirt, shorter lives, and vulnerability to violence. Association with blackness came to be dangerous for white workers, who asserted their racial supremacy and therefore their qualification for better treatment. White workers demanded all-white worksites. Working-class whites, blacks, and Mexicans became competitors rather than comrades. Employers could more easily play white and black workers against each other, depressing the wages of all three groups, whether they toiled as farmworkers or labored in the urban industries that became more important to the Texas economy by the 1920s and 1930s.[34]

In addition to segregation, in the early twentieth century the Texas Right embarked on another radical project to serve the maintenance of Anglo political and economic hegemony. Starting in the first three decades in the twentieth century, many elites sought to scientifically prove the racial inferiority of so-called whites of lower income to rationalize their poverty in a state supposedly dedicated to white supremacy. Prior to 1900, "white" meant not having African descent, a definition that by the segregation era starting in the 1890s meant not having the famous metaphorical "drop" of black blood. The rise of eugenicist thought in Texas at the beginning of the twentieth century greatly narrowed the definition of whiteness.

Lewis Dabney, a Dallas lawyer and son of a philosophy professor at the University of Texas at Austin, argued that no degree of education or acculturation would make southern and eastern Europeans real Americans. If nothing was done soon, he warned in a December 1922 speech to the Dallas Critic Club (an influential civic organization), the United States would be overwhelmed by "mongrelized Asiatics, Greeks, Levantines, Southern Italians, and sweepings of the Balkans, of Poland and of Russia."[35] Dabney told his audience that the United States faced a political takeover by racial inferiors that could be prevented only by encouraging "superior men and women" to increase their families, promoting birth control among the lower classes, sterilizing "criminals, lunatics, idiots, defectives and degenerates," and ending "promiscuous immigration."[36]

Hiram Wesley Evans, the energetic Dallas dentist who became the "grand titan" (district leader) of the Texas Ku Klux Klan in 1922, just before he seized the office of "imperial wizard" (national leader) of the revitalized KKK the following year, echoed Dabney's themes.[37] Evans, who would reign as imperial wizard until 1939, fanned the fears of many wealthy, powerful Texans who worried that racially degenerate immigrants would overwhelm the city and the nation.[38] Only Anglo-Saxons could become truly functioning citizens in a country built on capitalism and democracy, Evans insisted. "[G]enerations, or centuries, cannot school the Latin, the Greek, the Balkan and the Slav to that fundamental conception [responsible citizenship in a democracy]."[39] Such immigrants were as "utterly and eternally hopeless from the American point of view" as any black person.[40]

In the minds of men like Dabney, society would collapse were the expansion of democratic rights allowed to expand unchecked. Elites questioned the racial status of poor "whites" and immigrants. Dallas school superintendent Justin Kimball worried about the influence of a lower-class electorate who might be unfit for full citizenship. "Ignorant or corruptible citizens can always be counted on to vote, although they usually vote wrong," he wrote.[41] Dabney also thought the franchise should be sharply restricted for poor whites, as it was for African Americans. "The trouble about a democracy is that things are settled by voting and ninety-five percent of the voters, not having the sense of an ant or squirrel in the summer, but having the vote, will ravage the stores of those who have laid up a few nuts when they could," he wrote. Democracy, he warned, "by its very nature rejects the best and seeks the worst and is stumbling down into the mire."[42]

Textbooks widely used in Texas, such as *Our World Today and Yesterday:*

A History of Modern Civilization, praised authoritarian regimes such as Benito Mussolini's Fascist government in Italy for crushing labor unrest and restoring law and order. "He [Mussolini] has chosen a ministry made up of capable men and has straightened up the badly demoralized finances of the country," the textbook told its high school readership. "He and his followers are accused of suppressing liberty and downing the communists by violence. Nevertheless, he has done much to do away with strikes and to reestablish conditions as they were before the economic demoralization of the war [World War I] set in."[43]

Texas students were also told that Founding Fathers like George Washington, John Adams, and Thomas Jefferson abhorred letting the wrong people vote. Texas school textbooks praised the Founders for resisting demands for "radical democracy" when they wrote the Constitution. According to *The Record of America*, published in 1935, the wisdom of the Constitution lay in its protection of elite rule against the shortsighted demands of the unpropertied. The authors of the Constitution, the textbook said, "had little faith in the ability of people as a whole to maintain self-control and wisdom in government. They had no confidence in the man without property . . . a man who had failed to [accumulate property] . . . would be regarded as shiftless, lazy, or incompetent, and not deserving a voice in the government of others."[44]

By the 1920s some of the best-educated Texans called for restricting immigration, and hoped they could improve the state's stock by encouraging the biologically promising to breed and by reducing reproduction by the biologically and racially backward. The supposed science of breeding better humans, called eugenics, enjoyed a heyday in Texas in the first three decades of the twentieth century, though it would never achieve the grip it held in other states. For many years of the early twentieth century, "Better Baby" contests proved a crowd-pleasing event at the Texas State Fair in Dallas. In 1914 a committee of doctors measured the skulls and other traits of the five hundred entrants, and awarded fifteen dollars to the parents of the "best" child, any class, and five dollars for the best twins and triplets.[45] The children in such contests, as historians have observed, were judged on eugenic fitness and awarded in a similar way that prize "cattle, chickens, and pigs" also received blue ribbons elsewhere on the fairgrounds.[46]

Winners were white, blond, and often the scions of elite families. Hoping to evangelize the Dallas crowds to the gospel of better breeding, A. Caswell Ellis, an educational psychologist at the University of Texas (later a national leader in the eugenic movement and long a popularizer of science[47]) took the opportunity of a 1914 contest to evangelize for his favorite cause and "lightly touched on eugenics" for his Dallas audience.[48] Prompted by eugenicists like Dr. Ellis, the Texas Mental Hygiene Society in the early 1920s undertook to assess the effects of biological degeneracy on the state's mental health.

According to the society's 1924 published report *Psychiatric Study of Public School Children in Eleven Counties, Children in State and County Institutions for Delinquents and Dependents, Inmates of Eleven County Poor Farms [and] Inmates of Eighteen County Jails*, an alarming number of Texas schoolchildren rated as mentally defective. A survey covering 3,208 children in all (including 122 African Americans, 421 "Mexicans," and 2,665 "others" whom the report defined loosely as "white'), found that 24.7 percent rated as mental defectives or suffered from "borderline mental defect" (meaning they "tended toward the feeble-minded") and another 8.3 percent suffered from "gross personality defect." According to the report: "5.6 percent of total, 20.5 percent of Negroes, 20.4 percent of Mexicans, and 5.4 percent of whites tested more than two years below grade. 32.7 percent of total, 46.7 percent of Negroes, 30.9 percent of Mexicans, and 32.3 percent of whites tested one or two grades below grade."[49] The report reaffirmed the eugenicist assumptions of white supremacy. No black schoolchildren, only 1.9 percent of the Mexican males, and 0.9 percent of Mexican females ranked as mentally "superior" (compared to 2.4 percent of all whites). Meanwhile, the mental hygiene survey team ranked an extraordinary 34.4 percent of African American schoolchildren and 23.4 percent of Mexican children as mental defectives, compared to a still high 5.7 percent for whites.[50] If believed, the study held chilling implications for the state's future. Elsewhere the report established a firm link between mental defectiveness and crime. According to the researchers, 22.8 percent of the inmates contacted at state penitentiaries were mentally defective or suffered from borderline mental defect, while 41.1 percent of those held in county jails belonged to these two categories.[51] These numbers seem less disturbing when one considers the flawed methodology and assumptions eugenicists used to measure intellect in that era.

In his papers collected at the Dolph Briscoe Center for American History in Austin, Ellis kept copies of the *National Intelligence Test, Scale B, Form I*, designed by nationally prominent eugenicists like L. M. Terman and R. M. Yerkes[52] and used by psychologists and psychiatrists in Texas in the 1920s. These tests actually measured knowledge rather than intellect. A typical question asked who wrote the poem "Hiawatha." The possible answers were James Fenimore Cooper, Henry Wadsworth Longfellow, Edgar Allan Poe, and John Greenleaf Whittier. (The correct answer is Longfellow.) Another asks who was among Robin Hood's men, Allan Breck, Natty Bumppo, Galahad, or Friar Tuck? (The answer is Friar Tuck.)[53] Clearly, one could be misinformed, poorly educated, or lack English skills and miss such questions, but still be intelligent.

When the Texas Mental Hygiene Society published its report in 1924, it called for improved mental health care and rehabilitation for the mentally deficient but didn't seem to consider that the poor scores on the "IQ" tests actually gauged the inadequacy of Texas schools. The year the report was issued, progressives had only recently passed a school reform law to modernize an education system still dominated by rural one-teacher, one-classroom schools. State spending on education ranked near the bottom nationally, and regarding quality, one survey in 1920 rated Texas thirty-ninth of the forty-eight states.[54] With eugenicists dominating the national dialogue in the early 1920s, however, many in Texas concluded that the state faced a biological crisis more than an education crisis.

In the early twentieth century, eugenics laws went on the books across the country. During the time between the turn of the century and World War II, twenty-seven states passed mandatory sterilization laws aimed at preventing the poor, epileptics, and the supposedly unintelligent and mentally ill from passing their dysgenic natures to another generation.[55] However, in spite of the strong influence of eugenicists in Klan-dominated Texas, the Lone Star State did not rank among the states that passed sterilization laws or other eugenics measures. A major reason may have been the influence of cotton growers in the state who had begun importing Mexican farmworkers in large numbers. The urban population of Texas grew steadily in the early twentieth century, but by the 1920s Texas was still an overwhelmingly rural state, meaning that big growers in rural Texas House districts had disproportionate influence over the state legislature. Partly as a result of increased urbanization and economic modernization, which would accelerate in the 1930s and 1940s, a split developed within the Texas Right. Growers benefited from a segmented but multiracial workforce in which white, African American, and Mexican-descended sharecroppers and farmer laborers ruthlessly competed and lowered each other's wages; and for this reason growers fought eugenics and immigration restriction. Urban members of the Klan and city-based academics, however, saw Mexicans, Jews, and Italians as politically radical by their racial nature and as agents of biological degeneration.[56]

Cotton growers in particular worried that eugenics legislation nationally and at the state level might make it harder to find cheap labor to compete with white and black farm labor. After passage of the nativist 1917 Immigration Act, Texas planters and growers successfully lobbied Secretary of Labor William B. Wilson to allow the temporary entry of "otherwise inadmissible aliens" to offset labor shortages created by the American entry into World War I. Eugenicists led a chorus of protest against the quota waivers, leading Wilson after the war to rescind his exemptions of Mexican workers. Once again, the big planters and growers insisted they needed the cheap labor of Mexicans (whom they argued were uniquely suited physically for farm labor), and the exemptions were extended until 1920. When the US Congress passed a new Quota Act in 1921 further restricting the immigration of southern and eastern Europeans, Mexican farm labor became even more important in Texas, and again the rich landowners got all the poorly paid migrant workers they wanted.[57]

Many Anglos in the state, like Chester Rowell, insisted that "the Mexican peon is not a 'white' man. He is an Indian . . . who embodies no part of the fine Latin American culture which charms visitors to Mexico City." F. E. Jackson, president of the Ysleta Farm Bureau, described Mexicans as "creatures somewhere between a burro and a human being."[58] One opponent of the use of Mexican labor in Texas declared, "To Mexicanize Texas or to Orientalize California is a crime."[59]

The last sentiment suggests a basic eugenic fear—that once planted in Texas, Mexican immigrants would overwhelm the Anglo population and pollute the racial stock. Cotton growers used racist arguments to defuse the opponents of Mexican labor. Texas could never be "Mexicanized" by such a backward people, they said. As a cotton farmer put it, "Have you ever heard, in the history of the United States, or in the history of the human race, of the white race being overrun by a class of people with the mentality of the Mexicans?"[60] Fears of a Mexican invasion of Texas farm regions, coupled with the anxiety already felt in cities like Dallas and Houston over increased immigration of Jews and Italians, became so pervasive that the politically dominant growers had to fight a pitched battle to assert their economic interests.

In 1923 the Texas House debated a concurrent resolution introduced by Dallas representative Lewis Carpenter requesting the US Congress to allow the governor of a state or the state legislature to draw up a quota "of the kind and character and number of immigrants which any given State is willing and ready to receive for any given year or period of years."

The quota would then be forwarded to federal immigration authorities in Washington, and the national quota of immigrants from a nation like Mexico could be raised to that number to meet a state's economic needs. As a sop to the nativists and eugenicists, Carpenter and his allies included a provision requiring immigrants to remain in the custody of the state until they returned home or became United States citizens. Such a requirement would guarantee the "preservation of a homogeneous race" in Texas and the rest of the country, Carpenter argued. Such arguments didn't calm lawmakers fearing a rising tide of color washing northward from the Texas border. House Concurrent Resolution 15 was referred to the Committee on Federal Relations, which ultimately rejected the proposal.[61] Nevertheless, in 1924 when Congress passed the most restrictive immigration legislation in American history, the Johnson-Reed Act, the law focused on shutting down what had been since the 1880s massive southern and eastern European immigration while planters in Texas and elsewhere could still import low-wage Mexican farmworkers.

The Texas Right from the 1880s to the 1930s failed to pass a eugenics law because the racial purification agenda threatened the economic interests of some elites. The eugenics movement also tangled with the growing influence of a new force in Texas society, a religious movement known as "premillennial dispensationalism." Promoted by Dallas minister Cyrus Scofield, dispensationalists believed that the Bible represented a prophetic text that predicted the imminent "Second Coming" of Jesus. Intensely anti-Catholic because they believed that the Vatican represented a satanic false Christianity, such Protestants might have been expected to represent a force for eugenics legislation aimed at controlling the population of Catholic Mexicans, Italians, and other aliens in Texas. Critical issues nevertheless separated the growing dispensationalist movement and eugenicists. The eugenics movement generally was anti-Semitic, while Scofield and his followers believed Jews were critical actors in the events leading to Christ's return. Scofield preached that anti-Semitism was a sin that would bring divine wrath. Dispensationalists also adamantly rejected the theory of evolution, a concept central to eugenicists' worldview. Dispensationalism, furthermore, discouraged political activism, believing that faith in human institutions like legislatures represented a rejection of God as the ultimate arbiter of human affairs. "The true mission of the church is not the reformation of society," Scofield preached. "What Christ did not do, the Apostles did not do. Not one of them was a reformer."[62] This growing apolitical religious movement denied eugenicists a potentially key group of supporters.

In any case, eugenics and the whole of "race science" peaked in the 1920s. It would be a gross understatement to say the growing awareness of the professional ties between American, British, and German eugenicists, and the role Nazi eugenicists played in the Holocaust, became a serious public relations problem for advocates of American "race science" after World War II. Following the war, most scholars embraced a "populational" concept of human difference, shifting analysis from variation between large, artificial categories like "white" and "black" to variety between networks of "interconnected breeding populations." After World War II, one no longer heard of the Polish or Greek or Jewish "race." Ethnicity displaced race for such groups.[63]

The period from the New Deal to the Great Society, from the 1930s to the late 1960s, saw the erection of the modern social welfare state. Much of the reform effort of that period, from school desegregation to programs like Head Start, aimed at purging the toxic impact of racism and its role in creating economic inequality. Yet even after the period of liberal ascendancy, poverty, disease, poor education, and crime continued to disproportionately affect African Americans and Texans of Mexican descent. In the first decades of the twenty-first century, Census Bureau data indicated that the median income for African American families stood at $33,916, compared to a median income of $54,920 for non-Hispanic white families. According to a 2007 report by the Federal Reserve Board, for every dollar of wealth held by a white family, a Latino family held twelve cents and an African American family ten cents. Almost a quarter of African American families lived in poverty, compared to 8.2 percent of whites. Whites were more likely to have at least a high school diploma (with 89 percent of whites graduating compared to 80 percent of African Americans). Only 16 percent of black women held bachelor's degrees and 14 percent of black men, compared to 24 percent of white women and 25 percent of white men. Only 48.5 percent of African Americans earning between 80 percent and 120 percent of the median income in their area own their homes, significantly less than the 70.5 percent rate for whites. Hispanics with similar incomes enjoy a homeownership rate of only 51.2 percent.[64] Beginning in the 1990s, the modern American Right—in national best sellers such as *The Bell Curve: Intelligence and Class Structure in American Life* and *The End of Racism: Principles for a Multiracial Society*—cited such continued racial disparities as evidence of the futility of big government liberalism and the cultural and genetic inferiority of African Americans and those of Mexican descent.

Like earlier eugenicists, the authors of *The Bell Curve* argued that blacks and Mexicans were less intelligent than whites and that this difference was due to biology. Written by conservative activists Richard J. Herrnstein and Charles Murray, the book called for dismantling welfare programs because, the authors suggested, such expensive programs could not undo defective DNA. *The Bell Curve*, published in 1994, received a hearty endorsement from elites in Texas, including four top members of the psychology departments of the University of Texas and Texas A&M University and one A&M business professor.[65]

Much of the alleged documentation for *The Bell Curve*'s conclusions came from early twentieth-century eugenics research. Armed with ostensibly scientific data, many conservatives after the turn of the century argued that Mexican immigrants in particular represented a threat to the state, not an asset. In November 2006 the city council of the Dallas suburb of Farmers Branch passed Texas' most severe anti-immigrant ordinance. Ordinance 2903 made English the official language of the city and prohibited landlords from renting to undocumented workers, with daily five-hundred-dollar fines imposed on property owners until they complied. (The law failed to pass constitutional muster in the federal courts.) Farmers Branch city council member Tim O'Hare, the measure's chief proponent, claimed that undocumented workers "come from poor conditions, get . . . free medical care, get a free education, [don't pay] taxes, and compared to their living conditions before . . . live like kings and queens." O'Hare argued that immigrants brought crime, declining public schools, and welfare dependency to the once prosperous suburb. O'Hare complained that undocumented workers lowered property values: "When that happens, people move out of our neighborhoods, and what I would call less desirable people move into the neighborhoods, people who don't value education, people who don't value taking care of their properties."[66]

Implicit in O'Hare's comments is the notion that nationhood is a matter of blood. This is the rhetoric of John H. Reagan, Pat Neff, and Hiram Wesley Evans given new clothes. In Texas, the Reconstruction-era reforms giving African American men citizenship and voting rights destroyed an old order in which poor whites could claim membership in a racial elite exempt from the status of slavery. After Reconstruction, elite whites sought to eliminate the threat of biracial rebellion that had been posed by Populism in the 1880s and 1890s. Disenfranchisement laws politically crippled blacks, immigrants, Mexicans, and poor whites. However, from

1920 until the end of World War II, a more flexible concept of race arose in which some disenfranchised whites could regain a measure of power by compliance with the economic and political status quo. The concept of race itself briefly faced a fierce challenge after the grim facts of the European Holocaust became public knowledge in the late 1940s, and liberal Democrats in Washington initiated a host of social welfare programs designed to correct the economic inequalities produced not by genetic inequality but by discrimination and intolerance. When these programs failed to eradicate black and brown poverty, the Right synthesized a century of racial thought and, in Texas, used pseudoscience to roll back the legislative accomplishments of the left. By 2012 everything old in Texas' racial rhetoric was new again.

Notes

1. For events in South Texas, see Benjamin Heber Johnson, *Revolution in Texas: How a Forgotten Rebellion and Its Bloody Suppression Turned Mexicans into Americans* (New Haven, CT: Yale University Press, 2003).

2. The most important works on race in Texas are Chandler Davidson, *Race and Class in Texas Politics* (Princeton, NJ: Princeton University Press, 1990); Arnoldo De León, *They Called Them Greasers: Anglo Attitudes toward Mexicans in Texas, 1821–1900* (Austin: University of Texas Press, 1983); Neil Foley, *The White Scourge: Mexicans, Blacks, and Poor Whites in Texas Cotton Culture* (Berkeley: University of California Press, 1997); Jacquelyn Dowd Hall, "'The Mind That Burns in Each Body': Women, Rape, and Racial Violence," in *Powers of Desire: The Politics of Sexuality*, ed. Ann Snitow, Christine Stansell, and Sharon Thompson (New York: Monthly Review Press, 1983); David Montejano, *Anglos and Mexicans in the Making of Texas, 1836–1986* (Austin: University of Texas Press, 1987); Cynthia Skove Nevels, *Lynching to Belong: Claiming Whiteness through Racial Violence* (College Station: Texas A&M University, 2007); and Michael Phillips, *White Metropolis: Race, Ethnicity, and Religion in Dallas, 1841–2001* (Austin: University of Texas Press, 2006).

3. Delegates of the People of Texas, "A Declaration of the Causes Which Impel the State of Texas to Secede from the Federal Union" (Dallas: Basye Brothers, Printer, n.d.), 4, Texas State Library, Archives Division, Austin (hereafter TSL).

4. Letter, John H. Reagan, Fort Warren, Boston Harbor, to the People of Texas, August 11, 1865, typescript copy, John H. Reagan Collection, Miscellany File 2–23/1079, John H. Reagan Letters, Folder 31, TSL.

5. "Necessary Measures to Reconstruction," letter, John H. Reagan, Fort Houston, Palestine, Texas, to Governor J. W. Throckmorton, October 12, 1866, Jefferson Davis Reagan Collection A4674, Folder 10, Dallas Historical Society (hereafter DHS).

6. Lawrence Goodwyn, *The Populist Moment: A Short History of the Agrarian Revolt in America* (New York: Oxford University Press, 1978), 44–53. An excellent, more recent account of the populist and socialist movements in Texas can be found in Kyle Wilkison, *Yeoman, Sharecroppers, and Socialists: Plain Folk Protests in Texas, 1870–1914* (College Station: Texas A&M University Press, 2008).

7. Goodwyn, *Populist Moment,* 6, 15, 18–19, 122–23, 131–32, 137–38, 210, 280–83.

8. For more on the use of terrorism to suppress black voting, see Randolph Campbell, *Gone to Texas: A History of the Lone Star State* (New York: Oxford University Press, 2003), 336; and Lawrence Goodwyn, "Populist Dreams and Negro Rights: East Texas as a Case Study," *American Historical Review* 76, no. 5 (December 1971): 1435–56.

9. For more on the racist and sometimes reactionary nature of the progressive movement in Texas, see Lewis L. Gould, *Progressives and Prohibitionists: Texas Democrats in the Wilson Era* (Austin: Texas State Historical Association, 1992.) Regarding Texas' modern, restrictive voter ID law, see Daniel Setiawan, "After Six-Year Fight, Perry Signs Voter ID into Law," *Texas Observer,* May 27, 2011, http://www.texasobserver.org/component/k2/item/17879-voter-id-signed-into-law (accessed June 4, 2011).

10. Dorothy and Terrell Blodgett and David Scott, "Legislating: Serving in the Texas House of Representatives, 1899–1905," copy in the author's possession, 10. This manuscript was subsequently been published as *The Land, the Law, and the Lord: The Life of Pat Neff, Governor of Texas, 1921–1925, President of Baylor University, 1932–1947* (Austin: Home Place Publishing, 2007.)

11. Blodgett and Scott, "Legislating," 18; Worth Robert Miller, "Building a Progressive Coalition in Texas: The Populist-Democrat Rapprochement, 1900–1907," *Journal of Southern History* 52, no. 2 (May 1986): 172–74; Blodgett and Scott, "Legislating," 34; Alwyn Barr, *Black Texans: A History of African Americans in Texas, 1528–1995* (Norman: University of Oklahoma Press, 1996), 79–80.

12. Robert A. Calvert and Arnoldo De León, *The History of Texas* (Wheeling, IL: Harland Davidson, 1996), 272.

13. Gould, *Progressives and Prohibitionists,* 49.

14. Blodgett and Scott, "Legislating," 41.

15. Barr, *Black Texans,* 135–36. For more on the Texas "white primary" law and its impact on African Americans, see Darlene Clark Hine, *Black Victory: The Rise and Fall of the White Primary in Texas* (Millwood, NY: KTO Press, 1979). In one of her more interesting passages, Hine describes how elites modified franchise restrictions to allow continued voting by the state's significant Mexican American population in South Texas.

16. United States Bureau of the Census, Population Division, "Table 13. Nativity of the Population, for Regions, Divisions, and States: 1850 to 1990," http://www.census.gov/population/www/documentation/twps0029/tab13.html (accessed July 13, 2011); Calvert and De León, *History of Texas,* 186; Johnson, *Revolution in Texas,* 26; Terry G. Jordan, "A Century and a Half of Ethnic Change in Texas, 1836–1986," *Southwestern Historical Quarterly* 89 (April 1986): 418; and Robert McCaa, "Missing Millions: The Human Cost of the Mexican Revolution," report by the University of Minnesota Population Center

(2001), http://www.hist.umn.edu/~rmccaa/missmill/mxrev.htm (accessed July 13, 2011).

17. Cindy C. Smolovik, "A Tradition of Service: Early Synagogues in Dallas," *Heritage News* 12, no. 2 (Summer 1987): 12.

18. Gerry Cristol, *A Light in the Prairie: Temple Emanu-El of Dallas, 1872–1997* (Fort Worth: Texas Christian University Press, 1998), 19–25; Leonard Dinnerstein, *Anti-Semitism in America* (New York: Oxford University Press, 1994), 177; Jonathan D. Sarna, "The Evolution of the American Synagogue" in *The Americanization of the Jews*, ed. Robert M. Seltzer and Norman J. Cohen (New York: New York University Press, 1995), 215–29.

19. James Diego Vigil, *From Indians to Chicanos: The Dynamics of Mexican American Culture* (Prospect Heights, IL: Waveland Press, 1980), 129.

20. Vigil, *From Indians to Chicanos*, 129.

21. See W. J. Durham, "Citizens' Committee to Abolish Discrimination against Negro Women in Dallas Department Stores," circular letter, July 27 1953, John O. and Ethelyn M. Chisum Collection, Box 1, Folder 2, Texas/Dallas History and Archives Division, J. Erik Jonsson Central Library (Dallas Public Libraries); Claudia Feldman, "Their Road to Freedom: In 1960, a Group of TSU Students Helped Change Houston's Future by Standing Up—and Sitting Down—For Their Rights," *Houston Chronicle*, May 12, 2011, http://www.chron.com/disp/story.mpl/life/main/7562396.html (accessed June 4, 2011).

22. Patricia Evridge Hill, *Dallas: The Making of a Modern City* (Austin: University of Texas Press, 1996), 116–22. The Marcus quote is from Marilynn Wood Hill, "A History of the Jewish Involvement in the Dallas Community" (master's thesis, Southern Methodist University, 1967), 81.

23. "Strike Leader Takes Stand in Contempt Case: Perlstein, Russian-Born Jew, Says Didn't Urge Street Fighting but for Peaceful Result," *Dallas Morning News*, September 19, 1935, p. 1, sec. 1; Hearing Number 1 before the Industrial Commission of Texas, "Garment Industry in Dallas County: Statement of Facts," August 1935, 262–63, George and Latane Lambert Collection, AR 127-11-1, Labor Archive—University of Texas at Arlington Library.

24. Letter, Rabbi David Lefkowitz, Dallas, to Dr. J. M. Dowis, Acting Director, Department of Public Health, City Hall, Dallas, May 7, 1942, Anti-Semitism in Dallas/Anti-Defamation League, B'nai B'rith Folder, Dorothy M. and Harry S. Jacobus Temple Emanu-El Archives, Dallas.

25. Foley, *White Scourge*, 209–10.

26. Pancho Medrano, interview by George Green and Carr Winn, August 4, 1971, Dallas, Transcript OH55, Labor Archives, Division of Archives and Manuscripts, Central Library, University of Texas at Arlington. For more on the politics of Mexican American identity in this period, see Rodolfo Acuña, *Occupied America: A History of Chicanos* (New York: HarpersCollins Publishers, 1988); Juan Gómez-Quiñones, *Chicano Politics: Reality and Promise, 1940–1990* (Albuquerque: University of New Mexico Press, 1990); David G. Gutiérrez, *Walls and Mirrors: Mexican Americans, Mexican Immigrants, and the Politics of Ethnicity* (Berkeley: University of California Press, 1995); and George J. Sánchez, *Becoming Mexican American: Ethnicity, Culture, and Identity in Chicano Los Angeles, 1900–1945* (New York: Oxford University Press, 1993).

27. Calvert and De León, *History of Texas*, 252; Barr, *Black Texans*, 137.

28. Jacquelyn Dowd Hall, *Revolt against Chivalry: Jessie Daniel Ames and the Women's Campaign against Lynching* (New York: Columbia University Press, 1993), 134–35; Patrick Cox, *The First Texas News Barons* (Austin: University of Texas Press, 2005), 34–38; Barr, *Black Texans*, 137. See also Patricia Bernstein's detailed analysis of the Washington lynching in *The First Waco Horror: The Lynching of Jesse Washington and the Rise of the NAACP* (College Station: Texas A&M University Press, 2005). On the disputed number of lynchings in Texas, see Cynthia Skove Nevels, *Lynching to Belong: Claiming Whiteness through Racial Violence* (College Station: Texas A&M University, 2007); and William D. Carrigan, *The Making of a Lynching Culture: Violence and Vigilantism in Central Texas, 1836–1916* (Urbana: University of Illinois Press, 2004). For information on the South Texas anti-Mexican pogrom, see Johnson, *Revolution in Texas*, 86, 113–18, 115, 147, 155, 201.

29. Barr, *Black Texans*, 80–85.

30. David G. McComb, *Houston: A History* (Austin: University of Texas Press, 1981), 93, 96–97.

31. Robert Prince, *A History of Dallas: From a Different Perspective* (Dallas: Nortex Press, 1993), 29–30; Robert Fairbanks, *For the City as a Whole: Planning, Politics, and the Public Interest in Dallas, Texas, 1900–1965* (Columbus: Ohio State University Press, 1998), 29–30, 151–52; Barr, *Black Texans*, 140; W. Marvin Dulaney, "Whatever Happened to the Civil Rights Movement in Dallas, Texas?" in *Essays on the American Civil Rights Movement*, ed. W. Marvin Dulaney and Kathleen Underwood (College Station: Published for the University of Texas at Arlington by Texas A&M University Press, 1993), 69; McComb, *Houston*, 108, 159. The best study on how African Americans dealt with segregation and racism in Houston is Howard Beeth and Cary D. Wintz, *Black Dixie: Afro-Texan History and Culture in Houston* (College Station: Texas A&M University Press, 1992).

32. See, for instance, Jim Schutze, *The Accommodation: The Politics of Race in An American City* (Secaucus, NJ: Citadel Press, 1986), 9–10; Robert Fairbanks, *For the City as a Whole: Planning, Politics, and the Public Interest in Dallas, Texas, 1900–1965* (Columbus: Ohio State University Press, 1998), 192; Dennis Hoover, "Razing Slums Would Leave Many Homeless," *Dallas Morning News*, January 21, 1962, sec. 1, p. 5.

33. See the report "Civic Responsibility: An Appeal Addressed to the Thoughtful Citizen for Better Housing Conditions and Environment of the Poor in Dallas," 1910, George Dealey Papers, A6667, Folder 332, 2–3, Dallas Historical Society.

34. The classic work explaining how Jim Crow represented a dramatic break in Southern history remains C. Vann Woodward's *The Strange Career of Jim Crow* (New York: Oxford University Press, 1974). The embrace by the white working class of racism received an innovative and thoughtful treatment in David Roediger, *The Wages of Whiteness: Race and the Making of the American Working Class* (New York: Verso, 1991). How the Texas working class embraced white supremacy in Texas is intelligently explored in Foley, *White Scourge*, 92–117. I explore the same dynamic in *White Metropolis*, 77–102.

35. Lewis Meriwether Dabney, *A Memoir and Letters* (New York: privately printed by J.J. Little and Ives Company, 1924), 214.

36. Ibid., 232.

37. Darwin Payne, *Big D*, 77.

38. "Imperial Wizard Evans' Great Speech," *The Texas 100 Per Cent American*, October 26, 1923, 3–4.

39. "Imperial Wizard," 3–4.

40. E. Haldeman-Julius, *Is the Ku Klux Klan Constructive or Destructive? A Debate between Wizard Evans, Israel Zangwill, and Others* (Girard, KS: Haldeman-Julius Company, 1924), 12.

41. Justin F. Kimball, *Our City—Dallas: A Community Civics* (Dallas: Kessler Plan Association of Dallas, 1927), 218.

42. Dabney, *Memoir and Letters*, 88.

43. James Harvey Robinson and Emma Peters Smith with James Breasted, *Our World Today and Yesterday: A History of Modern Civilization* (Dallas: Ginn and Company, 1924), 620.

44. James Truslow Adams and Charles Garrett Vannest, *The Record of America* (Dallas: Charles Scribner's Sons, 1935), 702.

45. For newspaper coverage leading up to the contest, see "Better Babies Show," advertising copy, *Dallas Daily Times Herald*, October 11, 1914, sec. 1, p. 14; "Prizes Offered for the Baby Show," *Dallas Daily Times Herald*, October 26, 1914, sec. 1, p. 1; "Wednesday Is Big Day for Baby Contest," *Dallas Daily Times Herald*, October 27, 1914, sec. 1, p. 3; "Bright Sunshine and Varied Features Bring Big Crowd to the Fair: Better Baby Contest Is Drawing Card," *Dallas Daily Times Herald*, October 28, 1914, sec. 1, p. 1. For more on the contest, see Nancy Wiley, *The Great State Fair of Texas: An Illustrated History* (Dallas: Taylor Publishing Company, 2000), 73. For more on how eugenics influenced American thought on race, see Jonathan Peter Spiro, *Defending the Master Race: Conservation, Eugenics, and the Legacy of Madison Grant* (Burlington: University of Vermont Press, 2008).

46. Chip Berlet and Matthew N. Lyons, *Right-Wing Populism in America: Too Close for Comfort* (New York: Guilford Press, 2000), 94.

47. Edward T. Downer, "A. Caswell Ellis," *Skyline: A Quarterly of the Cleveland College of Western Reserve University* 13, no. 4 (May 1940): 19–20.

48. "Girl Child Makes Best Test Marks: Grace Gulden, Dallas County, Winner of Sweepstakes. Two Perfect Boys," *Dallas Daily Times Herald*, October 28, 1914, sec. 1, p. 4.

49. Elmer V. Eyman, *Report of the Texas Mental Hygiene Survey, 1924: Psychiatric Study of Public School Children in Eleven Counties, Children in State and County Institutions for Delinquents and Dependents, [and] Inmates of Eleven County Poor Farms Inmates of Eighteen County Jails* (New York: National Committee for Mental Hygiene, December 1924), 19, 53, 55. Alexander Caswell Ellis Papers, Box 2P49, Dolph Briscoe Center for American History, Austin, TX.

50. Eyman, *Report of the Texas Mental Hygiene Survey*, 53.

51. Ibid., 19.

52. The careers of Terman and Yerkes and the deep flaws of their work are described in Gould, *The Mismeasure of Man*, 172–233.

53. M. E. Haggery, L. M. Terman, E. L. Thorndike, G. M. Whipple, and R. M. Yerkes, *National Intelligence Test, Scale B, Form 1*, Alexander Caswell Ellis Papers, Box 4P347.

54. Calvert and De León, *History of Texas*, 277–78.

55. Edwin Black, *War against the Weak: Eugenics and America's Campaign to Create a Master Race* (New York: Thunder's Mouth Press, 2003), xv, 3–6.

56. Allen Duckworth, "Redistricting Long Overdue: Law Governing Membership of Legislature Unobserved," *Dallas Morning News*, January 7, 1951.

57. Foley, *The White Scourge*, 45–46.

58. Ibid., 52–53.

59. Ibid., 55.

60. Ibid., 58.

61. *Journal of the House of Representatives of the Regular Session of the Thirty-Eighth Legislature Begun and Held at the City of Austin, January 9, 1923* (Austin: Von Boeckmann-Jones Co., 1923), 587–88, 614, 643.

62. C. I. Scofield, "The Millennium: A Sermon Preached at the First Congregational Church, Dallas, Texas, Oct. 29, 1893," Scofield Memorial Church Archives, Dallas; Paul Boyer, *When Time Shall Be No More: Prophecy Belief in Modern American Culture* (Cambridge, MA: Belknap Press, 1992), 298.

63. Marek Kohn, *The Race Gallery: The Return of Racial Science* (London: Vintage, 1996), 11.

64. "African American Profile," Office of Minority Health, US Department of Health and Human Services, http://minorityhealth.hhs.gov/templates/browse.aspx?lvl=2&lvlID=51 (accessed February 2, 2011); "Income Gap between Whites, Blacks Continues to Grow," March 23, 2009, http://www.npr.org/templates/story/story.php?storyId=102233746 (accessed February 2, 2011); "America's Home Ownership Gap," United States Conference of Mayors, http://www.usmayors.org/publications/home.htm (accessed February 2, 2011).

65. "Mainstream Science on Intelligence," *Wall Street Journal*, December 13, 1994, 18. The UT professors were psychology department members David B. Cohen, Joseph M. Horn, John C. Loehlin, Del Theissen, and Lee Willerman. The Texas A&M professors were psychology department member Cecil R. Reynolds and business professor Lyle F. Schoenfeldt. Systematic debunking of *The Bell Curve* can be found in Bernie Devlin, Stephen E. Fienberg, Daniel P. Resnick, and Katherine Roeder, eds., *Intelligence, Genes, and Success: Scientists Respond to the Bell Curve* (New York: Springer-Verlag, 1997); Steven Fraser, ed., *The Bell Curve Wars: Race, Intelligence, and the Future of America* (New York: Basic Books, 1995); and Joe L. Kinchloe, Shirley A. Steinberg, and Aaron D. Gresson III, *Measured Lies: The Bell Curve Examined* (New York: St. Martin's Press, 1997).

66. Stephanie Sandoval, "FB Studies Tough Provisions Aimed at Illegal Immigrants," *Denton Record Chronicle*, August 21, 2006, DentonRC.com, http://www.dentonrc.com/sharedcontent/dws/news/city/carrollton/stories/DN-fbimmigration_21met.ART.North.Edition1.3e0478e.html. (accessed May 15, 2011).

"The Evils of Socialism"

The Religious Right in Early Twentieth-Century Texas

KYLE G. WILKISON

The Battle of Armageddon is on, and our rulers are slumbering. . . . Destruction will come!" Thus warned Church of Christ preacher William F. Lemmons, writing in 1914 of the menace of socialism facing Texas and America. From his East Texas home in Tyler he had witnessed the rapid growth of the Texas Socialist Party into a second-place finish in 1912 ahead of the Republicans and Prohibitionists in the governor's race. Although the movement was still small (second place to the dominant Democrats did not mean much), Socialist inroads among his neighbors and coreligionists prompted Lemmons to pen two books attacking "the evils of Socialism." These two early twentieth-century publications furnish a glimpse into the "plain folk" pulpit's defense of the contemporary social order. Lemmons and like-minded preachers among the early twentieth-century Texas religious Right provide an illuminative starting point for understanding the better-known religious Right that followed in the mid- to late twentieth century.[1]

American politics and American churches have been always intertwined to greater or lesser degrees. Historians of American politics, however, tend to leave the pulpit to the historians of religion, perhaps underestimating the political influence of American preachers. This neglect seems most pronounced when the pulpit supported the status quo. As historian Kim Phillips-Fein observed, analysis of religion's role in American conservatism has "received more lip service than sustained engagement from political historians."[2]

Indeed, preachers have been the ordinary poor majority's most immediate leadership. That most poor people's preachers appear to have lent their considerable influence to the cause of cultural and political conservatism is perhaps less remarkable than historians' neglect of that influence. Understandably, when preachers behave unexpectedly and defy elements of the social order, as in the case of Martin Luther King Jr.'s generation of dissenters, they come to the attention of political historians. Thus, while we know a good deal about the political might of the clergy in the civil rights struggle, the political might of the preachers on the other side is only now beginning to be explored. When religious authority figures endorse the mainstream social, political, or economic structure, it may be unremarkable but it is not unimportant.[3]

Like much of the rest of the country, especially in traditional rural settings, religion played a central role in the lives of nineteenth- and early twentieth-century Texans. The church was often the center of community life and its pastor one of the community's respected authority figures. We know very well that their early twentieth-century sermons successfully shaped public policy in campaigns against alcohol. But what do we know of their positions on the dramatic restructuring of the early twentieth-century Texas economy with its newly high levels of farm tenancy, rural poverty, and other matters of daily bread? Except for the case of Prohibition, much of their political influence remains unexamined in the Lone Star State's political history.[4]

Although Thomas Jefferson aimed his oft-quoted warning that history supplied no examples of a "priest-ridden people maintaining a free civil government" at Catholic Latin America, it is sometimes interpreted as his argument against the influence of American preachers. Jefferson made no such argument against "sectarian" (Protestant) preachers, however, because he believed the disestablished church was a voluntary association from which individuals might withdraw if the preacher chose to instruct them in politics.[5]

Jefferson placed a great deal of faith in individual prerogative and reason, allowing less leverage to the power of culture. Indeed, as others have shown, New Englanders failed to withdraw from their churches when instructed in politics by their Federalist pastors. The cause Jefferson and the Federalists held in common—the struggle for US independence—supplies many examples of local congregants being instructed in politics by their pastors. Might America's "sectarian" preachers have been more influential than Jefferson estimated?[6]

Historian Harry S. Stout makes a masterful case for the paradox lying at the heart of American political religion from the first generation of the new republic. "If Americans were to inherit the millennial promise, they must keep the covenant." While the conservative Federalist clergy accepted the new Constitution, they saw it only as a temporal adjunct to an older, more important covenant between their communities and God. For them, the Constitution's secular republic was a neutral-at-best vehicle that permitted contemporary society's perpetuation of a timeless and, to them, more real "Christian America," which could retain God's conditional blessing only as long as it maintained fidelity to that "original" covenant. For them, national doom lurked around the corner of each election if ungodly men—especially Thomas Jefferson—seduced the new, frail, secular, constitutional republic away from its godly purposes.[7]

Measuring the power of the pulpit in political affairs is a tricky business that hinges in part on accurately understanding the ordinary preacher's position in relation to other loci of power and influence. In some respects, the local preacher's influence was quite limited, at least if pointing up the social pyramid. After all, members of the economic elite were frequently the financial mainstay of the church, thus embodying another, potentially competing, locus of authority. Preachers who defied such authority did so, most likely, in obscurity or in another line of work. So, to argue that preachers were influential has to account for the social direction of their influence. It was mostly downward.[8]

Regardless of cause or party, evidence of the political influence of the American pulpit abounds. As Patricia Bonomi has shown, Christian ministers helped fuel the fires of the American War for Independence as illustrated in this despairing English report: "your Lordship can scarcely conceive what Fury the Discourses of some mad Preachers have created in this Country." One persuasive pastor, Bonomi writes, "preached all the young men of his congregation into the army," and the Continental Congress explicitly sought out the help of clergy in trying to win over skeptical frontier dissidents. American colonials and their descendants were accustomed to political pronouncements from the pulpits.[9]

The American War for Independence would not be the last occasion for American preachers to weigh in on war. As Drew Gilpin Faust has noted, the blessing of institutional Christianity provided the "most fundamental source of legitimization for the Confederacy." And the record is replete with religious Northerners' vision of the Union role in the Civil War in the most sacred terms possible. Preachers in 1898 Texas responded to the

Spanish-American War with sermons "calculated to kindle the fires of patriotism and arouse the military spirit."[10]

Jefferson might well have looked askance at the American political landscape of the early twentieth century. Perhaps at no other time in American history has the politics of the nation so reflected the influence of the Protestant pulpit in the Constitutional prohibition of alcohol. But, it was a peculiarly fragile influence, most successfully wielded in the interests of the established order. That the liquor lobby lost the war to the preachers may speak as much to the newly mechanized national market's need for a sober workforce as to the political leverage of the men of the cloth. In sharp contrast, the "social gospel" preachers failed in their hopes for a child labor amendment.

It may be, then, that successful preachers owe their "power" or influence—measured roughly by the size or influence of their congregations—to the financial pillars of such institutions. On the critical point of social power, the "Federalist clergy" seemed to hold the temporary upper hand, feeling free to lecture politicians and other elites about the meaning of the covenant. But power relationships between clergy and elites are slippery and easily misread. There are few examples in early twentieth-century Texas of "successful" preachers assailing the cultural and economic mainstays of their day.[11]

Church culture, like society's as a whole, changes. Early 1900s Texas Baptists and Methodists of the prosperous new cotton and railroad towns and cities consciously reached for middle-class respectability and status. Formerly the denominations of the frontier poor and rural plain folk, now urban Baptists and Methodists sought to spruce up their image. The *Baptist Standard*, organ of Texas Baptists, lectured its readers on "church manners" and lamented that "there is more rudeness, in and around, the church in the country, than in town." Likewise, Texas Methodist congregations proudly became "more and more the churches of the professional man, the business leader, and the landowners."[12]

Such developments came at a cost, and church attendance among the rural poor majority declined. This declension coincided with soaring farm tenancy and rural poverty as well as the persistent radical critique of the status quo coming from Texas' Populist and Socialist movements that emphasized the role of plain folk preachers as lecturers and candidates.

In 1900 one rural Texas county's Baptist Association brought in J. R. Barrett, a "missionary evangelist" thought to possess special skill in "preaching to the destitute," a growing demographic as cotton sharecropping tightened its grip on the countryside.[13] There Barrett found himself in active competition with Socialists for the attention of poor people. Shocked by their claims that socialism and Christianity were compatible, Barrett eventually took on the task of defending the existing social order with a powerful combination of scripture and cultural precept by challenging Socialist preacher Morgan A. Smith to a weeks-long written debate appearing on the front page of the local newspaper. Barrett began with a biblical defense of the acquisition of private property, especially land. Socialist preachers sought to "pervert" scripture in this regard when, Barrett argued, the Bible showed plenty examples of the righteous buying, selling, and owning land.[14] His Socialist opponent denied perverting scripture but focused his reply on the "theft" of the people's "natural inheritance" by greedy capitalists such as C. C. Slaughter, prominent Dallas banker and Baptist philanthropist who owned over 600,000 acres of land.[15] Thereafter Barrett shifted tactics and invoked the powerful cultural appeal of white supremacy, knowing the Left's vulnerability on that issue. Barrett accused the Socialists of promoting African American equality and signed his missive "A Democrat to the Bottom."[16]

The Socialist's response attempted to finesse the race issue by accusing Barrett of "asking some irrelevant question concerning 'the negro.'" Smith and Texas Socialists only wished the issue of race to be irrelevant. In reality, he dared not answer Barrett's question with damning admission to a belief in racial equality within an electorate overwhelmingly committed to white supremacy. Instead, the Socialist attempted a diversion by poking fun at Barrett's ringing declaration of partisan loyalty with a series of sly observations on the myriad divisions and factions within the Democratic Party of Texas. Was Barrett a gold or silver, prohibition or anti-prohibition, tariff or anti-tariff Democrat? And, most insulting of all, Smith had heard some Texas Democrats proclaim themselves for Theodore Roosevelt, and he asked Barrett, "Is that what kind of democrat you are?"[17]

This tactic backfired badly, allowing a resounding rebuttal in which Barrett summed up the mainstream church's defense of wealth, the economic status quo, and white supremacy by contrasting true preachers like himself to those who preached socialism. True preachers preach "that it is sinful and wicked and wrong to rob or steal or lie or defraud or to be covetous or envious or jealous or dishonest" while the Socialists' "so-called preachers" unjustly scorn "the class of men that have accumulated this world's goods and speak of them as capitalists owning and controlling the world and oppressing the poor people." Such false prophets urged their listeners to "rise up and vote for a party that would result in creating laws that would demand these rich capitalists to give up all their lands and industries that they have paid for, teaching your children a spirit of dishonesty, cramming down them the spirit of theft and covetousness and envy." God had ordained class structure; far from being the thieves and robbers described by Socialists, "rich men" were some "of the most Godly and saintly characters in the Bible." Finally, stepping into the opening provided by his opponent, Barrett invoked the power of faith, white supremacy, social conservatism, and partisan loyalty. "Mr. Smith wants to know what kind of Democrat I am. Well, I am not the kind that believes in the social equality with Mr. Negro in any shape, form or fashion." With that, the debate was over.[18]

White supremacy sat squarely at the center of mainstream cultural conservatism in early twentieth-century Texas. Preachers defended it with full confidence of the support of the overwhelming majority of their congregants. Powerful Baptist preacher, Prohibition leader, and sometime *Baptist Standard* editor J. B. Cranfill even worked it into his campaigns against liquor, warning northern Prohibitionists not to attempt to "break down" the "color line" in the South, further cautioning them to not waste their efforts on African Americans. Some measure of Cranfill's influence can be had by the fact that he published his preferred slate of "moral" (dry) Democrats running in that party's primary.[19]

The early twentieth-century Texas *Baptist Standard* consistently supported conservative principles. J. B. Cranfill solved the paper's financial difficulties early in the century by selling partnerships to C. C. Slaughter and George W. Carroll, Baptist businessmen. Cranfill exulted: "We suppose that it has never happened in Christian history before that two millionaire Baptist laymen were joint proprietors of a religious and denominational paper." Cranfill clearly articulated the new religious-business creed of his increasingly middle-class denomination. Baptist preachers should be good businessmen because of "the people to whom the modern preacher is to minister." The good Christian businessman "knows how to make money in a righteous way" and could be trusted to support his church. In fact, wealth followed piety, especially giving to the church and its efforts. In illustration, the *Standard* related the story of a businessman suffering losses because he had "not been honest financially towards God." Immediately he corrected this error with a large donation, and "from that very day, aye, from that very hour, I saw the change, and he did gather a fortune."[20]

Perhaps the *Standard* reached the height of its defense of business interests in an editorial supporting banks and railroad corporations against left-wing critics. Prominent prohibitionist preacher J. B. Gambrell lamented the people's "attitude of decided unfriendliness" toward railroad companies. For Gambrell, the injustice lay in how much the railroads had done for the people, increasing the value of their farms and spreading civilization and the gospel. Yet Gambrell reported that it had become "difficult, lawyers tell me, for railroads to get justice in the courts" because of "agitation" by "demagogues" who managed to stir up in "the masses an evil disposition." Banks, too, were being mistreated for the same reason. "No good comes to a people by keeping alive prejudices such as have made it difficult to develop the country." In an interesting admission that invites further scrutiny, Gambrell noted that railroad corporations "are liberal to religion . . . because morality and business are close friends." In the spring of 1912, during the height of the Socialist agitation of "the land question" growing up around soaring rates of sharecropping, the *Standard* attacked the single-tax theory of land redistribution and associated it with Mexican revolutionary Francisco "Pancho" Villa, an almost archetypal bogeyman for many Anglo Texans. According to the *Standard*, the "greasers" following this "chimerical" plan failed to appreciate its dangers. A few weeks later the newspaper attacked those who attempted to use the Bible to show that "Jesus decried wealth." Quite the contrary was true, as shown in early twentieth-century Texas where the largest fortunes of the day "have fallen to religious men." After all, Christ himself had "died among poor villains" but had been "buried by rich Christians." In order for the church to win over the practical-minded businessman, it must become "sensible about things."[21]

Leaders of the Disciples of Christ denomination, dominated by urban middle-class interests, likewise defended the religious basis of wealth. One Disciples of Christ minister averred that "the most beautiful souls" he had ever known were "not among the poor but the rich." In fact, he doubted that Christianity could "flourish in the wretched, filthy, vermin-besieged houses of the poor."[22]

Early twentieth-century Texas denominational newspapers and pulpits reflected the energetic optimism of a Texas economy booming—for the few—with cotton, cattle, and oil. Because representative run-of-the-mill Sunday sermons mostly have not been preserved, we are left with elite preachers or a minority of those who published their works. Among the latter, a stouter bastion of conservative defense of the established economic, gender, and racial status quo would be harder to find than in the published work of early twentieth-century Texas plain folk evangelist William F. Lemmons.

Lemmons, an Arkansas-born Church of Christ evangelist, spent most of his life in Texas preaching, publishing religious newspapers and, during the heyday of the Texas Socialist movement, denouncing socialism. In 1912 and in 1914 he published two books repudiating the notion that socialism was compatible with Christianity.[23]

The Churches of Christ in Texas and elsewhere in the country (predominating in the rural South), was the rural wing of the "Restorationist" movement founded by Alexander Campbell that split from the more urbane Disciples of Christ over the issue of ornate church buildings and, most famously, the inclusion of instrumental music (organs) in worship. Fiercely independent and congregational, the Churches of Christ opposed denominational structure and were clearly a plain-folk-friendly church, albeit in numbers a distinct minority compared to rural Baptists and Methodists. The "Campbellite" movement's goal was a restoration of primitive Christianity and the dissolution of denominationalism. Relative newcomers to the field and holding to an exclusive "closed communion," the Churches of Christ were viewed by many as something of an outsider's movement in early twentieth-century Texas. They came by that reputation honestly. Not only did they reject the potential for salvation to be had in any other group (often requiring ex-Methodist or -Baptist converts to be rebaptized), some of their founders had laid a firm foundation for rejecting much else about mainstream culture.

Within Church of Christ culture there ran a strain, by the early twentieth century a minor but still vibrant strain, of quietism, of Christian rejection of the world. Much of this was embodied in the career of Tennessean David Lipscomb, who called for Christians to eschew all participation in worldly politics, including voting, serving on juries, and fighting in wars. In spite of Lipscomb's quietist rejection of voting and military service, he also rejected passivity when witnessing what he saw as injustice. Through the pages of his newspaper he regularly denounced worldly acquisitiveness by both individuals and corporations (to whom he presciently denied personhood) writing that "corporations do not have souls" but existed only to give the business elite cover to exploit labor in a fashion that he believed they "would not do as individuals." He even sympathized with Jacob Coxey's 1894 march on Washington with unemployed workers and affirmed a positive role for labor unions. Lipscomb thought the prosperous drove the working class from their churches through their efforts "to gratify the culture of the world in artistic speaking, music and surroundings that indicate wealth and luxury." He further asserted that the great wealth accrued by Gilded Age families such as the Rockefellers and Vanderbilts "had been gained illegally and unscrupulously." In stark contrast to the Federalist clergy of the state-supported churches of New England, as a "restorationist" calling for Christian primitivism, Lipscomb completely rejected "the mistaken idea of a Christian America" whose central institutions he believed were in league with greed and worldliness. His indictment of wealth and his pointed reference to the working class as the "true nobility" stand in sharp contrast to his cohort of preachers on the Texas Right. Church of Christ preacher W. F. Lemmons and Baptist preacher J. Frank Norris, as will be seen in the next chapter, both used Lipscombesque appeals to poor people but for significantly different purposes.[24]

The Churches of Christ's congregational makeup promoted disputation. Not only did these congregations reject denominational organization and hierarchical discipline, they avoided the use of prescribed Sunday School literature or like material. Thus, their ministers regularly debated the true meaning of scripture in the pages of the *Firm Foundation*, the most prominent Texas Church of Christ newspaper. Even more congregational than Baptists in matters of church governance, no bishops or conferences could silence dissident clerics. When Church of Christ preachers began endorsing Socialism, their heresy had to be confronted individually. Lemmons seized the challenge.

In 1912 Lemmons worried over the number of "good brethren" who had adopted socialistic beliefs. "You would be surprised if I were to publish the names of preachers who claim that Socialism is the true religion of Jesus Christ." He objected that churches were "calling just such preachers to hold their meetings" instead of conservatives.[25]

Lemmons engaged in several celebrated debates with Texas Socialists and wrote an anti-Socialist article for the *Firm Foundation*. His article blasted Socialists for trying to hide their atheistic materialism under the cloak of biblical language. Further, socialism represented only the latest Eastern decadence to beset the pristine West. British oppression of the colonies and northern oppression of the South had come from the East as had a comprehensive—if paradoxical—list of other social evils, including slavery, child labor, "tainted" money, stock fraud, political corruption: "higher criticism, socialism, and other evils are eastern relics, injected into the west to poison the nation."[26]

Consisting mainly of a compilation of damning quotations from the most blatantly godless Socialist writers, *The Evils of Socialism* meant to correct the error of fellow believers who were devoting themselves to "the doctrine of this eighteenth century twaddle." Chief among the blights of socialism were its atheistic roots growing from the writings of Karl Marx and, according to Lemmons, Charles Darwin—two rank infidels. Socialism sought to supplant all religious creeds, even as its adherents falsely portrayed it as primitive Christianity. Socialism promoted free love, female equality, anarchy, and violence; failed to respect the flag and the Constitution; pushed impractical economics; and denied the God-ordained nature of private ownership and the class system. Socialism broke a number of biblical injunctions against the "mingling" of nations, worker discontent, and contempt for temporal authorities. Finally, socialism would mean "social equality" with African Americans.[27]

Lemmons's first book focused on debating the issues of primitive Christianity, the correct moral basis for landownership, the causes of landlessness, and concluded with a lengthy denunciation of socialism's threat to white supremacy. While Socialists sought to represent their critique of capitalism as resurgent primitive Christianity, Lemmons denied the legitimacy of any such claims. In fact, socialism embraced atheism and drained away attention from the spiritual life. "Look at the many who have gone into Socialism. . . . I could cite you to [*sic*] preachers, as well as 'Lay members,' who have lost all interest in Christianity, and are giving their life's work" to spreading the heresy of socialism. In fact, the economic practices Socialists claimed were primitive Christianity were really only their "trying to make it [the Bible] apply where it has no application." In addressing the moral basis for landownership, Lemmons used the same kind of language Texas Socialists used to question private ownership. According to Lemmons, socialism meant theft. Here Lemmons carefully acknowledged that "capital" could be put to both good and evil purposes; this position reflected the conventional plain folk critique of capitalists rather than capitalism. But from the very beginning, God had decreed private ownership of property. "Adam and Eve were capitalists" and doing just fine until Satan's arrival. "But the Devil was a Socialist" who persuaded Eve to expropriate fruit to which she was not entitled.[28]

Lemmons made a special appeal to farmers. Private ownership represented the only claim to land upon which farm families could depend. Socialists, on the other hand, sought to fool farmers with their propaganda, but, Lemmons warned, "the farmer is just a Government renter under Socialism."[29]

Landlessness and poverty existed because the poor did not use their wealth "judiciously." Lemmons claimed the Texas economy grew so fast that property values rose 600 million dollars a year or forty-one dollars a second. "With these figures before us, what is to hinder every family owning a farm?" The poor, especially "Socialist inclined people" and "negroes," simply did not want to work. "If these poor people in New York and Chicago and other cities would get out into the country and dig, as God ordained, they would not suffer. . . . If their wages do not suit them, why don't they get out and settle on a farm and raise their own hog and hominy and be independent?"[30]

But Lemmons realized that discussions of primitive Christianity, the sanctity of private property, nor the dereliction of poor white people carried as much immediate emotional appeal as white supremacy. Consequently, Lemmons devoted an eighth of the first book to a denunciation of socialism's "brotherhood of man" as "a system of 'nigger' equality." If socialism continued to grow, the purity of the white race, and thus true religion and civilization itself, would be destroyed. The subtext of African American men as sexual rivals, as well as an apparent fear of white women "freed to do as they please," ran throughout Lemmons's essay. In one particularly revealing section Lemmons warned that—if the Socialists won—their white daughters might accompany "a colored gentleman to church at high noon on Sunday, or on the dark of the moon at night, because . . . it will be no stigma on society."[31]

Leftists within the Church of Christ wrote Lemmons attacking "monopolization of land" and his opposition to the Socialist Party. One annoyed "brother" lectured Lemmons on socialism's true religious character by referring him to the popular St. Louis socialist newspaper edited by Frank P. and Kate Richard O'Hare, the *National Rip-Saw*: "Better read the *National Rip-Saw* and post up." Lemmons retorted: "That is your trouble. You have read the *Rip-Saw* until you think it is the gospel of Jesus Christ."[32]

In 1914 Lemmons published his second defense of capitalism, entitled *The Devil and Socialism*. This much larger work revisited many of the same themes as *The Evils of Socialism* and reproduced many of the same copious quotations appearing in the first. But here Lemmons attempted to reach a national audience while remaining focused on the locale he knew best, East Texas. If anything, in the intervening months, his positions appear to have hardened toward both racial and gender equality. Yet in regard to both, he was safely in the mainstream of Texas culture.

The innovations in *The Devil and Socialism* were to emphasize the "infidelity" of scientific materialism, to occasionally conflate the disparate worldviews of Darwin, Marx, and Spencer, to establish the biblical underpinnings of capitalism and specifically the American state, and to make even more pointed appeals to white supremacy and early twentieth-century notions of masculinity.

With language that would provide a template for the next century of the American religious Right, Lemmons crossed into new territory by laying claim to a sacrosanct status for the American nation and economic status quo. Leaving Lipscomb's rejection of nationalism far behind, Lemmons averred that the American nation and its government were both God-ordained and a fulfillment of specific biblical prophecy. Washington's defeat of the British ushered in "the entering wedge of universal freedom." American nationhood was "a strong chain that was thrown around the power of Satan, and the binding is still going on." Indeed, if Americans resisted socialism and remained true to their godly mission, the world was on the brink of indefinite peace. Writing with unknowing irony in 1914, Lemmons assured his readers that soon, through the work of former president William Howard Taft and American millionaires "contributing their fortunes to international peace," international war "will be impossible." God had chosen the current structure and "has worked through the 'powers that be' for the purpose of accomplishing his work."[33]

God had ordained the capitalist structure of the American economy as well. Lemmons reminded his readers that the Bible instructed believers to be content with their station in life, to avoid coveting, to obey without complaining or criticizing their "rulers." Socialism fostered such sins. The Bible, Lemmons wrote, shows "conclusively" that socialism "is of the devil, and its end destruction." Nations prosper according to their obedience to God's will. America was prosperous in 1914 because of that. On the other hand, in 1914 Palestine and many other countries were backward, poverty-stricken places. The "sins of the Jews, or other nations, is the direct cause of the conditions that prevail in those countries today." Lemmons's anti-Semitism here and elsewhere in the book stands in sharp contrast to the rhetoric of his post–World War II successors on the Right. But, in 1914 America, prosperity was available to all. Texas cotton sharecroppers were accumulating wealth so rapidly that "they scarcely know how it came about" and had begun investing their surplus income in the stock market. Poverty existed, but only through the failures of dissolute individuals. The poor were profligate, lazy, or stupid. As a group, farmers were "extravagant" and wasted their money, failing to maintain their implements and purchasing farm wagons more often than necessary. Much was wasted on picture shows, candy, chewing gum, liquor, tobacco, patent medicines, and automobiles. "Poor people make thousands of unnecessary trips on railroads." With land so plentiful and cheap, a Texas farmer had "little excuse" for remaining a tenant.[34]

Lemmons believed that man's place in the home, church, and society was that of God-ordained preeminence. While lauding the femininity of true women, Lemmons suffered no Victorian delusions about her inner nature. For example, he rejected social reformers' pleas that poverty forced poor women into prostitution. Instead he offered the unusual—in that time—explanation that in "most cases" women entered into prostitution because "they allowed their lust to overcome their judgment, and flee to the red-light district to hide their shame."[35]

Appealing to the manliness of his readers, if not their misogyny, Lemmons argued that socialism would unleash women's latent desire to rule. Once liberated from male restraints, women would insist on becoming "boss of the whole goose nest." Under socialism, women's pride would become so unmanageable that they would "have to put on bloomers and ride in air ships for the ground will be too dirty for them to walk on." Woman suffrage was unfeminine, un-American, and against scripture. No true woman would support it; the idea had come from foreigners in "the slums" and the naturally discontented "old maids" seeking "authority under their apron string." Indeed, Lemmons could not imagine what more women could want. "Every law on the statute book, where men and women are involved, favors women."[36]

Even the widespread tenancy on Texas cotton farms might be traced to women's frailties. Women's weakness for labor-saving conveniences "accounts for the reason that many farmers rent all their lives, and never own a home." Further, such women "fool away enough time in fool society, and useless lodges, to make enough hominy to run the family a year round." Women were "more extravagant than men. . . . They will buy hundreds of things a man would not think of buying." He accused the socialists of attempting to establish a female-dominated society under the "petticoat government of Socialism." This would be ungodly because God had "never selected a woman as leader in the affairs of men."[37]

Once more he reminded his readers that socialists were guilty of favoring racial equality. Here Lemmons assured his readers that he had no personal ill will for "the negro" toward whom he believed in "dealing out justice." Justice did not preclude Lemmons's use of racial epithets in both books, nor did it, in his view, include equality with white people. Because socialists refused to make distinctions based on race, their victory would "mean the impossibility of a Jim Crow law, or the impossibility of a law to prohibit the intermarriage of blacks and whites." Lemmons understood the efficacy of racist language in an outspoken defense of white supremacy because each was a privileged and commonplace feature of mainstream public culture in 1910s Texas.[38]

While the Texas religious Right that followed Lemmons found it necessary to revise the specifics of his rhetoric in order to remain in the mainstream of an ever-changing culture, Lemmons's template has held up well over the past century. His arguments that faithful Christians must also respect social hierarchy, believe in the justice of the free market, reject government intervention against economic inequality, and protect traditional family and gender roles would resonate with most, if not all, twenty-first-century Texas conservatives. While the arrival of modern Israel revolutionized conservative American Christian attitudes toward Jews, and midcentury social revolutions meant overt appeals to white supremacy had to be replaced, nevertheless, the appeals that he developed to piety, tradition, hard work, and social values tied to deeply held emotions (such as manhood and racial identity) stood his successors in good stead throughout the twentieth century.

In order to better comprehend the cultural and political landscape of early twentieth-century Texas, more historical work must be done. Darren Dochuk has provided a valuable guide with his exploration of plain folk religion's marriage to conservative politics in postwar California.[39] In his splendid study of the rise of the mid- to late twentieth-century religious Right, Dochuk does much to increase our understanding of the linkage between displaced Southern plain folk culture in California and the triumph of "evangelical conservatism." And indeed, the "old-time" gospel often proved irresistible to the new Sunbelt suburbanites when they heard it preached in the cadences and accents of their rural Southern grandparents and parents. But as early as the 1910s the battle lines had been drawn. The difference then was that there were still preachers on the other side. The equally plain-folk preachers of the early twentieth-century Texas Left also preached in the same cadences and accents but denounced the structure of the ascendant economic order.[40]

Historians have grappled with correctly dating the birth of the American Right. The first historians of conservatism had mostly focused on the era of Barry Goldwater and William F. Buckley Jr., and later, seeing in the movement a rejection of the 1960s counterculture and civil rights revolutions. Eventually, the roots of contemporary conservatism were identified by some writers as beginning one generation earlier with organized resistance to the New Deal. More recently, historian Chad Pearson and others have argued for an even earlier start, pointing out evidence of an organized Right in pre–World War I America. The example of W. F. Lemmons and the Texas religious Right of the early twentieth century certainly supports the notion of a long movement of American conservatism as well as its special relationship with the American church.[41]

Notes

1. William F. Lemmons, *The Devil and Socialism* (Cincinnati: F. L. Rowe Publisher, 1914), 270; W. F. Lemmons, *The Evils of Socialism* (Austin: Firm Foundation Press, 1912).

2. Kim Phillips-Fein, "Conservatism: A State of the Field," *Journal of American History* 98 (December 2011): 733.

3. Two excellent examples of the growing scholarly literature on American politics and religion is Darren Dochuk, *From Bible Belt to Sunbelt: Plain-Folk Religion, Grassroots Politics, and the Rise of Evangelical Conservatism* (New York: W. W. Norton, 2011), and Mark A. Noll and Luke Harlow, eds., *Religion and American Politics: From the Colonial Period to the Present*, 2nd ed. (New York: Oxford University Press, 2007). For a magisterial review of the "state of the field" in conservatism studies, see Phillips-Fein's "Conservatism," 723–43.

4. Joseph Locke, "Conquering Salem: The Triumph of the Christian Vision in Turn-of-the-Century Texas," *Southwestern Historical Quarterly* 115 (January 2012): 233–57.

5. It is plain, however, that he sought to cut off formal clerical political power by arguing for school board elections to be held in the smallest local unit possible to avoid the county-level tyranny of "fanaticizing" preachers. "Letter to Baron Von Humboldt" [1813], *The Jeffersonian Cyclopedia* (Funk and Wagnalls, 1900), 827; "Letter to Joseph C. Cabell," [1820], *Jeffersonian Cyclopedia*, 791.

6. Patricia U. Bonomi, *Under the Cope of Heaven: Religion, Society, and Politics in Colonial America* (New York: Oxford University Press, 1986), 211.

7. Harry S. Stout, "Rhetoric and Reality in the Early Republic: The Case of the Federalist Clergy," in Noll and Harlow, *Religion and American Politics*, 73, 65–76.

8. Joseph Locke argues in "Conquering Salem" that nineteenth-century Texas political culture had a strong "anticlerical" bent that early twentieth-century preachers such as J. B. Cranfill had to overcome before they could enact their "Christian vision" of Prohibition (233–45). Richard Hofstadter flirts with the topic of preacher clout but does not develop it. He does note the disproportionately large role of preachers in the mid-twentieth-century

"right-wing movement." Richard Hofstadter, *The Paranoid Style in American Politics* (Cambridge, MA: Harvard University Press, 1965), 73–75.

9. Bonomi, *Under the Cope of Heaven*, 209–211.

10. Drew Gilpin Faust, *The Creation of Confederate Nationalism: Ideology and Identity in the Civil War South* (Baton Rouge: Louisiana State University Press, 1988), 22, quoted in Luke E. Harlow, "Slavery Race and Political Ideology in the White Christian South before and after the Civil War," in Noll and Harlow, *Religion and American Politics*, 205). For one example of Northern zeal, see Richard Cowardine, "Methodists, Politics, and the Coming of the American Civil War," in Noll and Harlow, *Religion and American Politics*, 193–94; J. L. Hicks, *Christianity, War, and Politics: Can a Man Be a Christian and Kill His Fellow-Man? The Christian's Relationship to Christ and the World* (Abilene, TX: Self-published, 1898), 2, 10, 20.

11. The radical dissenters among poor people's churches have been chronicled elsewhere. See Kyle Wilkison, *Yeomen, Sharecroppers, and Socialists: Plain Folk Protest in Texas, 1870–1914* (College Station: Texas A&M University Press, 2008), 125–60.

12. *Baptist Standard* (Dallas, TX), August 26, 1904, 2; Walter N. Vernon, *Methodism Moves across North Texas*, (n.p.: Historical Society, North Texas Conference, Methodist Church, 1967), 151.

13. *Baptist Standard*, February 22, 1900, 8; *Minutes of the Hunt Baptist Association, 1911*, p. 29, microfilm edition, Southern Baptist Historical Archives, Nashville, TN.

14. J. R. Barrett, "An Article on Land Ownership," *Commerce (Texas) Journal*, November 18, 1910, 3.

15. Morgan A. Smith, "Ownership of Land," *Commerce Journal*, November 25, 1910, 1.

16. Barrett, "Reply from J. R. Barrett," *Commerce Journal*, December 2, 1910, 1.

17. *Commerce Journal*, December 9, 1910, 1.

18. Barrett, "Barrett Replies to Smith Again," *Commerce Journal*, December 16, 1910, 1.

19. J. L. Hicks and J. B. Cranfill clippings, Box 1, Folder 228-1-3, Scrapbook 1, pp. 153–57, Hicks Family Papers Collection, Texas Labor Archives, Special Collections Division, University of Texas at Arlington Libraries, Arlington, TX.

20. *Baptist Standard*, May 9, 1901, 3; May 16, 1901, 4; December 12, 1901, 1; January 11, 1900, 4.

21. *Baptist Standard*, January 11, 1900, p. 1; June 6, 1912, 25; Harrell, "Sectional Origins of Churches of Christ," 273–74. Lemmons also worried about injustice to railroad corporations in *The Devil and Socialism*, 212–15.

22. A North Carolina denominational newspaper expressed the logical conclusion of this line of thinking when it asserted that "poverty resulted 'directly or indirectly from some transgression of divine law.'" Frederick Bode, "Religion and Class Hegemony: A Populist Critique in North Carolina," *Journal of Southern History* 37 (August 1971): 425.

23. Boyd E. Morgan, *Arkansas Angels* (Paragould, AR: College Bookstore and Press, 1967), 45–46.

24. Robert C. Hooper, *Crying in the Wilderness: A Biography of David Lipscomb* (Nash-

ville: David Lipscomb College, 1979), 11, 228, 231, 233. For an example of remaining quietism among the Texas Church of Christ, see G. H. P. Showalter to T. A. Hickey, *The Rebel*, February 28, 1914, 2.

25. William F. Lemmons, *The Evils of Socialism* (Austin: Firm Foundation Press, 1912), 3, 64.

26. *Firm Foundation*, February 13, 1912, 6; Lemmons, *Evils of Socialism*, 68.

27. Lemmons, *Evils of Socialism*, 4–5, 8–9, 12–13, 16, 29–30, 31–32, 35, 40–42, 76–86.

28. Ibid., 12–15, 40–41, 63.

29. Ibid., 49.

30. Ibid., 51–52, 57, 69.

31. Ibid., 21, 76–86.

32. Ibid., 66–67. The Socialist *Rebel* printed a spate of rebuttals from nineteen of Lemmons's fellow Church of Christ ministers, defending their support of the Socialist Party. They argued that in spite of its "infidel" founders, the Socialist Party's demands represented the best chance for the fulfillment of their hopes for an economy based on primitive Christianity. They also pointed out that churchgoing Democrats seemed to have no trouble supporting "infidel" Thomas Jefferson's party. Shortly after the appearance of *The Evils of Socialism*, a major left-wing newspaper retorted with Henry M. Tichenor's *The Evils of Capitalism: A Reply to W. F. Lemmons' Book, "The Evils of Socialism"* (n.p.: National Rip-Saw Publishing Company, 1912). The *Rebel*, Texas' official Socialist Party organ, launched repeated rebuttals and attacks on Lemmons from May 1912 through October 1915 that ran the gamut of the entire range of debating technique, including ad hominem. The *Rebel*, March 14, 1914, 2; August 26, 1911, 3; March 30, 1912, 2; April 13, 1912, 1; May, 11 1912, 1–3; June 29, 1912, 4; May 17, 1913, 2; September 10, 1915, 4; Peter H. Buckingham, *Rebel against Injustice: The Life of Frank P. O'Hare* (Columbia: University of Missouri Press, 1996).

33. Lemmons, *Devil and Socialism*, 280–81.

34. Ibid., 77, 202, 215, 220, 226–28.

35. Ibid., 78.

36. Ibid., 91, 253–55.

37. Ibid., 220, 255, 21, 262–63.

38. Ibid., 108, 246.

39. Dochuk, *From Bible Belt to Sunbelt.*

40. Wilkison, *Yeomen, Sharecroppers, and Socialists*, 125–60.

41. Chad Pearson, "What's So New about the 'New Right'? Rethinking the Origins of Postwar Anti-Unionism," presented at the Organization of American Historians, Washington DC, April 2010, cited in Phillips-Fein, "Conservatism," 738.

"He, Being Dead, Yet Speaketh"

J. Frank Norris and the Texas Religious Right at Midcentury

SAMUEL K. TULLOCK

J. Frank Norris's attention-grabbing rhetoric from the pulpit both carried on the old traditions and provided new models for Texas political preachers of the Right. His themes mixed old warnings of threats to constitutional government, warnings against alien influence and socialism, accusations of disloyalty against opponents, and the old appeals to traditional values and use of biblical imagery to frighten voters into action. But Norris was flexible enough to curtail his anti-Catholic pronouncements once he decided the Catholic Church was a stalwart anticommunist ally, and even earlier, he rejected the anti-Semitism of reactionary allies. His early support for the new nation of Israel became a significant contribution to the rhetoric of the politically conservative Texas pulpit. Likewise, Norris had lent tacit support to the New Klan in Texas during its 1920s heyday but backed away once their popularity faded. The constant throughout his career was adherence to Christian fundamentalism.

American fundamentalism emerged from the nineteenth-century Bible Conference Movement, and in its early years centered leadership and activism in the North. The South, already steeped in social and religious conservatism, did not provide a ready breeding ground for fundamentalist reformers. Modernism seemed but a distant threat, and conservative leaders were the norm. In the 1920s, Frank Norris, pastor at Fort Worth's First Baptist Church, changed all that. Convincing his enthusiastic followers that modernists and political liberals had infiltrated Dixie, Norris devoted himself to immunizing the South from, as he perceived, these ungodly and un-American contaminants. His efforts helped transform the social, political, and religious milieu of Texas.

John Franklyn Norris was born to an Alabama farming family on September 18, 1877.[1] His parents, Warner and Mary Norris, moved to Hill County, Texas, in the late 1880s. According to Norris, his father's alcoholism condemned the family to poverty; nevertheless, young Frank overcame the deprivation and violence, aided in part by a religious conversion during his teen years, at a local revival meeting. Sensing a call to pastoral work, he attended Baylor University while pastoring small churches in Hill County. Financial assistance from a family doctor and the kindness of Baylor professor John S. Tanner enabled Norris to graduate in 1903.[2] After his Baylor years, Norris earned a master of divinity from Southern Baptist Theological Seminary in Louisville, Kentucky.[3]

After graduating as valedictorian of his seminary class, Norris accepted the pastorate of the McKinney Avenue Baptist Church in Dallas, Texas, and for a time edited the *Baptist Standard*, Texas Baptists' flagship periodical.[4] His early successes opened the door for Norris to assume the pastorate of First Baptist in Fort Worth in 1909, and during his early years in Fort Worth, Norris played a significant role in the founding of Southwestern Baptist Theological Seminary. For several years it appeared that Norris would become a respected, influential leader among Texas Baptists; however, following a mysterious experience during a revival meeting in Owensboro, Kentucky, in 1910 his ministry underwent a remarkable transformation.[5] Norris lieutenants later claimed that the Owensboro revival persuaded Norris to abandon the staid ministry strategies that characterized his early professional years, in favor of sensationalism and public controversy.

Always quarrelsome and combative, the "Texas Tornado" returned to Fort Worth determined to use conflict and bombast to garner attention.[6] His campaigns against Fort Worth's Hell's Half Acre and the increasing melodrama of his sermons alienated his more demure church members, and Fort Worth elites left the church in droves. Nonetheless, thousands of the "folks between the forks of the creek" poured into the membership.[7] Newspapers filled their pages with spectacular stories about Norris, including news of felony indictments for arson, perjury, and even murder.[8]

As Norris's renown grew, he became a centerpiece, along with Northern fundamentalists, in a dizzying array of new fundamentalist organizations, including the World's Christian Fundamentals Association and the Bible

Baptists Union of America. By 1924 his involvement with non–Southern Baptists and his constant irritation of Texas denominational leaders caused an acrimonious break with the Tarrant Baptist Association and the Baptist General Convention of Texas. Nor did Norris restrict himself to intramural controversies. He began to weigh in on local politics as well. In 1926, during a particularly rancorous Fort Worth mayoral campaign, an incensed supporter of the incumbent burst into Norris's church office. Norris, claiming to believe his life was in danger, drew a pistol from his desk and killed D. E. Chipps. The murder trial held in Austin exonerated Norris on the grounds of self-defense.[9]

The murder trial marked a critical turning point in Norris's career. Though occasionally involved in local controversies, he increasingly focused his political involvement on state or national concerns, perhaps in an effort to draw attention away from residual public preoccupation with Chipps. The 1928 presidential campaign gave Norris such an opportunity, and New York Democrat Alfred Smith provided a convenient target for the Fort Worth fundamentalist's newest crusade, a crusade that foreshadowed this nominal Democrat's support for the Texas Right and the national Republican Party. He was, above all, an opportunist with an uncanny talent for identifying issues and trends that fostered his own brand of self-promotion and sensationalism.

The 1928 election pitted Republican Herbert Hoover against Democrat Al Smith in a campaign largely focused on religion and Prohibition. Norris perceived Smith, a Catholic and opponent of Prohibition, as a puppet of Tammany Hall and an agent of liberalism and corrupt "machine politics." Few of Norris's sermons or articles extolled the Republican candidate's qualifications or experience; instead, they focused on the supposed danger of a Smith presidency.

The Democrats selected Smith to run against Hoover because they believed he could unite the wet and dry factions of the party. Though personally opposed to Prohibition, Smith promised to uphold the law. Fundamentalists like Norris distrusted Smith's public stand on the issue because of the candidate's Catholic background. To little avail, Smith defended his Catholicism and called for religious tolerance. Many Southern conservatives, including Norris, feared a Catholic president would be a pawn of Rome.[10]

Norris cataloged his opposition to Smith in a pamphlet entitled "Six Reasons Why Al Smith Should Not Be President of the United States." Norris projected that Smith's opposition to the Eighteenth Amendment revealed a conspiracy to undermine the Constitution of the United States. Conjuring sinister images such as that of Sacco and Vanzetti, Norris argued a Smith presidency would tend toward anarchy and lawlessness. "The same process of reasoning that would nullify one part of the Constitution will nullify any or every part of the same authority."[11] This portion of the pamphlet verges on incoherence, bouncing from one example to the next of "liberalism and anarchy" while trying to convince his readers that Smith embodied these unsavory qualities.

Norris opposed Smith's connection with Tammany Hall, which the pastor equated with foreign influence and corrupt big-city politics. He claimed that New York was no longer an American city; rather, it floundered under foreign ownership and control. Tammany Hall, and its minions like Smith, reflected this alien, anti-American mind-set and prompted political corruption and graft.[12]

Furthermore, Norris disapproved of Smith's supposed allegiance to an alien power, the Roman Catholic Church. This fundamentalist argument was standard fare against Catholics. The pamphlet recounts Cardinal Bonzano's visit to the United States during Smith's governorship of New York, and it recalled accounts of Smith bowing before the cardinal, kissing his ring. "This act of obeisance, of subservience to a foreign potentate was the most un-American act ever flung in the face of liberty-loving American citizens."[13]

The pamphlet reached its crescendo when Norris challenged Smith's views on religious tolerance. Norris poured out a litany of charges that ranged from the allegation that Smith would refuse to kiss the inaugural Bible, as had previous presidents, to charging that the Democratic nominee would not recognize the legitimacy of marriages performed outside the Roman Catholic Church. He even suggested that Catholics, emboldened by a Smith presidency, might engage in the execution of their enemies: "Yes, if Rome had it in her power every Protestant church would go up in smoke and every Protestant minister would be burned at the stake, for Rome never changes."[14]

Norris's fifth argument raised concern about the separation of church and state. He marshaled several quotations from Catholic leaders who asserted the right of the church to utilize the power of the sword and included a lengthy quotation from William Gladstone expressing concern over Catholic entanglement in nineteenth-century British politics.[15]

Norris's final argument focused on Prohibition. The pamphlet rehearsed Smith's record on the alcohol issue from 1907 to 1927 and called on the women of the country to take up militant opposition to the liquor traffic. Norris concluded with a call for fundamentalist solidarity, equating Protestantism with American identity: "Come on, all you infidels, on all you bootleggers; come on all you gamblers: come on all you anarchists; come on all you Bolsheviks; come on all you Roman Catholics—Protestantism will meet you and be your Waterloo."[16]

Regularly, anti-Smith articles appeared in the *Searchlight*, Norris's weekly newspaper. Throughout the summer and fall of 1928 he peppered the paper's pages with articles with such titles as "Will the South Sell Its Soul to Tammany Hall?"; "First Hand Facts on Al Smith's Wet Record"; and "The Baylor University Al Smith Club: They Have Defiled the Oldest and Greatest Baptist University."[17] The pamphlet did not introduce race into the campaign rhetoric, but on other occasions, Norris railed against Tammany Hall and Smith for appointing African Americans to governmental positions and promoting racial intermarriage. Elsewhere during the campaign he warned that the Democratic Party was becoming untrustworthy in the battle "to maintain our white supremacy."[18]

In addition to his publications, Norris initiated an impressive personal correspondence in opposition to Smith. Norris pledged to work with Republican National Committee leader Rentfro Barton Creager to persuade Texas Baptist preachers to support Hoover. Moreover, he expressed hope the Democrats would nominate Smith, thereby weakening their hold on Texas. He promised to declare for Hoover from the pulpit on the following Sunday and expressed optimism his announcement would strengthen the resolve of Republicans in other parts of the country.[19] Creager, for his part, seemed welcoming but cautious in dealing with the master controversialist.[20]

After Hoover's nomination in the Kansas City Republican National Convention, Norris corresponded with the candidate, and after winning the election, grateful Republicans gathered at First Baptist Church to present the pastor with a wristwatch that bore the inscription "The man who did more than any man to carry the state for Hoover."[21] They also invited the contentious minister to attend the inauguration. No doubt, Norris believed he had secured his rightful place as a moving force in national politics.

Norris's vitriolic rhetoric and admixture of religion and politics foreshadowed significant developments in Texas fundamentalism: fears of threats to the Constitution, suspicions about alien influences, portrayal of political opponents as socialists, questioning the patriotism and allegiance of candidates, the appeal of conservative social issues to persuade voters, and the use of biblical imagery to alarm the citizenry. While Norris certainly took advantage of long-held Southern proclivities, such as the anti-Catholic bias, he introduced new elements into Texas conservatism.

George Marsden characterized fundamentalism's 1920s political involvement as haphazard and "drifting rather than moving purposefully."[22] Aside from issues such as evolution and Prohibition, fundamentalists evidenced little coherence as a political movement. The career of Frank Norris signaled a change in that trend. From the 1928 presidential campaign to the end of his life, he evidenced a clear political agenda that set the stage for the highly organized fundamentalist groups that emerged in the 1970s and 1980s. He contributed to the weakened hold of the Democratic Party on Texas politics, emphasizing conservative social issues over economic policy, and blurred the lines of the separation of church and state, a time-honored principle of Baptist life. Though he affected a homespun populism, appealing to the "folks between the forks of the creek," he also conversed with the country's highest political figures and interacted with international politicians as well. It proves difficult, however, to assign ideological motives for his political involvement. Inconsistent support of Republican candidates after 1928 indicates that he was an opportunist rather than an ideologue.

With the coming of the Great Depression, Norris defended Hoover for a time; however, the increasingly dire economic circumstances finally subdued his support. During the 1932 presidential campaign, the *Fundamentalist* concentrated its attention elsewhere. Caught between the growing unpopularity of Hoover and the liberal, anti-Prohibition stance of Roosevelt, Norris simply chose to remain silent throughout the campaign. However, during the early years of the new presidential administration Norris voiced support for the New Deal.

Though encumbered with staggering financial burdens of its own, the First Baptist Church tried to meet the overwhelming needs of the Fort Worth poor during the early stages of the depression. The *Fundamentalist* announced that the church provided baths, cots, clothes, and food for more than seven thousand people over a two-week period.[23] By March 1934 Norris estimated the church had given away "132,790 meals, 130,297 gallons of milk, and 12,125 articles of clothing."[24]

In this March 23, 1934, edition of the *Fundamentalist*, Norris compared Roosevelt to the Old Testament statesman Nehemiah. Though rambling and difficult to follow, the article endorsed Roosevelt and his New Deal policies. Norris lamented the fact that, in spite of First Baptist's herculean efforts to meet the needs of the poor, the church had failed to sustain the relief programs. Norris rejoiced that "the government came to our relief and has taken over the feeding of the hungry thousands, and they can do it far better than any church."[25]

Furthermore, Norris scolded the Supreme Court for opposing various aspects of the president's economic program. He reminded the Court that "there was a higher law, the law of humanity. . . . That is the Roosevelt program—humanity." Amazingly, Norris even called for the country to yield dictatorial powers to the president and set in motion policies that would redistribute wealth: "There must be a redistribution of the wealth of this country, for it isn't fair for 35 million men, women, and children to be on the bread line, when there is plenty and enough to spare."[26] These surprising views apparently grew from Norris's frustration with the depression and the inability of First Baptist to cope with the astounding needs of the city's poor. Like many Americans, he was desperate enough to accept help from any quarter. Also, Norris seemed to fear violent social unrest if the government did not provide some safety valve to release economic pressure. Nevertheless, Norris did not espouse these views for long, perhaps eighteen months. By August 1935 Norris dramatically revised his views of the New Deal to see it as a communist plot that threatened the foundations of American democracy.[27]

On August 6, 1935, Norris addressed several hundred Detroit businessmen in a speech entitled "The New Deal Uncovered." Norris charged: "The New Deal comes to us with the hands of democracy, but with the voice of Moscow; it comes like Absalom sitting in the gates stealing the hearts of the American people. While at the same time it reaches forth and tears the Stars and Stripes from its mast and unfurls the Red flag of Communism . . . it comes with a smile like Joab, only to thrust the sword of treachery into our vitals. That's the New Deal."[28]

In addition, Norris severely criticized Eleanor Roosevelt as a "socialist sympathizer and associate" and "pacifist," then listed more than thirty connections of Mrs. Roosevelt with alleged "Red" organizations.[29] According to Norris, the Supreme Court was the only barrier against the New Deal carrying the country into socialism. Reversing his position from a year earlier, Norris vilified the president for "defying the courts" and called for Roosevelt's impeachment if he continued.[30] What changed?

Clovis Gwin Morris surmises that Norris's close association with Detroit industrialists, beginning in late 1934, occasioned a reconsideration of the pastor's perspective.[31] While acknowledging that Norris had much to gain from a relationship with Ford and General Motors, Barry Hankins argues that Norris's political reversal was based primarily in his objections to Northern Baptist modernism (which had coincidentally embraced the social gospel) and that Norris felt compelled, when attacking modernism, to attack the left-leaning social gospel along with the New Deal. Powerful opposition to the New Deal in Texas may have influenced Norris as well. In any event, Norris turned on the New Deal with a rhetorical vengeance.[32]

Detroit hosted an annual fundamentalist Bible conference beginning in the mid-1920s, and the 1934 meeting boasted an impressive docket of preachers that included Billy Sunday and J. Frank Norris. Supporters raised a huge tent, provided by anti–New Dealer Henry Ford, and for weeks thousands flocked to the evening meetings. In September, Norris preached the concluding sermons of the great revival.[33]

His eloquence impressed the members of the pulpit committee of Detroit's Temple Baptist Church, who urged the combative Texan to become their pastor, but he returned to Fort Worth without giving them an answer. In fact, Norris might never have accepted their invitation if not for a controversy that seemed to suit Norris's insatiable appetite for attention. Norris agreed to return to Detroit to lead an evangelistic campaign for the Temple Baptist Church, and the Detroit congregation spared no expense in promoting the meeting and arranged for crowds to gather at a local high school auditorium. The first Sunday proved a great success, but trouble—the kind Norris relished—awaited the second night of the revival.[34] Norris's paper reported that on Monday evening school board members turned away more than two thousand people from the school auditorium, claiming that a "mistake had been made."[35] Norris and his Detroit supporters believed they saw the hand of the Detroit Baptist Union at work to close the doors on Norris. As members of the Northern Baptist Convention, the Detroit Baptist Union anticipated that Norris might create the same denominational turmoil in the North that he had fostered in Texas. They were right. The master controversialist seized the opportunity to re-create in Detroit something of his old Texas melodrama. At the conclusion of the meeting, the Temple Church pulpit committee renewed their efforts to persuade Norris, and the deacons enthusiastically recommended the church extend a formal "call" to come to Detroit. Norris accepted with the conditions that he retain his position in Fort Worth and that the Temple congregation yield absolute control of the church to him. Amazingly, the church accepted his terms.[36]

Several considerations may have persuaded Norris to assume the dual pastorates of First Baptist in Fort Worth and Detroit's Temple Baptist. Norris savored controversy; however, his combativeness had grown stale in Texas, especially after the Chipps trial. Also, it proved increasingly difficult to bait Texas Baptists into contention, and Norris floundered without a war to fight. The new pastorate provided Norris an arena to spar anew with modernists.

The fundamentalist-modernist controversy in the Northern Baptist Convention provided Norris an opportunity to reenact glorious battles with the Southern Baptist Convention. Northern religious conservatives like William Bell Riley, while remaining faithful to fundamentalist ideology, had increasingly withdrawn from the public fray. Northern fundamentalists needed a shot in the arm, and Norris believed he was just the prescription needed. When Northern Baptist leaders criticized him, he sought to rally his supporters with the bombastic language of warfare against the "political whip" and their "little machine" trying to conquer his church for "modernism."[37] Norris persuaded Temple Baptist Church to withdraw from the Northern Baptist Convention in 1935.[38]

In addition, Norris found the Detroit opportunity irresistible because large numbers of transplanted Southerners attended the Temple Baptist Church, and many others made their homes in Detroit, working in the automobile plants and other heavy industry. Norris therefore had a ready-made audience for his brand of Southern revivalism. Labor shortages during World War I forced automakers to hire large numbers of African American workers, and in the late 1920s many poor, Southern whites found jobs in Detroit as well. Labor unrest and racial tension followed this migration. Men like Frank Norris no doubt added to the white supremacy rhetoric of Detroit.[39]

Temple Baptist Church furthermore gave Norris a platform, long sought and heretofore unsuccessful, to extend his influence into the North. Years earlier he had attempted to expand his authority northward by building alliances with Northern fundamentalists; unfortunately for Norris, these uneasy alliances proved fragile and did not stand the test of time. He intended now to sustain his work in Fort Worth while extending his religious and political empire without the encumbrance of rival leaders.

A third factor in Norris's attraction to Detroit centered on his associations with industrialists. Prior to his dramatic reversal on the New Deal, Norris portrayed himself as the champion of the "people between the forks of the creek." Beginning in 1934 Norris came to have significant interaction with Detroit industrial leaders, and he relished the attention brought by these associations. Perhaps these business leaders, aware of the significant labor unrest of the mid-1930s, sought to anesthetize their workforce by bringing in culturally appealing Southern religious leaders whom they hoped would calm some of the labor storm of the period. It does not take much imagination to conceive of Norris as one of these "anesthetic" ministers. The question, it seems, is whether Norris consciously participated in this unsavory misuse of religion or, like others, he simply succumbed to the money and flattery of the industrialists. Also, his association with industrial leaders opened new political doors for Norris, especially as seen in his correspondence with Congressmen Tom Connally and Sam Rayburn. By 1938 Norris was explicitly claiming that only his brand of religion could save America and its industries. In an interview with the *New York Times* the "flying pastor" informed the reporter that "American industrialists" wanted a religious revival because they—and he, presumably—thought it the only way to save the country from communism. Norris claimed that Detroit was even then "in the throes of a revolution" and advocated that "foreign subversive groups" should be "smashed." Chief among those to be smashed, he named the Congress of Industrial Organization (CIO), the militant parent union of the United Auto Workers, and specified its founding president, John L. Lewis, "as our greatest threat."[40]

Above all, for Norris, his affiliation with Temple Baptist relieved the financial burdens of the First Baptist Church, the *Fundamentalist*, and the Bible Baptist Seminary. Royce Measures asserts that Norris needed Temple Baptist more than it needed him. Because of the 1929 fire that destroyed First Baptist and the devastation of the Great Depression, Norris's Texas kingdom stood on the brink of financial ruin. According to Measures, the economic strength of the Detroit congregation provided much-needed capital for the church in Fort Worth, and Norris siphoned large amounts of money from Detroit to Fort Worth.[41]

The administration of the daily affairs of the two large congregations fell largely to the hands of two capable Norris associates, Louis Entzminger in Texas and G. Beauchamp Vick in Michigan. Indeed, within a few years, for all practical purposes, Vick pastored the Detroit church. Norris functioned more as a figurehead for his expansive empire than as a pastor of a local church. In this sense, he created an organizational model for late twentieth-century and early twenty-first-century megachurches. But in the late 1940s the unwieldy structure proved unstable, and a conflict arose over the leadership of the Detroit church and the Bible Baptist Seminary, causing an irreparable breach between Norris and Vick. Yet for sixteen years the dual pastorate enabled Norris to accomplish critical achievements. In addition to relieving the financial constraints of the empire, this arrangement empowered Norris to shift the epicenter of fundamentalism from the North to the South with both religious and political repercussions.[42]

Ironically, at the height of the New Deal controversy, Norris associated himself with the popular Texas governor James V. Allred, a vigorous supporter of Roosevelt. It appears that Norris's love of the spotlight trumped political consistency. On the other hand, despite his connection to Allred, Norris also had ties to the Jeffersonian Democrats, a right-wing national and Texas group committed to ending the New Deal and defeating Roosevelt in 1936. Led in Texas by such Texas Right stalwarts as John Henry Kirby and J. Evetts Haley, the Jeffersonian Democrats considered nominating a third-party candidate; however, in the end they refrained from leaving the Democratic Party, instead deciding to endorse some Republicans in local and state campaigns. While failing to defeat Roosevelt on the national stage, in Texas the Right triumphed in the 1938 gubernatorial race with the victory of the conservative W. Lee O'Daniel. Norris noisily congratulated the governor-elect with a bold prophecy. "Texas will give the nation its next President," Norris wrote to O'Daniel. The country, Norris assured the next governor of Texas, was "looking for a Moses to lead it back to such fundamentals as home and God." Like Norris, much of O'Daniel's popularity was based in the new technology of radio broadcasts. With his brilliantly constructed persona as a Texas country boy, O'Daniel could have been an even less authentic secular version of Norris himself. The new governor of Texas claimed his election was the work of God and "a great victory for the clear-thinking Christian people of Texas."[43]

During the late 1940s, Norris seemed desperate to remain relevant. Roosevelt's death in 1945 robbed the old controversialist of his liberal presidential foil, and Norris never seemed to know how to respond to Harry Truman. At times the Texas fundamentalist expressed support for Truman, especially in regard to the president's anticommunist policies; however, to the degree Truman continued New Deal programs, Norris balked. Surprisingly, Truman's plan to appoint an ambassador to the Vatican met with Norris's approval, a step the old fundamentalist saw as a safeguard against the spread of communism. Fellow fundamentalists like T. T. Shields roundly criticized Norris's position, but the old anticommunist warrior remained steadfast, now convinced that Catholics would prove valuable allies against communism. His opportunism clearly trumped the anti-Catholicism of the Smith versus Hoover campaign.

On April 20, 1949, Frank Norris addressed the Texas state legislature. Tarrant County representative Doyle Willis had introduced a resolution to recognize the anticommunist contributions of Norris, and the state legislature tepidly approved the motion. Norris's legislative speech identified three enemies to America: radical labor leadership, liberal university professors, and mainstream clergymen. Norris was careful to legitimate some labor organizations, placing the blame for the radicalization of unions on a few unnamed leaders while—ironically—commending John L. Lewis. He then turned his guns on certain state university professors who, abusing their privileged tenure status, undermined democracy and capitalism. The state legislature, Norris opined, should fire these professors. Finally, he addressed modernist clergymen like Atlanta's Louie Newton (unnamed in the speech), who tacitly endorsed Joseph Stalin. Newton made a much-publicized journey to the Soviet Union, and, somewhat naively, observed the high quality of life and religious freedom enjoyed by Soviet citizens. He acknowledged his limited exposure to Russian life, but Norris, not given to nuance, seized the opportunity to impugn Newton. Norris, near the conclusion of his talk, blamed Northern African Americans for the alleged growth of communism in the United States, a trend, he avowed, which grew from blacks' desire to intermarry with whites. Norris concluded the speech with, "To hell with Joe Stalin!" The legislature responded with prolonged applause.[44]

Norris died a few months before the 1952 election, but in the weeks before his death, the old warrior embraced the Eisenhower candidacy. Health concerns limited Norris to radio pronouncements, but he endorsed Eisenhower's wartime leadership and Nixon's anticommunist record. Since 1928, Norris had evidenced Republican sympathies, but the hardship of the depression and Roosevelt's World War II popularity erected insurmountable obstacles for a preacher who liked being on the winning side. Rather than face the embarrassment of supporting losing candidates, he simply remained silent, or he played both sides against the middle. Had he lived, Norris would have enjoyed the 1952 election.

The political legacy of J. Frank Norris centers on a few critical issues. First, Norris helped loosen the South's Democratic Party moorings. Other factors, of course, contributed to the South's political transformation, but those changes had their genesis in Norris's opposition to Al Smith and the perceived liberal drift of the Democrats, a trend Norris interpreted as evidence of encroaching communism and modernism. He saw Smith's anti-Prohibition politics as an attack on family values, a familiar theme in future Republican campaigns in Texas. Also, Norris's racial views—reflecting the prevailing attitudes of many other white Southerners—clashed with Northern Democrats' increasing willingness to endorse racial equality.

Second, and particularly critical, Norris made political involvement the norm. Traditionally, Southern Baptists carefully guarded the separation of church and state, though at times, temperance concerns pushed some leaders to engage in political activism. However, Norris exceeded the boundaries of Baptist polity and historical example. Baptist leaders like George W. Truett (1867–1944), longtime pastor of First Baptist Dallas, refused to address political issues from the pulpit, but Truett's successor, W. A. Criswell, followed the example of Norris. The Fort Worth fundamentalist justified his actions by pointing out the religious implications of political decisions, but he set few boundaries to protect the separation of church and state.

Like Norris, Criswell presided over the largest Baptist congregation of his generation. More genteel than Norris, Criswell nonetheless provoked a great tempest within Southern Baptist circles on more than one occasion. Both men came from hardscrabble agrarian backgrounds, attended Baylor University and Southern Baptist Theological Seminary, pastored large urban churches, espoused biblical inerrancy, and profoundly blurred the lines of church-state separation.[45]

Third, Norris pioneered the megachurch movement. He extended his influence by wielding the power of an enormous ecclesiastical domain. His sensational sermonizing, social combativeness, flamboyant personality, and the massive utilization of the media (print and radio) contributed to his empire building. The move to Detroit extended his influence into the North and provided much-needed capital to sustain the Fort Worth ministries. In time, Norris's work took on a near-denominational outlook. Many young ministers, influenced by Norris, founded new churches, thus adding to the Norris legacy. Contemporary megachurches, following Norris's example, are often characterized by powerful, charismatic leaders, and as history reveals, these churches struggle to maintain stamina when the charismatic leader dies. Such was certainly the case with First Baptist. Nevertheless, the sheer size of these churches fosters the wielding of great social influence, often supported by mass media access.

Norris always alloyed his political actions with personal advancement and ambition. He remained combative but consistently postured himself to end up on the winning side. In addition, after the Chipps murder trial, his political combat took on a different tone and strategy. Norris, while retaining his blustering, sensational bombast, aimed his attacks at more distant and thus safer targets. He never acknowledged retreat or defeat because of the Chipps fiasco, but he never again allowed himself entanglement in unmanageable confrontations with local opponents.

Marsden makes a cogent point that deserves commendation. He asserts that fundamentalists often constructed their political appeals around a variety of conspiracy theories. And quite correctly, Marsden cites Norris as one of the most effective practitioners of this tactic.[46] Norris delighted in dividing the world into dichotomies of evil and righteousness. No gray areas cluttered his mind. His cause was always a righteous one; therefore, those who opposed him did so as part of a larger conspiracy to destroy the moral and religious foundations of the country. His followers developed a siege mentality that strengthened their allegiance to and dependence on Norris. Dragon slayers need dragons. If threats did not seem apparent, the dragon slayer must conjure a danger to maintain relevance. Consequently, fundamentalists like Norris not only did not shun conflict, they thrived on it.

Notes

1. United States Federal Census, 1870, 1880, and 1900. Reports of Norris's early childhood most often came from sermonic accounts, retold by Norris supporters. These men often uncritically accepted the accounts of the Norris family poverty; however, they may have exaggerated the dire circumstances. The census reports indicate that the family owned land, both in Alabama and in Texas.

2. William Frasier, *Fundamentalist*, December 7, 1938, 1. Norris Papers, micro-film collection, A. Webb Roberts Library, Southwestern Baptist Theological Seminary (hereafter SWBTS). Dr. W. A. Wood lent Norris money to cover enrollment fees, and throughout his years at Baylor, Norris boarded with New Testament professor John S. Tanner.

3. Barry Hankins, *God's Rascal: J. Frank Norris and the Beginnings of Southern Fundamentalism* (Lexington: University Press of Kentucky, 1996), 11. Lillian Gaddy Norris was the daughter of prominent Texas Baptist leader J. M. Gaddy and mother of the four Norris children.

4. Joseph Martin Dawson, *A Thousand Months to Remember* (Waco, TX: Baylor University Press, 1964), 95. Norris purchased the paper from T. B. Butler in 1907. Joseph M. Dawson, an old Baylor classmate, assumed editorship of the *Standard*, thus initiating a

combative relationship that never healed. The two leaders met in the household of John S. Tanner at Baylor University, and many years later, Dawson recalled he had no personal difficulties with Norris until their years at the *Standard.*

5. Dwight A. Moody, "The Conversion of J. Frank Norris: A Fresh Look at the Revival of 1910," *Baptist History and Heritage*, June 22, 2010. Moody, former minister at Third Baptist Church in Owensboro, has concluded that the revival occurred in 1910, not 1911, as reported by Norris biographers, in particular Louis Entzminger's *Inside the Cup or My 21 Years in Fort Worth.* According to Moody, Entzminger conflated stories of three revival meetings, one in Kentucky and the others somewhere in Central Texas.

6. The origins of the term "Texas Tornado" remain obscure. Norris's lieutenants frequently used this term of endearment, but Norris may have coined the appellation.

7. Norris frequently used this term in reference to his followers, displaced rural folk who gravitated to cities like Fort Worth. The term clearly was meant to refer to isolated rural dwellers cut off from urban influences.

8. David Stokes, *Apparent Danger: The Pastor of America's First Megachurch and the Texas Murder Trial of the Decade in the 1920s* (Minneapolis: Bascom Hill Books, 2010), 40–46. After fires at the Norris home and First Baptist Church, a 1912 grand jury leveled indictments for perjury, based on Norris's alleged lies about threatening letters, and for arson, based on accusations that Norris set the fires. In 1926 Norris shot D. E. Chipps, a supporter of H. C. Meacham. Juries exonerated Norris in each case. Stokes provides an engaging, popular treatment of Norris's legal woes.

9. Tarrant Baptist Association Minutes, 1922, unpaginated, Roberts Library, SWBTS. The constant conflict between Norris and Southwestern Seminary president Lee R. Scarborough and Norris's unrelenting criticism of seminary faculty led to the Tarrant Association expelling the First Baptist Church. Minutes of the Baptist General Convention of Texas, 1924, pp. 24–25. Similar circumstances, plus Norris's opposition to the Seventy-Five Million Campaign, an effort to centralize Southern Baptist funds, led to First Baptist's exclusion from the Baptist General Convention of Texas in 1924. "Norris Acquitted in Swift Verdict: Jury after Two Ballots Decides Pastor Not Guilty," *New York Times*, January 26, 1927, 1.

10. Robert A. Slayton, *Empire Statesmen: The Rise and Redemption of Al Smith* (New York: Free Press, 2001), 251–62; Norman Brown, *Hood Bonnet and Little Brown Jug: Texas Politics, 1921–1928* (College Station: Texas A&M University Press, 1984); William A. DeGregorio, *The Complete Book of U.S. Presidents: From George Washington to Bill Clinton* (New York: Wings Books, 1993), 468–69.

11. J. Frank Norris, "Six Reasons Why Al Smith Should Not Be the Next President of the United States," p. 1, self-published pamphlet, 1926, Norris Papers, Roberts Library, SWBTS. The Roberts Library has organized and indexed most of the Norris Collection; however, some of the materials remain in boxes, unindexed.

12. Ibid.

13. Ibid., 2.

14. Ibid., 5–7.

15. Ibid., 9.

16. Ibid., 11.

17. These articles appeared on the front page of Norris's weekly paper, *Searchlight*, on the following dates: "Will the South Sell Its Soul to Tammany Hall?," July 13, 1928; "First Hand Facts on Al Smith's Wet Record," August 17, 1928; "The Baylor University Al Smith Club: They Have Defiled the Oldest and Greatest Baptist University," October 26, 1928. The periodical also went by the names *Fence Rail* and *Fundamentalist.* From 1917 to 1927 he called the paper *Searchlight.* Norris Papers, SWBTS.

18. J. Frank Norris, *Fundamentalist*, October 26, 1928, 1, Norris Papers, SWBTS; Hankins, *God's Rascal*, 164.

19. J. Frank Norris to R. B. Creager, January 19, 1928, Norris Papers, SWBTS.

20. R. B. Creager to J. Frank Norris, March 21, 1928, and September 6, 1928, Norris Papers, SWBTS.

21. *Searchlight*, November 9, 1928.

22. George Marsden, *Fundamentalism and American Culture: The Shaping of Twentieth-Century Evangelicalism, 1870–1925* (New York: Oxford University Press, 1980), 208.

23. J. Frank Norris, *Fundamentalist*, January 6, 1933, 1, Norris Papers, SWBTS.

24. J. Frank Norris, "Fifteen Bible Reasons Why [*sic*] Support Roosevelt's Recovery: We Have Mortgaged Our Land—Roosevelt a Modern Nehemiah," *Fundamentalist*, March 23, 1934, 1–2, 5–7, Norris Papers, SWBTS.

25. Ibid., 2.

26. Ibid.

27. Hankins, *God's Rascal*, 99–101.

28. J. Frank Norris, "The New Deal Uncovered," self-published pamphlet, August 6, 1935, 11–12. Norris Papers, SWBTS.

29. Ibid., 13–14.

30. Ibid., 16.

31. Clovis Gwin Morris, "He Changed Things: The Life and Thought of J. Frank Norris" (PhD diss., Texas Tech University, 1973.

32. Hankins, *God's Rascal*, 99–103.

33. J. Frank Norris, "Frank Norris Stirs Detroit," *Fundamentalist*, September 28, 1934, Norris Papers, SWBTS.

34. William Fraser, *Fundamentalist*, December 7, 1941, 1, Norris Papers, SWBTS.

35. Ibid.

36. Homer G. Ritchie, "The Life and Legend of J. Frank Norris: The Fighting Parson" (PhD diss., Texas Christian University, 1991), 183.

37. Ibid., 184.

38. Hankins, *God's Rascal*, 90.

39. Robert H. Craig, *Religion and Radical Politics: An Alternative Christian Tradition in the United States* (Philadelphia: Temple University Press, 1992), 168. Discerning Norris's connection with the Klan proves difficult. No evidence indicates his formal involvement, but he allowed the Klan to use First Baptist facilities for Klan activities.

40. The Norris Papers, SWBTS, contain numerous letters and telegrams from Norris

to Rayburn and Connally. "Religious Revival Held the Only Hope: 'Flying Pastor' Says Nation Faces a Minority Dictatorship," *New York Times* June 19, 1938, *ProQuest Historical Newspapers: The New York Times (1851–2007)*, 2.

41. Undoubtedly, the fire and the depression stifled First Baptist's work, and Norris did funnel substantial amounts of money from Detroit into the printing operations of the *Fundamentalist*; however, he exerted great effort in raising funds while conducting revival meetings throughout the country. Measures largely based his conclusions on the charges of Beauchamp Vick, Norris's "lieutenant" in Detroit; however, as is discussed in this chapter, Vick's motives for such claims may have resulted from a personal rupture that ended their friendship. Whatever the case, it seems reasonable that Norris's handling of Temple Baptist's money contributed to the deteriorating relationship between the two congregations. Royce Measures, "Men and Movements Influenced by J. Frank Norris" (ThD diss., Southwestern Baptist Theological Seminary, 1976).

42. Entzminger worked with Norris, off and on, for many years. Indeed, much of the Sunday school success at First Baptist depended on Entzminger's leadership and considerable organizational skills. In addition to his managerial expertise, he proved an able motivator for the army of volunteer workers needed to staff a large Sunday school, and despite the steady parade of controversies, he remained a loyal supporter and friend when many others turned on Norris in the late 1940s and early 1950s. After a short period of organizational work in Detroit, "Entz" returned to Fort Worth to assume the primary administrative role at First Baptist. Vick, on the other hand, had served as a youth worker in Fort Worth during the mid-1920s, and from 1928 to 1936 he directed music in the large crusades of Southern evangelist Mordecai Hamm. In this capacity he visited Temple Baptist Church in a crusade in 1936–37. After Entzminger returned to Fort Worth, Norris named Vick superintendent of Temple Baptist Church. Norris continued to spend most of his time in Fort Worth but came to Detroit for extended periods of ministry. As his health began to fail, however, and outside preaching responsibilities demanded more of the old man's energies, he gradually yielded more authority to Vick. Morris, "He Changed Things," 373.

43. George N. Green, *The Establishment in Texas Politics: The Primitive Years, 1938–1957* (Norman: University of Oklahoma Press, 1984), 25, 30; "Maverick Appears Defeated," *New York Times*, July 25, 1938, 1.

44. J. Frank Norris, Address to the Texas State Legislature, Norris Papers, SWBTS. Norris delivered this speech April 20, 1949, in Austin.

45. Oran P. Smith, *The Rise of Baptist Republicanism* (New York: New York University Press, 1997), 40–41, 84–85; Chandler Davidson, *Race and Class in Texas Politics* (Princeton, NJ: Princeton University Press, 1990), 212–16. These works provide helpful summaries of Criswell's influence on Baptist politics, particularly Criswell's opposition to John Kennedy's presidential aspirations.

46. George Marsden, *Fundamentalism and American Culture: The Shaping of Twentieth-Century Evangelicalism, 1870–1925* (New York: Oxford University Press, 1980), 210–11.

The Far Right in Texas Politics during the Roosevelt Era

KEITH VOLANTO

On June 28, 1934, Franklin Roosevelt delivered his fifth fireside chat to the American people. The president chose this opportunity to openly address growing criticism of his administration's efforts to combat the Great Depression. Chastising the bombastic rhetoric often employed by Far Right dissenters to his policies, Roosevelt famously stated: "A few timid people, who fear progress, will try to give you new and strange names for what we are doing. Sometimes they will call it 'Fascism,' sometimes 'Communism,' sometimes 'Regimentation,' sometimes 'Socialism.' But, in so doing, they are trying to make very complex and theoretical something that is really very simple and very practical." The president related his belief that the large array of programs and the means by which they were implemented, while unprecedented, was still consistent with cherished American ideals: "All that we do seeks to fulfill the historic traditions of the American people. Other nations may sacrifice democracy for the transitory stimulation of old and discredited autocracies. We are restoring confidence and well-being under the rule of the people themselves. We remain, as John Marshall said a century ago, 'emphatically and truly, a government of the people.' Our government 'in form and in substance . . . emanates from them. Its powers are granted by them, and are to be exercised directly on them, and for their benefits.'"[1]

While mainstream conservatives, whether Republicans or Democrats, decried much of the New Deal, what distinguished members of the Radical Right at this time from other Roosevelt opponents was the matter-of-fact manner in which they equated the president's initiatives with communism and the vehemence with which these views were propagated, reflecting an often paranoid suspicion of communist subversion of the government.

Early in his presidency, Roosevelt did not have to concern himself much with accusations of being an un-American radical. The president had a mandate for change as exemplified by his large margin of victory over Herbert Hoover and the existence of strong Democratic majorities in both houses of Congress. Opponents had to be wary about denouncing the new president too strongly, lest they face a public backlash. While not necessarily giving Roosevelt and congressional Democrats carte blanche to do anything they wished, the public nevertheless wanted and expected action after the grinding economic downturn entered its fourth year. Thus, during the "Hundred Days" of Roosevelt's presidency when the first phase of the New Deal was enacted, opposition was disorganized and largely muted.

Most conservative Democratic congressmen from the Lone Star State voiced their displeasure with certain aspects of the administration's course of action, refusing to be typecast as a rubber stamp for the president, but in most cases they voted for the measures after making speeches and public statements expressing their reservations. In many ways, the reaction of House Committee on Agriculture chairman Marvin Jones of Amarillo was typical. Though he was a strong believer in fiscal responsibility and a restrained federal bureaucracy, the reality of the depression encouraged the congressman's desire to help Texas farmers through greater government aid. Still, his vision generally entailed help in the form of lower taxes, reduced freight costs, mortgage relief, and an almost religious zeal for government support of agricultural exports rather than through the production control measures of the New Deal's Agricultural Adjustment Administration (AAA). Nevertheless, despite dramatically walking out of a heated committee hearing on the farm bill that would create the AAA and otherwise refusing to take responsibility for the measure, Jones allowed the bill to reach the House floor and spoke strongly on its behalf, albeit with reservations. In one speech, Jones declared that in normal times, he would not support the farm bill and reiterated his preferred formula to aid the farmers, but then stated:

> That is my program, but I am only one out of 435 members. . . . We are in a desperate emergency. . . . We are at war, and war is the grimmest business that ever engaged the attention of mankind. While this war is on, I am going to follow the man at the other end of the Avenue,

> who has the flag in his hand. . . . I am in favor of giving these strong government powers in this tremendous emergency in accordance with the desires of the President of the United States, and I am going down the line on that, notwithstanding my personal views.[2]

The most notable exception to this prevailing view among the Texas delegation was at-large representative George B. Terrell. A former state agriculture commissioner and a staunch conservative, Terrell harshly attacked the measure and its supporters, stating that "the strongest argument and the only argument that has weight in favor of this bill is the call to arms to follow our leader." Without the president's prestige, he asserted, "this bill would not command a corporal's guard." In objecting to the wide power given to the executive branch, the congressman proclaimed, "We should stop conferring dictatorial powers upon administrative officers, for when these powers are once conferred they are seldom withdrawn." Despite Terrell's opposition and the protests from Republicans, the farm bill passed easily.[3]

Some business groups in Texas voiced displeasure with the New Deal because of the adverse effect of these policies upon their companies. Again, the agricultural situation provides a ready example. The production control aspects of the AAA were extremely detrimental to the interests of volume-oriented middlemen, such as the ginners and shippers of cotton. No wonder that the Texas Cotton Ginners Association and the Texas Cotton Association (the group representing the state's export merchants) vociferously opposed the AAA. The head of the state's leading shipping firm, Will Clayton of Anderson, Clayton and Company, denounced the AAA from its inception, arguing that the farmers' problem was not a national overproduction problem, but rather a global underconsumption problem that could be rectified with the promotion of agricultural exports. Urging government restraint before employing "artificial means" to solve the nation's cotton surplus crisis, Clayton in the summer of 1933 reaffirmed his belief in market forces by asserting that "those things have a way of settling themselves."[4]

Apart from the perfunctory negative votes of Republican (and occasionally, conservative Democratic) congressmen during the Hundred Days, the first organized resistance to Roosevelt did not occur until 1934, when a group of wealthy businessmen and prominent conservative politicians formed the American Liberty League. With an original executive committee that included the two previous presidential nominees of the

Democratic Party, John W. Davis and Al Smith, and Republican congressman James Wadsworth and former Republican New York governor Nathan Miller, the group attempted to exude a bipartisan image of concerned citizens who wished to protect the rights of persons and property from the huge unconstitutional assumption of power by the federal government that threatened the liberties of the hardworking and patriotic American people. However, the American Liberty League was never able to shake the correct view that the organization was merely a device for disgruntled corporate elites to attack the Roosevelt administration in an attempt to turn the tide against further regulation of their business activities. Indeed, much of the league's funding came from a relatively small number of donors, with a sizable proportion coming from the Du Pont family.[5]

The American Liberty League provided much of the inspiration and funding for the first organized efforts in Texas to resist the New Deal. The actual catalysts for this work in the Lone Star State, however, would be wealthy Texas oilmen and their retainers. These powerful business interests were not only galvanized by the belief that Roosevelt and his backers had undertaken an unconstitutional power grab, but also by the sneaking suspicion that the president and his cohorts were opening the door for socialism and communism to undermine the entire capitalist system in America. The relatively recent Bolshevik takeover of Russia and the subsequent post–World War I "Red Scare"—caused by politicians and others who linked labor unrest to an international communist plot to overrun America—was still fresh in their minds. As one Texas millionaire later stated about the frame of mind of his wealthy colleagues: "We all made money fast. We were interested in nothing else. Then this Communist business burst upon us. Were we going to lose what we had gained?"[6]

Among the most noted Texas oil barons who dedicated much of their energies to countering the New Deal were Hugh Roy Cullen and John Henry Kirby. Cullen's major influences seem to have been his South Carolina–born mother's hatred for the North after the Union army burned down her family's plantation as well as the fact that, because he largely self-educated himself (never attending school beyond the fifth grade), he never broadened his worldview. Starting at the turn of the twentieth century at the age of nineteen, he worked for seven years as a cotton buyer in Oklahoma before spending four years as a real estate agent in Houston. A business associate then offered to pay him to travel around the state and acquire oil-leasing rights from landowners. Knowing nothing about the geology of oil, Cullen characteristically went to the Houston Public

Library to read up and learn whatever he could about the topic rather than receive any form of formal training before entering the frenzied world of Texas oil. In 1920 Cullen arranged an oil drilling operation of his own on a tract of land south of Houston that he had his eyes on, convincing some investors (including John Henry Kirby) to help with financing. The success of that effort, followed by major discoveries in other Gulf Coast fields, led to a massive accumulation of wealth in a very short period of time (he became one of the richest men in America), sealing his reputation as "King of the Wildcatters." Starting in the 1930s, Cullen began to use that oil-generated wealth to provide expression for his already-cultivated states rights and anticommunist views.[7]

John Henry Kirby took a different path before his wealth and ideas found him in the same company as Cullen and other ultraconservative Texas oil magnates. Born on a small farm near Tyler and educated in his youth by his mother and rural public schools, Kirby studied law under state senator Samuel Bronson Cooper, eventually passed the bar exam, and moved to Houston with his family. Along with Boston and New York investors, the young lawyer bought up extensive timberlands in East Texas, helping to develop the area into a major producing region. Kirby amassed a fortune as head of the giant Kirby Lumber Company, which owned more than three hundred thousand acres of East Texas pinelands and operated thirteen sawmills, as well as the Houston Oil Company (holder of the lumber company's oil rights). He held the paternalistic views of a consummate welfare capitalist by paying high wages and providing social services, but he expected complete obedience in return. Labor unions should be opposed because their organizers and leaders were "latter-day carpetbaggers" who unnecessarily misled contented workers. By the 1920s the "Prince of the Pines" was Texas' leading businessman, serving as president of the National Association of Manufacturers and living in style in one of Houston's finest mansions. Then, by 1933 and at the age of seventy-three, much of his fortune was gone—a by-product of the Great Depression. When his liabilities and outstanding loans could not be paid by liquidating property and securities, Kirby filed for bankruptcy, and the Kirby Lumber Company came under the control of the Santa Fe Railway.[8]

While still drawing a salary as president of the Kirby Lumber Company, Kirby increasingly channeled his personal bitterness toward Franklin Roosevelt and the New Deal. In 1934 he hired Vance Muse, a frenetic publicist who had worked with the lumber baron on many other probusiness lobbying enterprises, to start up a host of anti–New Deal organizations to operate out of downtown Houston's Kirby Building. In *The Big Rich*, Bryan Burrough describes these front organizations with such names as the "Texas Tax Relief Committee," the "Sentinels of the Republic," and the "Order of American Patriots" as little more than "the Ku Klux Klan in pinstripes, a kind of corporate Klan," which promoted white supremacy, disparaged labor unions, railed against communism, and devoted themselves to defeating Franklin Roosevelt in the 1936 election. The best known of all these Kirby-inspired groups was the Southern Committee to Uphold the Constitution (SCUC). Formed in late summer 1935, the SCUC served as the Southern version of the American Liberty League. Most of its funding came from Northern Liberty Leaguers such as the Du Ponts, Alfred P. Sloan, and John Raskob. The SCUC counted numerous Texas oilmen as members, including Roy Cullen, and sought to stop the supposed encroachment on American liberties by the New Deal. An official SCUC letter sent to its members explained the group's fears: "Every informed American knows that if Mr. Roosevelt is re-elected in 1936, the sovereign rights of the states will be completely demolished and power over all their affairs little and big will be consolidated in Washington."[9]

Kirby and Muse had hoped to recruit Huey Long to lead the public face of the SCUC. The Louisiana governor's assassination in September 1935, however, led them to seek out Georgia governor Eugene Talmadge, who seemed a perfect fit for the organization given his rabid anticommunist bent and devotion to racial segregation. In late January 1936, the SCUC held its first convention in Macon, Georgia, with Talmadge slated to be the keynote speaker. About three thousand attendees were fed "red meat" by a slew of speakers appealing to their worst racial and political fears. Underneath a large Confederate battle flag, introductory speakers attacked Roosevelt as a "nigger-loving Communist" and the NAACP as "the worst communist organization in the United States." Interspersed were demands for an end to the supposed gradual tearing down of states' rights and allegations that federal government spending was holding back the inevitable natural recovery. After Kirby introduced Talmadge as a "plumed knight on an errand for the Republic, refusing to bend his knee to dictatorship," the governor incited his fellow Southerners to drive the communists from Washington. On every seat in the auditorium, attendees found a magazine that included articles with the same type of rhetoric as well as photos of Eleanor Roosevelt being escorted by two black ROTC officers before a speech at Howard University, deliberately designed to inflame racial prejudices. The photos, which began to be known as the "nigger pictures" in the press, and the whole spectacle of the convention soon caught the attention of liberal Democratic senator Hugo Black of Alabama, who called Kirby, Muse, and other SCUC organizers before a Senate committee to answer questions about the group. Black succeeded in his task of embarrassing the SCUC to the point of extinction when, under questioning, Muse had his racism on full display and admitted under oath that most funding for the organization came from Northern financiers.[10]

Despite the SCUC's decline, Kirby was not deterred from joining with others to fulfill his dream of defeating Roosevelt in the 1936 election. Meeting at Dallas's Adolphus Hotel, Kirby, former congressman Joseph W. Bailey Jr., and twenty-six other staunch Roosevelt opponents formed a new organization known initially as the Constitutional Democrats of Texas, creating the first organized political effort to challenge Roosevelt in Texas. The group named J. Evetts Haley, a rancher and historian of the Texas cattle industry, to be their chairman. Kirby, Bailey, and Haley soon traveled to Detroit as the Texas representatives to a national convention of disaffected conservative Democrats who formed an alliance that assumed the name "Jeffersonian Democrats." With the election only three months away, the delegates, who refused to officially endorse Republican nominee Alf Landon, decided to leave the details of how to oppose Roosevelt to the individual state affiliates. After the Detroit gathering, the Constitutional Democrats of Texas held an organizational meeting in Waco, changed their name to the Jeffersonian Democrats of Texas to show unity with the national umbrella group, and made plans to establish a state headquarters in Austin.[11]

The Jeffersonian Democrats had limited appeal in Texas, with perhaps no more than five thousand active members, primarily disgruntled conservative lawyers, big businessmen, and large ranchers and landowners. Roy Cullen lent his support, as did Will Clayton and Lamar Fleming Jr., both partners in Anderson, Clayton and Company. Attorney T. J. Holbrook joined the Jeffersonian Democrats because of his belief that "[t]he Constitution has been ground to dust, and the courts, which form the last paladium [*sic*] of the people's liberty, have been mocked and spat upon. If the new dealers are not soon stopped, in their mad rage of communistic experiments, there won't be much left of our original form of government, which was the first to recognize the value of individual freedom."[12]

Though only active for the three months leading up to the November election, the Jeffersonian Democrats unleashed a large-scale publicity campaign designed to appeal to all opponents of Roosevelt, especially in the state's rural areas. Diatribes against Roosevelt numbered in the thousands, largely in the form of distributed pamphlets or articles appearing in the *Jeffersonian Democrat*, the official newspaper of the movement, which boasted a first-edition run of 250,000 copies. Coke Stevenson, the speaker of the Texas House of Representatives and future governor, believed a copy of the treatise "Roosevelt's Red Record," sent to him by the Jeffersonian Democrats, was "an excellent publication." Rabid supporters of the movement, such as former congressman George B. Terrell, also contributed member-generated content.[13]

Most of these pieces asserted a direct link between the New Deal and socialism, communism, the destruction of private enterprise, and the end of local self-government. As a front-page item appearing in the *Jeffersonian Democrat* proclaimed:

> THE ISSUE
> *Democracy vs. Communism*
>
> The issue is not Roosevelt vs. Landon, it is not the Democratic Party vs. [t]he Republican Party. The issue is [the] Socialism of Roosevelt and his brain trust vs. Democracy.
>
> We are now confronted with a change in our government from a Democracy in which the government is the servant of the people to a communistic state in which one loses all of his rights in personal freedom and property rights, and becomes the servant of the state.[14]

In their dogged pursuit of votes, the Jeffersonian Democratic press deliberately sought to appeal to base human emotions. Frequently, it sought to play on many citizens' latent racial prejudices, such as when chairman Haley commented in one editorial appearing in the *Jeffersonian Democrat*: "The New Deal Party is consorting with the Communist Party. The Communist Party believes in tearing down all racial lines and [in the] amalgamation of all races. Does the South want legalized marriages between negroes and whites?" An untitled Jeffersonian-produced circular predicted that the United States would soon be infused with ideas of equality and a person walking down the street might well hear the "horrifying" call of "Nigger Grab Your White Woman." Appeals to anti-Catholic bias also appeared, as when another pamphlet circulated by the Jeffersonians asserted: "Control of the Postal Service is vitally important to the Roman Catholics, mobilizing as they are, to increase their domination over American politics and wipe out Protestantism. It affords such a splendid opportunity for espionage that the pope laughs up his sleeve every time Roosevelt appoints another Roman Catholic postmaster." In one article appearing in the *Jeffersonian Democrat*, Haley managed to succinctly combine all paranoid strains of their movement's message into an assault upon some professors at the University of Texas he purported to know, describing them as "[a] bunch of so-called liberals who damn the profit system that supports them; who advocate communistic doctrines destructive to all religion; who stand for loose morals and free love instead of the rigid relations upon which the Christian home is built; who believe in the communistic doctrine of racial equality and practice it in the University neighborhood on occasion."[15]

The degree of resonance of such attacks measured whether one was a mainstream conservative opponent of FDR or sympathized with the Far Right. Readers who picked up the *Jeffersonian Democrat* and found no problem with the views expressed, or excitedly experienced a "Give 'Em Hell!" moment, were safely in the ultraconservative camp. Others who supported the movement, however, eventually balked at the use of such vitriolic verbiage. Lamar Fleming Jr., Will Clayton's partner at Anderson, Clayton and Company, proved to be a prime example of the latter stripe of conservative. In a letter to the leadership, Fleming clearly stated his objections to such bombastic language and his belief that it was counterproductive:

> I agreed to serve on Mr. Moore's Financial Committee and solicit contributions from my friends, and subsequently find myself in the disagreeable situation of still wanting to help him but not feeling able to solicit help from my friends.
>
> The people that I could appeal to are people of temperate conservative type. They would contribute to help finance temperate publicity, and I would not hesitate in asking them to do so. But, at the moment, I was preparing to start approaching them, Mr. Haley's advertisement was published here, stating among other things that we believe that this debt is being piled up for the purpose of bankrupting the Nation and turning it over to the communists.
>
> My friends do not believe anything like that, nor do I, and I do not feel that I can solicit their enlistment and support in an organization

> that permits anyone to advertise that its members and supporters hold such views.[16]

On election night, the Jeffersonian Democrats received the devastating news that the American people not only overwhelmingly reelected FDR, but Texans also approved of Roosevelt by a seven-to-one margin over Alf Landon. Though their arguments fell on deaf ears in 1936, the Jeffersonian Democrats still hold importance in Texas political history because they laid the groundwork for future ultraconservative activity in Texas politics. Though John Henry Kirby retired from political involvement, most of the other founders of the organization joined the myriad of antiprogressive groups that appeared under different names over the next twenty years, including the Texas Regulars and the Dixiecrats.[17]

After the 1936 election, purveyors of Radical Right thinking briefly stepped aside from the limelight as traditional conservative Democrats in Congress rose to challenge Roosevelt. This challenge came early in the president's second term after he announced his plans to combat the active stifling of New Deal efforts by conservatives on the US Supreme Court through his proposal to add up to six new members to the high court for every justice that did not retire upon reaching the age of seventy. This "court packing plan," as opponents quickly dubbed it, caused many of FDR's former allies to call in their chips. With the crisis of the first term having passed and their willingness to sponsor further structural reforms at an end, three important Texans began to openly rebel against the administration, contributing greatly to the plan's ultimate demise: Vice President John Nance Garner, Senator Tom Connally (a member of the Senate Judiciary Committee), and Representative Hatton Sumners (chairman of the House Judiciary Committee). These men were not ultraconservatives, but rather, traditional limited-government politicians who believed the president's plan was unconstitutional and feared that the sacred separation of powers between the branches of the government would be forever altered if the measure passed.[18]

Another national political issue that contributed to renewed efforts by traditional conservative Texas politicians to stymie the New Deal was the series of sit-down strikes begun by the Congress of Industrial Organizations (CIO) in an effort to force automobile and steel companies to recognize their workers' right to bargain collectively. While Roosevelt disapproved of the tactic, he refused to send in federal troops to help dislodge the striking workers, thus earning the ire of conservatives of all types.

The sit-down strike provided the opportunity for one emerging Far Right politician from East Texas, Representative Martin Dies Jr., to take advantage of the tumult and emerge on the national scene. Despite support from John Henry Kirby, Dies actually cooperated with most of the relief and recovery efforts of the New Deal before 1937 as he helped to channel much-needed aid to his rural East Texas constituents. Nevertheless, from his father, former Congressman Martin Dies Sr., he inherited a strong animus toward foreigners and an abiding hatred of communism. As these feelings began to coalesce, the congressman became convinced that communist aliens were the driving forces behind the sit-down strikes. Wishing to publicize the issue (and himself in the process), Dies dramatically called for a congressional investigation of the CIO, though Roosevelt's allies were later able to defeat the resolution. After this initial splash, Dies became better known nationally when he began a six-year-long chairmanship of the House Un-American Activities Committee, established in 1938 to investigate foreign subversion. Though his committee spent time seeking out possible Nazi influences in the country, Dies was in his element trying to uncover evidence of communists in Hollywood, labor unions, universities, and the government, years before the even more paranoid Senator Joseph McCarthy made greater headlines undertaking the same types of activities on a grander scale during the 1950s. As later with McCarthy, Dies targeted liberals, made outrageous allegations against innocent people and institutions, and in the end had very little to show for the effort. Historian George Green summed up the congressman well while also tying him to the emerging Radical Right in Texas politics:

> Right-wing extremism was evident in Martin Dies' policies: racism, opposition to all immigration, slander against New Dealers and all opponents, violations of civil rights, extravagant and untrue findings of subversion, opposition to the existence of labor unions, attacks on academic freedom, and passionate religious fundamentalism. Just one or two or three of these policies might not constitute rightist extremism, but the combination of policies and the style in which he presented them revealed Dies to be an authoritarian similar to W. Lee O'Daniel.[19]

The successful election of W. Lee "Pappy" O'Daniel to the governorship of Texas marked the beginning of heavy Far Right influence on the government of the Lone Star State. A lifelong Republican born in Ohio and reared in Kansas, O'Daniel moved to Fort Worth in the mid-1920s to work as a sales manager with a local flour company. For advertising purposes, he began to host a daily noontime radio show heard across most of Texas with an orchestra known as the "Light Crust Doughboys" (which included for a while fiddler Bob Wills). By 1935 O'Daniel started his own company and began to tout his "Hillbilly Flour" on a new radio program with a new band, the Hillbilly Boys. He filled his shows with a mixture of hillbilly and religious music, self-composed songs and poetry, humorous anecdotes, moral stories, and business advice.[20]

In 1938 he announced that he would make a run for the governorship. At the very least, the race would provide free publicity for Hillbilly Flour, a benefit that he did not deny. Twelve other candidates entered the 1938 Democratic primary race for governor, and O'Daniel beat them all. On the campaign trail O'Daniel announced a simple platform: the Ten Commandments. When pressed for specifics, he called for state assistance to all elderly Texans and voiced opposition to a sales tax. The state government could get all the revenue it needed, he claimed, from rigid enforcement of existing tax laws. Large crowds turned out to see O'Daniel and his band. During his short musings posing as stump speeches, the candidate constantly railed against professional politicians and promised the return of a businesslike administration in Austin. The hillbilly country-boy image that O'Daniel cultivated, however, was purely an act he managed with help from a publicist. Far from a commoner trying to make ends meet in the midst of the depression, O'Daniel was a business college graduate worth a half-million dollars during the 1930s. And though he never admitted to the fact, his campaign received much financial support from big oil interests, including Roy Cullen. Nevertheless, his folksy image and popular message resonated with voters, who responded by turning out for O'Daniel by such a large margin that he did not need a runoff. In the November general election, he received 97 percent of the vote.[21]

O'Daniel proved to be an ineffective governor. Frequent combat between the governor and the "professional politicians" in the legislature led to stalemate. The governor vetoed numerous acts of the legislature. He refused to support higher taxes on natural resources and utilities, vetoed appropriations for new orphanages and mental health facilities, and slashed the budget of the Department of Public Safety. Though he received no major newspaper endorsements, O'Daniel easily received the Democratic nomination in 1940, again without the need of a runoff.[22]

Pappy O'Daniel's governorship is also noteworthy because of the marked influence of the Far Right on his administration. Many of his key advisers were ultraconservatives, such as Republican attorney Orville Bullington of Wichita Falls, Dallas oilman E. B. Germany, and Mayor C. K. Quin of San Antonio. Several of O'Daniel's appointments consisted of men of this persuasion. James M. West, an oil, cattle, and lumber millionaire from Houston, for example, received a nomination to the highway commission in 1939, though the state senate rejected him after West's active involvement with the Jeffersonian Democrats became known. Even more significant was the governor's successful appointments of Far Right businessmen and politicians to the University of Texas Board of Regents. After meeting with wealthy reactionary supporters about how best to counter the perceived influence of liberalism and communism in higher education, O'Daniel and the others in the cabal decided to seek control of college governing boards. Then, limits could be placed on academic freedom, restrictions on the teaching of certain subjects enacted, and unwelcomed radical professors could be removed. The appointment of Bullington and fellow ultraconservative oil and cattle millionaire Dan Harrison marked the beginning of a raucous period in the administration of the University of Texas as these board members, soon to be reinforced with additional appointees by the next governor, Coke Stevenson, began to impress their views upon the governance of the campus.[23]

When O'Daniel won election to the US Senate, Lieutenant Governor Coke Stevenson moved into the governor's mansion. Raised on a Kimble County ranch in West Texas, Stevenson self-educated himself while working as a freight hauler, janitor, bookkeeper, and bank cashier before passing the state bar examination. He rose to become a prominent local lawyer, businessman, rancher, and banker in Junction before his election to the state legislature. After serving two consecutive terms as Speaker of the Texas House, Stevenson won the lieutenant governor's race in 1938. A reserved and unpretentious conservative politician, Stevenson held strong anti–central planning beliefs that led him to oppose most of the New Deal, in addition to such wartime controls as the national speed limit and gasoline rationing.

The return of economic prosperity proved to be the major factor driving his popular support as he won reelection in 1942 and 1944. Beginning his governorship with a 34-million-dollar debt, he left office in 1946 with a 35-million-dollar surplus. While increased wartime business activity largely explains the reversal, Stevenson also refused to raise taxes, especially on the exportation of oil, and supported deep funding cuts for state government services. Though he favored increased funding for the state highway system and a building program for the University of Texas, most colleges and government agencies (especially mental health facilities, orphanages, and hospitals) received greatly reduced appropriations. The governor also endorsed a state constitutional amendment, passed by voters in 1942, requiring a balanced state government budget. On racial matters, Stevenson could display detached insensitivity, such as his reaction to the kidnapping and lynching of Willie Vinson, a black man accused of raping a white woman, by a Texarkana mob in July 1942. Replying to a letter sent by US attorney general Francis Biddle, the governor callously stated that "certain members of the Negro race from time to time furnish the setting for mob violence by the outrageous crimes which they commit."[24]

Many of Stevenson's appointments were men of ultraconservative beliefs, including those chosen to be members of the University of Texas Board of Regents. Together with O'Daniel's appointees, the reactionaries constituted a majority and began to pressure university president Homer Rainey to make wholesale changes. Rainey did not agree with the regents' requests, however, such as when he refused to fire three tenured professors of economics for alleged communist teachings when in fact they were guilty only of approving of New Deal fiscal policy. The president was further incensed by the board members' suspension of all funding for social science research, the "non-rehiring" of certain untenured instructors, and their decision to ban the use of John Dos Passos's *U.S.A.* in sophomore English classes. When Rainey brought his objections to an open faculty meeting, the regents fired him, leading to a student strike and a massive "funeral" march to memorialize the demise of academic freedom on campus. Governor Stevenson accepted the firing and stayed out of the entire affair. Indeed, his personal views on this issue were very much in accord with the regents, as indicated by a letter he wrote to one board member expressing his view that the state's colleges were dominated by such organizations as the American Association of University Professors, which he believed were "undemocratic" and "totalitarian."[25]

The height of the Far Right's anti–New Deal efforts in Texas occurred during the 1944 presidential election, when disfavor with Roosevelt among many wealthy business interests led them to create a movement to challenge the president's bid for an unprecedented fourth term—the "Texas Regulars." While much of their discontent revolved around the government's wartime restrictions on gas and oil prices and the New Deal's prolabor stance, another source of resentment originated with outrage over the Supreme Court's recent ruling in the *Smith v. Allwright* case against the constitutionality of Texas' white primary law. Roy Cullen emerged as the most influential leader of the Texas ultraconservatives after the death of John Henry Kirby in 1940. By this time, Cullen began to divert more attention away from his oil holdings in order to focus on politics as he began to throw his considerable financial weight behind numerous conservative candidates and causes. Refusing to run for office himself, Cullen believed that, as he wrote Kirby before the lumber giant's death: "I can do more good helping other candidates—doing what I can to see that the good men get into office and the bad ones are kept out." Cullen later bragged that he was the largest contributor to the Texas Regulars.[26]

Prior to the 1944 campaign, anti-Roosevelt Democrats in Texas gained success at their party's initial state convention in May. There, conferees selected a slate of delegates to the national convention who pledged to support the presidential nominee only if the party denounced the *Smith v. Allwright* decision and restored the requirement that the party's nominee had to receive the vote of two-thirds of the assembled delegates (the "two-thirds rule," which had been abolished in 1936). Because neither of these changes would occur, the delegates would become de facto uninstructed delegates free to support whoever they wished. After pro–New Deal Texas delegates arrived at the national convention, however, the party's credentials committee eventually diluted the field by allowing both groups to participate as voting delegates.[27]

The Regulars formed after New Deal supporters fought back at the second state convention held in September. By the narrow margin of 803 to 774, they succeeded in securing a slate of presidential electors who pledged to support the party's nominees for president and vice president. Refusing to accept the result and eschewing support for Thomas Dewey (the Republican Party nominee), Texas ultraconservatives united for a third-party effort to divert enough votes away from Roosevelt to deny him their state's electoral votes. Their platform demanded:

> 1. Restoration of the Democratic Party to the integrity which has been taken away by [labor union leader Sidney] Hillman, [American Communist Party leader Earl] Browder, and others.
>
> 2. Protection of honest labor unions from foreign-born racketeers who have gained control by blackmail.

3. Return of state rights which have been destroyed by the Communist-controlled New Deal.

4. Restoration of the freedom of education.

5. Restoration of the supremacy of the white race, which has been destroyed by the Communist-controlled New Deal.

6. Restoration of the Bill of Rights instead of rule by regimentation.

7. Restoration of government by laws instead of government by bureaus.

8. Restoration of the individual appeal for justice, instead of a politically appointed bureau.[28]

The Regulars ran a well-financed campaign with little trouble getting their word out. The movement received help on the stump from Pappy O'Daniel and Martin Dies. Money from Roy Cullen and other big oilmen allowed for statewide radio broadcasts heavily publicized ahead of time. Front-page advertisements in newspapers across the state further spread the group's message. All these efforts ultimately failed to defeat Roosevelt, who received 72 percent of the vote in Texas. (Dewey received 16 percent while the Regulars, who had no official candidate, received 12 percent.) The emergence of the Regulars nevertheless signified the continued resilience of the Far Right as a fixture in Texas politics, foretelling the continued divisions within the Texas Democratic Party in the postwar years.[29]

In seeking to evaluate the activities of the Far Right in Texas during the Roosevelt era, some noteworthy traits stand out. During these initial years of development, the leadership of the Radical Right in Texas consisted almost entirely of rich businessmen, especially recently minted oil magnates. Far from originating the grass roots, the movement owed its existence to its wealthy benefactors who had the money and motivation to express their views out of proportion to the ability of the common Texan without such funds to do likewise. While some of their opinions might seem outrageous and designed to appeal to the emotions of less-educated voters, one must not assume that the leadership of the Far Right was merely playing politics and that they did not adamantly believe in their words. These men were devout supporters of laissez-faire capitalism because the system provided the source of their empires and social standing. They believed that anything that threatened that status had to be resisted with tenacity. A large number of Far Right leaders in Texas were quite undereducated themselves. Some, like Roy Cullen, had a very little formal schooling. Many others were "self-educated" men whose thinking was subject to all the pitfalls that accrue from reading material that tends only to reinforce one's worldview. Further, though some ultraconservative leaders had law or business degrees, such training did not give them much experience in understanding the nuances of national economic policy, let alone allow them to truly comprehend communist theory and how the New Deal might be different from communism.

Perhaps one of the best quotations to reinforce this viewpoint comes from, of all people, Wendell Willkie—the 1940 Republican Party presidential nominee. Before the 1940 campaign began, Roy Cullen contacted Willkie and they exchanged a round of correspondence. When Willkie campaigned in Houston, Cullen told reporters that he had exchanged letters with the Republican nominee and told him that he disagreed with his foreign policy positions (which were similar in many ways to Roosevelt's). When reporters asked Willkie about Cullen's statements, he denied ever hearing of the oilman—a position he held until Cullen released his correspondence with Willkie to the media. Exasperated, Willkie responded: "You know the Good Lord put all this oil in the ground. Then someone comes along who hasn't been a success at anything else, and takes it out of the ground. The minute he does that he considers himself an expert on everything from politics to petticoats."[30]

Though ineffectual in defeating FDR, members of the Far Right in Texas exerted stronger influence at the state level. The activists within the Jeffersonian Democrat and Texas Regular movements supplied the leadership, inspiration, and funds to impact the Texas Democratic Party for years to come. Their efforts contributed to the later estrangement of less radical conservatives from the party, following them to support Dwight Eisenhower during the 1950s before the more permanent shift to the Republicans beginning in the 1960s.

Notes

1. Full text of Roosevelt's fireside chats can be found at the FDR Presidential Library and Museum website,: http://docs.fdrlibrary.marist.edu/firesi90.html.

2. *Congressional Record*, House, 73rd Cong., 1st sess., pt. 1, 673–74. For more on Marvin Jones's views and his role in promoting the passage of the farm bill in 1933, see Irvin M. May Jr., *Marvin Jones: The Public Life of an Agrarian Advocate* (College Station: Texas A&M University Press, 1980), 98–107, and Keith J. Volanto, *Texas, Cotton, and the New Deal*, 28–33. For the remarks of Texas congressmen Richard M. Kleberg, W. D. McFarlane, Wright Patman, and Hatton Sumners, who all gave support, with reservations, to the farm bill, see *Congressional Record*, House, 73rd Cong., 1st sess., pt. 1, 685–86, 736–37, 756–57, 764–65.

3. Ibid., 751–52. Both Texas senators and fifteen members of the House delegation voted for the farm bill while only three voted no—Terrell, Fritz D. Lanham, and Joseph W. Bailey Jr. The son of a former US senator, Bailey would later head the Texas-for-Willkie clubs consisting of conservative Democrats who opposed to a third term for Roosevelt.

4. Volanto, *Texas, Cotton, and the New Deal*, 37.

5. The definitive study of the American Liberty League is George Wolfskill, *Revolt of the Conservatives: A History of the American Liberty League, 1934–1940* (Boston: Houghton Mifflin, 1962).

6. George N. Green, *The Establishment in Texas Politics: The Primitive Years, 1938–1957* (Westport, CT: Greenwood Press, 1979), 9 (quotation).

7. Cullen's early life is well covered in Bryan Burrough, *The Big Rich: The Rise and Fall of the Greatest Texas Oil Fortunes* (New York: Penguin Press, 2009), chapter 2.

8. Ibid., 128–29. For details about Kirby's control of his lumber company, its labor conditions, and Kirby's anti-union activities, see Thad Sitton and James H. Conrad, *Nameless Towns: Texas Sawmill Communities, 1880–1942* (Austin: University of Texas Press, 1998), and Robert S. Maxwell and Robert D. Baker, *Sawdust Empire: The Texas Lumber Industry, 1830–1940* (College Station: Texas A&M University Press, 1983), chapters 7–9.

9. Burrough, *Big Rich*, 129 (first quotation); Wolfskill, *Revolt of the Conservatives*, 241 (second quotation).

10. Burrough, *Big Rich*, 132 (quotations); Wolfskill, *Revolt of the Conservatives*, 175–77, 242; Green, *Establishment in Texas Politics*, 59.

11. Lionel V. Patenaude, *Texas, Politics, and the New Deal* (New York: Garland Publishing, 1983), 111–12.

12. Ibid., 112–13; T. J. Holbrook to W. P. Hamblen, July 24, 1936, Jeffersonian Democrats Correspondence (hereafter cited as JDC), quoted in Lionel V. Patenaude, "The New Deal and Texas" (PhD diss., University of Texas, 1953), 151. Originally placed in the University of Texas Archives, the surviving papers of the Jeffersonian Democrats are currently housed in the Haley Memorial Library and History Center, Midland, TX.

13. Patenaude, *Texas, Politics, and the New Deal,* 114; Patenaude, "New Deal and Texas," 152–53 (quotation).

14. *Jeffersonian Democrat,* September 23, 1936 (quoted in Patenaude, "New Deal and Texas," 154).

15. *Jeffersonian Democrat,* October 6, 1936; untitled Jeffersonian Democrat circular; "Did Jim Farley Romanize the American Post Office System?"; *Jeffersonian Democrat,* October 22, 1936, all in JDC and quoted in Patenaude, "New Deal and Texas," 156–59.

16. Lamar Fleming Jr. to W. P. Hamblen, September 25, 1936, JDC, quoted in Patenaude, "New Deal and Texas," 162.

17. Patenaude, *Texas, Politics, and the New Deal,* 119–20.

18. For detailed coverage of these Texas politicians' views toward the court packing plan and their roles in killing it, see Lionel V. Patenaude, "Garner, Sumners, and Connally: The Defeat of the Roosevelt Court Bill in 1937," *Southwestern Historical Quarterly* 74 (July 1970): 36–51. See also James T. Patterson, *Congressional Conservatism and the New Deal* (Lexington: University Press of Kentucky, 1967).

19. Patterson, *Congressional Conservatism and the New Deal,* 166–69; Allan A. Mitchie and Frank Rhylick, *Dixie Demagogues* (New York: Vanguard Press, 1939), 55–67; Green, *Establishment in Texas Politics,* 69–76 (quotation).

20. Green, *Establishment in Texas Politics,* 22–24; Mitchie and Rhylick, *Dixie Demagogues,* 47–48.

21. Green, *Establishment in Texas Politics,* 24–25; Seth Shepard McKay, *W. Lee O'Daniel and Texas Politics, 1938–1942* (Lubbock: Texas Tech University Press, 1944), 32–53.

22. Green, *Establishment in Texas Politics,* 25–29.

23. Ibid., 25, 83–84; McKay, *W. Lee O'Daniel and Texas Politics,* 161–64, 359–61.

24. Green, *Establishment in Texas Politics,* 77–80.

25. Ibid., 86–87.

26. Ibid., 46; Burrough, *Big Rich,* 136 (quotation).

27. Green, *Establishment in Texas Politics,* 46–48.

28. Ibid., 49–50; Paul Pressler, *The Texas Regulars: The Beginning of the Move to the Republican Party in Texas* (Garland, TX: Hannibal Books, 2001), 153–54; *Austin American,* October 6, 1944 (quotation).

29. Burrough, *Big Rich,* 138–39; Green, *Establishment in Texas Politics,* 51–55; Sean P. Cunningham, *Cowboy Conservatism: Texas and the Rise of the Modern Right* (Lexington: University Press of Kentucky, 2010), 25–27.

30. Burrough, *Big Rich,* 137 (quotation).

Establishing the Texas Far Right, 1940–1960

GEORGE N. GREEN

The Far Right in post–World War II Texas was alienated from the mainstream by anger over rapid social change. Some of its leaders were possessed of recently made oil wealth and despised both taxes and regulations that might diminish that money or impede getting more. Others believed American institutions were threatened by the presence of allegedly inferior ethnic and religious groups. But apart from the ongoing racism against African Americans and Tejanos, ethnic prejudices, especially anti-Semitism, provided less and less fuel for the Far Right of the era due to the effects of national restrictions on European immigration and the bonding experience and prosperity generated by World War II. However, there were still plenty of anti-European and anti-Asian isolationists soon appalled by the specter of world government represented by the new United Nations. Communism absorbed much attention as the new target of both zealots and the genuinely fearful, whose ranks included a growing number of politicized evangelical and fundamentalist churchgoers. The latter's beliefs in a world eternally divided between good and evil, in a very particular kind of biblical literalism and a growing crisis culture absorbed with "end times" prophecy, made them fearful of and resistant to all manner of social changes. Yet another faction were the reactionaries, either intransigent or sentimental, who despised twentieth-century reforms, the growth of the federal government, and economic and political changes in general (many equated with communism), and who yearned for the days of President William McKinley. All claimed to be fervent patriots pessimistic about the future and deeply concerned about betrayal from within. But at least in this era they did not normally deploy rhetoric revolving around the use of guns or embrace violent tactics or openly advocate deportation of Jews or Mexicans or any group other than communist aliens.

The Far Right's ideas were presented under the banner of conservatism in the 1940s and 1950s by Texans affronted by the New Deal and Fair Deal. Some had earlier supported the New Deal because it dealt with the economic emergencies of the 1930s, then they soured on continued government intervention with the return of prosperity during the war. Texans on the Far Right were often energized by nouveau riche oilmen, who made money fast and felt insecure about keeping it. Distrustful of political pluralism, the democratic process, and of normal civil discourse, but empowered by their wealth, these leaders of the Texas Right were able to broadcast their beliefs in irrational and apocalyptic speech and writing. They exercised their newly minted power to push Texas politics to the right in the 1940s and 1950s, and in the process pushed their paranoid style close to the mainstream of Texas and American political history.[1]

By 1941 an organized antilabor campaign was under way in Texas, as the nation's industries—with massive government assistance—geared up for war, and the nation's unions fought to organize the workforce in these plants. The Texas Manufacturers' Association, Texas director of public safety Homer Garrison, and US congressman Martin Dies excoriated strikes as the weapons of revolutionary communism. In this atmosphere Governor W. Lee "Pappy" O'Daniel suddenly demanded an immediate joint session of the Texas Legislature to hear him on March 31, 1941. He delivered an emotional speech about "labor leader racketeers" who were threatening to take over Texas after having crippled Great Britain's struggle against the Nazis. He insisted that the legislature pass his proposed antiviolence bill before leaving the room, even though, of course, no one had read it. Even at that, the bill failed by only seven votes in the House. The original bill was such a legal monstrosity that the attorney general ruled it unenforceable and unconstitutional on ten different counts.[2]

The eventual O'Daniel antiviolence act provided that a picketer who used force to prevent a strikebreaker from entering a plant was committing a penitentiary-level felony, while a strikebreaker who beat up a picketer had committed only a misdemeanor. Freedom of assembly near any place where a labor dispute existed was illegal. O'Daniel's recent concerns for the nation's defense preparations and Britain's plight appear to have waned later that year when he denounced the draft and dismissed the war as European howling that should be ignored. Raised a Republican in the Midwest, O'Daniel was hewing to the GOP isolationist line that the Nazis were not a threat to America. Yet war anxiety coupled with an antilabor political culture continued to generate energy the governor could not ignore. Dallas congressman Hatton Sumners had already upped the ante by declaring of war industry strikers that it might become "necessary to send them to the electric chair in order to preserve liberty in this country." O'Daniel clearly yearned for an opportunity to appear on the national stage and ride the anti-union issue as far as he could take it. In the Lone Star State at least, the "issue" was simply manufactured for political purposes by the governor and others. A spokesman for the US Conciliation Service announced in mid-April 1941 that not a single man-hour of labor had been lost on any Texas defense job because of strikes or labor disturbances.[3]

It was O'Daniel who most shrewdly tapped into the growing corporate resistance to taxes and unions, and positioned himself on the Far Right in the process. A preference for regressive or flat taxation whereby the working and middle classes would be taxed at a heavier percentage of their wealth than businesses and wealthy individuals, and a preference for laws that placed restrictions on unions to limit their ability to persuade corporations to share their wealth and/or their ability to utilize all their assets in political campaigns, are by themselves frequently in the conservative mainstream. Nevertheless, regressive taxation is also invariably a part of the Radical Right package of beliefs and approaches. O'Daniel emotionally demanded a multiple sales tax and viciously lambasted all who opposed him. He demanded the passage of his antilabor bills before any legislator had read them, and in their original version they would have destroyed unions altogether.

O'Daniel and Dies soon had their chance to take their antilabor crusade to a higher level. During the special US senatorial election in June 1941, the governor pledged to introduce a national version of the O'Daniel Anti-Violence Act, and those senators who failed to vote for it would be subjected to his roll call on a national radio broadcast. He bragged that he had driven the radical labor agitators out of Texas, yet also claimed that they were supporting his opponents. Dies entered the contest, hurling spectacular charges of internal communist subversion but made the early mistake of sneering at O'Daniel's hillbilly music. His underlying problem was that his political base was largely the same as O'Daniel's—the fundamentalist or traditional evangelical non-union Anglo from rural areas and small towns. Moreover, he gave few speeches and made little effort to establish any organization outside his congressional district. Another entrant was Austin's New Deal congressman, Lyndon B. Johnson, who announced his candidacy from the White House steps. Johnson had the support of most urbanites, laborers, young people, and blacks (who were allowed to vote in general elections). Johnson ran the strongest race, and on election night with 96 percent of the ballots counted, he led by over five thousand votes.[4]

But there were powerful interest groups desperate to get O'Daniel out of Texas, including lobbyists for liquor, gambling, and horseracing, and friends of Lieutenant Governor Coke Stevenson (who wanted the governorship). O'Daniel and his millionaire corporate friend Carr P. Collins illegally pumped corporate money into the campaign and won a scant victory. Some Johnson advisors discussed challenging the election, but the investigation would have been conducted by state senators selected by Stevenson and O'Daniel, who already had their eyes on pro-Johnson state and federal employees who seem to have violated Hatch Act provisos against electioneering. And there were the Brown and Root Construction Company donations to the Johnson campaign, and those expenses far exceeded the twenty-five-thousand-dollar limit set by federal law (the company later paid a sizable fraud penalty).[5]

Senator O'Daniel submitted his antistrike bill several times, though it never mustered more than four votes from the ninety-six senators. He also urged the senate to cancel all draft deferments for "labor racketeers and other privileged classes," to eliminate overtime pay and the forty-hour week, and to ban picketing. All failed overwhelmingly. Needing to divert the electorate's attention from his dismal success rate, he suddenly became aware of more communist menace in Texas during the 1942 Democratic senatorial primary. "Pappy" eventually discovered that there was a conspiracy to defeat him by the *Dallas Morning News, Fort Worth Star-Telegram,* other politically controlled newspapers, professional politicians, his two primary opponents, and the ubiquitous "communistic labor leader racketeers," a phrase he used as many as sixteen times in a single speech. Even such conservative, antilabor, urban businessmen as C. K. Quin, Sid Richardson, E. B. Germany, and D. F. Strickland—appalled by O'Daniel's absurd lies, ineffectiveness, and paranoia—supported the mildly progressive Jimmie Allred in the runoff. O'Daniel was barely reelected, helped by some one hundred thousand crossover Republican voters.[6]

Corporate money financed a wave of newspaper and radio ads accusing workers of betraying Americans in uniform and castigating the administration as a pawn of labor. William Ruggles, editorial page chief of the *Dallas Morning News*, spawned the "right-to-work" campaign, born in a column in 1941. It was a plea for an open-shop amendment to the US Constitution, designed to outlaw compulsory unionism and dues. It was linked to racism at the time, especially in the South, where both white anxieties and black hopes were fanned by the Roosevelt administration's sporadic efforts to achieve racial equality in employment practices in wartime industries. Professional Far Right lobbyist Vance Muse and others sought to weaken unions by agitating tensions between white and African American union members. Muse declared that "I like the nigger—in his place" and that the proposed open-shop "right-to-work" constitutional amendment "helps the nigger. Good niggers, not these communist niggers." Inflammatory rhetoric and violence were also part of the campaign. A white organizer assigned to unionize black oil workers was publicly beaten in Port Arthur in 1942. Baytown's Humble Oil refinery management accused the CIO, Communist Party, and African Americans of forming an unholy alliance to take over control of the United States and charged that the effort to organize Mexicans would lead to a race war. But the race-baiting eventually failed.[7]

The labor issue spilled over into freedom of speech and academic freedom in universities. Millionaire businessmen Orville Bullington, Dan Harrison, Jim West, H. H. Weinert, Maco Stewart and Maco Stewart Jr., D. F. Strickland, Lutcher Stark, and Karl Hoblitzelle began strategizing with Governor O'Daniel, some of them as early as 1940, to bring Texas colleges to heel. Most were appointed regents, and they decided to ignore tedious and uncertain legislative solutions and take direct control of college governing boards and purge the universities, especially the flagship Austin campus. Their opportunity to strike came in 1942.[8]

In Dallas an anti-union meeting was ostensibly called in 1942 by the mothers of servicemen, who offered all citizens an opportunity to express their views. It was actually called by Hoblitzelle in a *Dallas Morning News* advertisement featuring big Japanese soldiers with rifles aimed at small US soldiers with popguns. The ad asserted that soldiers were dying needlessly because the union-dominated administration would not allow anyone to work more than forty hours per week. At the Dallas meeting, four University of Texas economics instructors were denied the opportunity to read the actual law being discussed. (It provided for overtime pay beyond forty hours. Even with overtime pay, wartime wages lagged behind wartime inflation, and by every conceivable measurement, far behind wartime profits.) The attending Texas economics faculty informed a reporter after the meeting that the agenda had been carefully managed with organized labor and the Roosevelt administration denounced by unopposed, preselected speakers. Six members of the board of regents soon interrogated the instructors, while taking at least two phone calls from Senator O'Daniel in Washington, and voted four to two to fire the untenured men. The *Dallas Morning News* denounced the instructors as part of its ongoing antilabor campaign, even descending to blaming Speaker of the House Sam Rayburn and President Roosevelt for contributing daily to "a fresh list of dead heroes killed in battle and never fully supported by our country's efforts."[9]

Meantime, in Austin, the regents responded to University of Texas president Homer Rainey's protests against the firings by searching for ways to abolish the tenure rules so that they could easily rid themselves of all undesirable professors, including two who had called for higher taxes on the wealthy. They could only weaken tenure, not abolish it, which was another example of constraints within the system that prevented a total takeover by extremists. University administrators, however, have never had tenure as administrators, and the regents soon found their excuse to dump Rainey. He defended the English Department's placement of John Dos Passos's *U.S.A.* on the supplementary reading list for sophomore classes. Unable to discover any individual who was responsible, so he could be fired, the board settled on banning the "obscene" and "perverted" novel, which soon won the Pulitzer Prize. It quickly became the most popular book in the state. The regents fired Rainey on November 1, 1944, citing no reasons.[10]

Regent Bullington then proceeded to smear the university with the new, sensational, and baseless charge that it had coddled a "nest of homosexuals" on the faculty (an accusation refuted by the director of the Texas Department of Public Safety). Regent Strickland accused Rainey of wanting to admit blacks to the university and told a university official—without citing any evidence—that over a thousand communists had infiltrated the university under Rainey. Regent Stark revealed his notion of academic freedom by asserting that university presidents were just general managers who reported to the corporate board of directors known as regents. O'Daniel's successor as governor, Coke Stevenson, appointed or reappointed some of the most reactionary regents, demonstrating the ease by which Far Right politicians, in the atmosphere of wartime jitters and backlash against the New Deal and organized labor, could take over institutions. But they were constrained by laws and bureaucracies on the one hand, and on the other, by their own failure to micromanage these institutions with moderation or even with intelligence. Several of these regents were part of the rebellious Texas "Jeffersonian" Democrats who sought to defeat Roosevelt's reelection in 1944.[11]

Internal political rebellions affected the four consecutive presidential elections of 1944 through 1956. Many prominent Southern Democrats either threatened to or actually did abandon the party in their presidential balloting, selecting a right-wing ideological approach instead. After each of the four elections, most dissidents returned to the Democratic fold, but the bitter contests had the cumulative effect of pushing Texas away from one-party rule.

By 1944 Texas oil and corporate interests had been preparing for three years to seize the machinery of the Texas Democratic Party and deny Roosevelt's place on the party's presidential ticket. Other Texans—including many small-town and rural merchants, farmers, ranchers, bankers, and editors—had gone along with the New Deal and accepted what many regarded as economic dictatorship during the emergencies of the Great Depression and the first year or so of the war. But by 1943 and 1944 many felt that the dictatorship was no longer necessary, but feared that it was becoming permanent. Various issues rankled these Texans, including Roosevelt's decision to seek a third term (which they believed denied the White House to Texan John Nance Garner), the strikes and the concessions to organized labor, and the US Supreme Court decision *Smith v. Allwright* that struck down the Texas law barring blacks from the Democratic primary. Anti–New Dealers, many from oil and gas companies, dominated the state convention in May, selecting presidential electors who were instructed to vote for the party's nominees only if the national party convention restored the two-thirds rule (requiring a supermajority to nominate a presidential candidate, thus giving the South a virtual veto) and renounced the *Smith v. Allwright* decision. Since the Democratic convention would never adopt these measures, Texas' Democratic members of the Electoral College would be free to vote for whichever anti–New Dealer appealed to them, perhaps the renegade Southern Democrat, Virginia Senator Harry Byrd, or even GOP nominee Thomas Dewey. The result of this ballot-nullifying tactic would have been the disfranchisement of Texans in the general election.[12]

But the Texas Democratic Party had long maintained the peculiar practice of holding two state conventions in presidential years, the second one in July, normally for the purpose of planning the fall campaign and writing the state party's platform. Aroused New Dealers now contested this second election of local delegates in many spirited conventions across the state. In the confusing and emotional second state convention, the New Deal delegates barely defeated the rebels and then replaced the renegade electors with Democrats pledged to support FDR. The anti–New Dealers promptly formed the Lone Star State's own political party, the Texas Regulars, who hoped their candidate would siphon off enough voters to deny Roosevelt a victory in Texas. The movement was led by a host of oil and gas company presidents, lawyers, and lobbyists such as Hugh Roy Cullen and many others on the Far Right, including Weinert, Strickland, Hoblitzelle, Stewart, Fleming, O'Daniel, and Dies. Although lavishly financed, they were unable, finally, to agree on a nominee. Nor could they cooperate with the Republicans, since most Regulars wanted to vote Democratic in state and local elections, and did not really favor Dewey. Besides, Texas Republicans wanted to keep their party identity in order to enjoy patronage (their main reason for existence) from future GOP administrations and in case a two-party system grew out of the political wars of 1944.

The Regulars nevertheless ran a campaign worthy of their beliefs. The Democratic Party and the New Deal were accused of communism, Judaism, and undermining the supremacy of the white race, among many other charges. But their economic planks—the loathing of federal regulations, government bureaucrats, and unions—were more important to most of them than the bigotry. The Regulars resented government intrusion in the marketplace even in the name of home-front sacrifices—after all, rationing impeded free enterprise. O'Daniel handled much of the speechmaking, while openly violating campaign finance laws. He no longer drew huge crowds, but with the support of the *Dallas Morning News* he gamely offered his latest insights, for example, that Roosevelt was a greater danger than Hitler and that virtually every high officeholder in the nation wanted to communize America. Receiving less than 12 percent of the vote, mostly from affluent urban precincts across the state, the Regulars quickly disbanded and, as a bloc, returned to the Democratic Party. Congressman Martin Dies retired, physically ailing and still heartsick over his dismal defeat in 1941. Also in the aftermath of Roosevelt's victory, Governor Stevenson managed to propose new regents appointees drawn exclusively from the state's tiny minority of Texas Regulars. But a Democratic backlash had set in, forcing the governor into unprecedented wheeling and dealing in the state senate for two weeks before he could secure confirmations.

It is not known what promises were made, but judging by the subdued results, the governor and his new regents seem to have concluded that the turmoil and perhaps the micromanagement had outlived its usefulness. Nevertheless, the most conservative faction of Texas Democrats had set the precedent of a bloc of party leaders bolting the party out of ideological conviction.[13]

The Texas Right defeated Homer Rainey's gubernatorial bid in the 1946 Democratic primary with none-too-subtle cultural appeals involving race, religion, and sex. His opponent, railroad commissioner Beauford Jester, accused Rainey of being the tool of labor, blacks, and communists. Anonymous circulars and rumors further charged Rainey with sexual degeneracy and of being a "nigger lover," though the greatest underground triumph may have been convincing the voters that Rainey, an ordained minister, was an atheist. The moneyed interests of Texas—not dominated by the Regulars but including them—were far less concerned about the supposed issues of race, sex, and religion, but were much more concerned about Rainey's advocacy of closing the state's deficit with a tax on corporations. That truly frightened the Texas Manufacturers' Association, the leading lobby for heavy industry and for "rigid economy in government," which spent a record half million dollars to ensure Rainey's defeat.[14]

In 1948 there was another internal revolt against the Democrats, ostensibly caused by President Harry Truman's civil rights program. Governor Jester charged that the president's proposal to make the wartime Fair Employment Practices Committee a permanent body was a violation of "racial purity laws," a message amplified by party-bolter Strom Thurmond in his presidential bid. But the greater material objection to Truman in Texas was his position that oil lands beyond the three-mile limit in the Gulf belonged to the United States, but oilmen preferred Texas' claim—because of the state's lower tax—that its boundary extended twelve miles out into the sea. State land commissioner Bascom Giles proclaimed that rather than surrender these misnamed "tidelands," Texas should secede from the union. In the end, most such right-wing bombast fizzled, and Truman carried Texas easily.[15]

Another highlight of the year was that polls revealed that Pappy O'Daniel's support had shrunk to 7 percent, surely an all-time low for an incumbent senator. His seat was contested by Coke Stevenson and Lyndon Johnson in the Democratic primary. Upon perceiving that he was losing, Johnson gained votes by accusing Stevenson of being a tool of the Communists, though he knew it was preposterous. It was so close that both camps clearly tried to steal the election, and Johnson succeeded. Hugh Roy Cullen backed young Republican oilman Jack Porter's senatorial campaign in that fall's general election, a portent of the GOP's eventual rise. In 1948 Johnson still won handily, but Porter did better than expected, and he and Cullen began devoting themselves to transforming the Texas GOP into an actual party and pushing it to the Far Right.[16]

Meanwhile, the Truman administration, numbed by years of false charges of spies, became aware that some government employees did have communist connections. The administration's severe loyalty investigation, along with the simultaneous campaign for the European Recovery Program, aroused strong anticommunist emotions. Just as the Truman administration was trying to damp down these emotions, the nation was assailed by a series of events in 1949 and 1950 that further provoked strong anticommunist reactions: Soviet acquisition of atomic weapons, the communist victory in China, the exposure of Alger Hiss, and the outbreak of war in Korea. These events on Truman's watch appeared to confirm both the dangers of communism and the failures of Truman, and played into the hands of the Republicans.[17]

Republican senator Joseph R. McCarthy of Wisconsin, who owed much to Martin Dies, burst on to the national scene in 1950 and injected the GOP with an extremist—but popular—serum. McCarthy tapped into the raw nerve of Americans' rising fears, even though he was repeating old charges for which he had no evidence. McCarthy's reckless accusations that Democrats tolerated internal communist conspiracies probably contributed to Republican congressional victories in the 1952 election. Finally, on this occasion in 1952, the Texas Democratic party bolters included mainstream conservatives as well as the Far Right oilmen and their allies. Although useful for motivating voters, the communist "issue" was incidental for most of them compared to tidelands oil. The national Republicans' support for Texas' ownership of the tidelands led Governor Allan Shivers and all but one statewide Democratic officeholder to endorse Eisenhower and also run on the state GOP ticket as well as the Democratic. "Ike" carried Texas strictly as a Republican. Encouraged by their tidelands victory, Texas oil tycoons—including Cullen, Clint Murchison, and H. L. Hunt—yearned to exert more power in the nation. But, inspired by McCarthyism, they soon considered President Eisenhower and other Eastern Republicans insufficiently reactionary. They were beginning to move openly into the GOP, and along with other corporate interests combined with libertarians, racists, and vehement anticommunists, were attempting to take over the national Republican Party. State officials in 1952, however, still won far more votes as Democrats than as Republicans, and below the presidential ballot, Texas remained solidly Democratic in the 1950s.[18]

McCarthy was an extremist, but even he, while on a visit to Dallas in February 1954, twice refused to comment on the announcement that Governor Shivers would ask the Texas Legislature to make membership in the Communist Party a crime punishable by execution; under federal law party membership at that time was not even a criminal act. This solution was too extreme even for McCarthy, perhaps because he needed his communists as live targets. McCarthyism clearly fueled Martin Dies's comeback as congressman-at-large in 1952. He made his customary promise to disclose startling information of subversion involving prominent people, then learned that the House Un-American Activities Committee did not want him back. The nation still awaits Dies's "startling information."[19]

Governor Shivers, who liked to portray himself as a moral force in Texas politics, was running for reelection in the 1954 Democratic primary, plagued by scandals that would have surely defeated a less adept politician. His campaign conjured up a phony "clear and present danger" red scare, highlighted by the false claim that Port Arthur was shut down by a communist strike. While the legislature balked at his recommended death penalty for communists, the state loyalty and subversion acts of 1954 made membership in the Communist Party a felony punishable by a maximum fine of twenty thousand dollars and as many as twenty years in prison. Shivers also rode the emotional race issue for all it was worth. While his son attended an integrated high school, the governor denounced the Supreme Court's *Brown* decision and pledged to fight for segregation and local control of schools—meanwhile dictating to school districts that they could not integrate. He defeated Judge Ralph Yarborough with crossover GOP votes providing the winning margin.[20]

The Texas GOP had overthrown the old patronage machine in 1952 and enjoyed another breakthrough in the election of hyperconservative Bruce Alger as congressman from Dallas in 1954. He did not race-bait, however, while running against a strictly segregationist Democrat for reelection in 1956. He was a reactionary except for the vital issue of race, and was quite ineffective during his ten years in Congress—once coming out on the short end of a 378 to 1 vote, trying to block free milk for schoolchildren. But the Eisenhower administration disregarded the Republican parties of Texas and the South and worked with the dominant Democrats, winning the public endorsements of many of them in 1952 and 1956 and appointing several Texas Democrats to the cabinet. By the late 1950s Texas Republican leaders, aghast at the array of federal programs maintained, as well as their own lack of patronage, had broken with the administration but were bereft of funds and to most observers did not appear to be a serious threat to the Democrats. Grassroots organizers rejuvenated and slowly constructed the Texas GOP in the 1950s, and while Eisenhower's and Shivers's popularity also rejuvenated Texas Republicans in the long run, in the short term Shivers's decision to remain a nominal Democrat also staved off meaningful growth in the party ranks. Not until 1961 did many prominent Shivercrats officially leave the Democrats, sometimes in dramatic "resignation rallies."[21]

Notes

1. These concepts were adapted from various sources, including Clinton Rossiter, *Conservatism in America*, 2nd ed. rev. (Westport, CT: Greenwood Press, 1962), 166–69; and John Redekop, *The American Far Right* (Grand Rapids, MI: William Eerdmans, 1968), preface, 180–88. See also Michael Miles, *Odyssey of the American Right* (New York: Oxford University Press, 1980), 24–27; David Bennett, *The Party of Fear* (Chapel Hill: University of North Carolina Press, 1988), 278–85; and Murray Levin, *Political Hysteria in America* (New York: Basic Books, 1971), 219. For additional discussions of these matters, see Leo Ribuffo, *The Old Christian Right* (Philadelphia: Temple University Press, 1983), 225–74, as well as Seymour M. Lipset and Earl Rabb, *The Politics of Unreason* (New York: Harper and Row, 1970); Daniel Bell, ed., *The Radical Right* (Garden City, NY: Anchor Books, 1964); and Richard Hofstadter, *The Paranoid Style in American Politics and Other Essays* (New York: Alfred A. Knopf, 1965).

2. Richard Gid Powers, *Not Without Honor: The History of American Anticommunism* (New Haven, CT: Yale University Press, 1998), 162; George N. Green, *The Establishment in Texas Politics: The Primitive Years, 1938–57* (Westport, CT: Greenwood Press, 1979), 31–32.

3. Miles, *Odyssey*, 58–59; Raymond Moley and Celeste Jedel, "The Gentleman Who Does Not Yield," *Saturday Evening Post*, May 10, 1941, http://www.hattonsumners.org/library/gentleman.pdf (accessed October 8, 2011); Green, *Establishment*, 23, 31–32.

4. Green, *Establishment*, 34, 36–37, 74; Robert A. Caro, *The Years of Lyndon Johnson: The Path to Power* (New York: Alfred A. Knopf, 1982), 688–89.

5. Green, *Establishment*, 36–38; see also Caro, *Years of Lyndon Johnson*, 695–753.

6. Green, *Establishment*, 38–42. For more on the Texas labor movement in this era, see chapters in James C. Foster, ed., *Labor in the Southwest: The First 100 Years* (Tucson:

University of Arizona Press, 1982); and David Cullen and Kyle Wilkison, eds., *The Texas Left* (College Station: Texas A&M University Press, 2010).

7. Green, *Establishment,* 61–62; Morris Akin, *Tales of a Texas Union Pioneer* (Austin: Morris Akin, ca. 1992), 10–12; Dennis McDaniel, "Martin Dies of Un-American Activities: Life and Times" (PhD diss., University of Houston, 1988), 484; Michael Botson, "We're Sticking By Our Union: The Battle for Baytown, 1942–1943," *Houston History* 8 (Spring 2011): 12–14.

8. Green, *Establishment,* 83–86. On the ensuing academic freedom issue, see Homer Rainey, *The Tower and the Dome* (Boulder, CO: Pruett, 1971); and Alice Cox, "The Rainey Affair: A History of the Academic Freedom Controversy at the University of Texas, 1938–1946" (PhD diss., University of Denver, 1960).

9. Green, *Establishment,* 62 (quote), 86.

10. Ibid., 86–87; Don E. Carleton, *A Breed So Rare: The Life of J. R. Parten, Liberal Texas Oil Man, 1896–1992* (Austin: Texas State Historical Association, 1998), 236–43, 302–6.

11. Green, *Establishment,* 88; Carleton, *A Breed So Rare,* 304, 311–13. Among the regents, H. H. Weinert, D. F. Strickland, Maco Stewart Jr., and Scott Schreiner were clearly identified by Roosevelt stalwarts as Texas Regulars or contributors to them, and Orville Bullington as a Roosevelt-hating Republican. See Green, *Establishment,* 49, 53, 83, 87; and *Dallas Morning News,* November 4, 12, 1944, and January 21, 23, 1945. Dan Harrison and Lutcher Stark were also suspected Regulars, but if so, they do not seem to have been as prominently involved.

12. Green, *Establishment,* 46–47; Jeff Roche, "Cowboy Conservatism: High Plains Politics, 1933–1972" (PhD diss., University of New Mexico, 2001), 105–10, 114–15.

13. Green, *Establishment,* 48–56; V. O. Key, *Southern Politics* (New York: Alfred A. Knopf, 1949), 256; McDaniel, "Martin Dies," 488–97; *Dallas Morning News,* February 4, 6, 11, 1945; Carleton, *A Breed So Rare,* 313–14, 322.

14. Green, *Establishment,* 90–96; quote in letter from Ed Burris, TMA Executive Vice-President, to Allan Shivers, January 30, 1951, Allan Shivers Papers, Texas State Archives, Box 73 (prior to collection's reorganization).

15. Green, *Establishment,* 108–12.

16. Ibid., 113–17; Robert A. Caro, *The Years of Lyndon Johnson: Means of Ascent* (New York: Alfred A. Knopf, 1990), 287–93, 303–84; Bryan Burrough, *The Big Rich: The Rise and Fall of the Greatest Texas Oil Fortunes* (New York: Penguin Press, 2009), 207. Much of the actual work of party building was accomplished by hyperconservative well-to-do women with time on their hands, who resented what they perceived to be the corruption and lack of choices in one-party rule; see Meg Grier, *Grassroots Women: A Memoir of the Texas Republican Party* (Boerne, TX: Wingscape Press, 2001), 3–19.

17. Powers, *Not Without Honor,* 191–225; Bennett, *Party of Fear,* 286–92; Richard Freeland, *The Truman Doctrine and the Origins of McCarthyism* (New York: Schocken Books, 1974), 334–60; Miles, *Odyssey,* 125.

18. Green, *Establishment,* 145–48; Mary Brennan, *Turning Right in the Sixties* (Chapel Hill: University of North Carolina Press, 1995), 5–13; Bennett, *Party of Fear,* 293–304; Burrough, *Big Rich,* 219, 222–23.

19. Miles, *Odyssey,* 136; Thomas Reeves, *The Life and Times of Joe McCarthy* (New York: Stein and Day, 1982), 319, 540; David Oshinsky, *A Conspiracy So Immense* (New York: Free Press, 1983), 302–4; Lipset and Rabb, *Politics of Unreason,* 220–24; Bennett, *Party of Fear,* 310; David Reinhard, *The Republican Right since 1945* (Lexington: University Press of Kentucky, 1983), 63 (quote); David Caute, *The Great Fear* (New York: Simon & Schuster, 1978), 72; Green, *Establishment,* 180.

20. Green, *Establishment,* 151–64; Ricky Dobbs, *Yellow Dogs and Republicans* (College Station: Texas A&M University Press, 2005), 101, 104–13; Patrick Cox, *Ralph W. Yarborough, the People's Senator* (Austin: University of Texas Press, 2001), 105–21.

21. Roger M. Olien, *From Token to Triumph: The Texas Republicans since 1920* (Dallas: Southern Methodist University Press, 1982), 139–46; Green, *Establishment,* 165; Dobbs, *Yellow Dogs and Republicans,* 121–23, 149–50; Sam Kinch and Stuart Long, *Allan Shivers: The Pied Piper of Texas Politics* (Austin: Shoal Creek Publishers, 1973), 215; John Knaggs, *Two-Party Texas: The John Tower Era, 1961–1984* (Austin: Eakin Press, 1986), 4.

The Paranoid Style and Its Limits

The Power, Influence, and Failure of the Postwar Texas Far Right

SEAN P. CUNNINGHAM

During one particularly memorable scene in Oliver Stone's 1995 pseudobiographical film *Nixon*, the title character finds himself in a dark, smoke-filled room on a ranch somewhere outside Dallas in 1963. There, he is confronted by a cabal managed by ultraconservative Texas businessmen—ostensibly real-estate tycoons and oil millionaires, subsequently identified in the film as "Birchers" and "extremists." Led by "Jack Jones"—a fictional composite archetype of Texas power and wealth (played, appropriately, by Larry Hagman)—the cabal tries to pressure Nixon into challenging John F. Kennedy in a 1964 rematch of their famed razor-thin presidential contest of 1960. It is his patriotic duty as an anticommunist, they say, but it is also his opportunity to make the right kind of friends in the Lone Star State. The room grows quiet, filled with unspeakable tension. Cautious and sweating through his response, Nixon, played by Anthony Hopkins, suggests that Kennedy will be virtually unstoppable in 1964, but he receives a jarring vote of confidence from the men who insinuate that JFK might not live to see 1964. The following scene splices newsreel footage and artful moviemaking to depict Kennedy's arrival at Love Field in Dallas on November 22, 1963, his fate already tragically sealed.[1]

In *Nixon*, as well as in the Oscar-nominated *JFK* (1991), Stone depicts a Texas Far Right willing and able to manipulate the nation's democratic processes and culpable not only for the death of John F. Kennedy but also for the destruction of rational, sane, democratic American liberalism. Later in *Nixon*, Stone reestablishes the relationship between Nixon and the Texas Far Right, this time through a meeting set in 1972 following the president's trip to China. During that encounter, the fictional Jones laments America's loss in Vietnam and threatens to destroy Nixon's reelection prospects if something is not done to thwart left-wing (always "communist") influence both at home and abroad. Jones's specific concerns include federal price controls on oil, the Environmental Protection Agency, court-ordered busing, Henry Kissinger's soft-headed internationalism, difficulties with "ragheads" in the Middle East, and the Allende regime in Chile. The scene further reinforces the notion that Nixon owes his presidency to the fictional Jones and the Texas Far Right cabal that put him there.[2]

Few would question the filmmaking talent of Oliver Stone, a Vietnam veteran and outspoken critic of American foreign and domestic policy during the post–World War II era. However, the care with which he seeks to responsibly retell history is another matter. Stone is hardly the only pop culturalist to capitalize on the stereotypical image of a criminally connected Texas Far Right. In fact, the image of greedy Texas oilmen conspiring to do all manner of evil in an effort to line their own pocketbooks has not only maintained resonance in the nation's popular consciousness but has actually gained momentum in recent years as a result of actions taken and accusations made during George W. Bush's presidency, primarily surrounding the administration's oil connections and military interventions in the Middle East.[3]

Perhaps more fairly than conservative critics might care to admit, such images reinforce stereotypes that conflate Dick Cheney and J. R. Ewing. But broadly speaking, are these stereotypes accurate? What, precisely, was the postwar Texas Far Right? Who was involved, how, why, and to what ends? Was Texas conservatism dominated by the Far Right in the decades after World War II? What is the legacy of the postwar Texas Far Right and does the modern Texas Republican Party stand as a testament to that influence?

This chapter contends that a Far Right element did exist in powerful and influential ways in Texas during the 1950s and early 1960s. During that time, the Far Right worked against national liberal Democrats as well as local ones, and sometimes advanced the cause of a conservative Democratic establishment, but it also contributed to the eventual destruction of one-party politics in the Lone Star State. Through all of this, the Texas Far Right reflected aspects of a radicalism with deep roots in the early twentieth-century Texas experience.

However, while acknowledging these realities, it is quite possible to overstate the influence of a Texas Far Right, particularly if trying to identify the origins of the modern Texas Republican Party. During the 1950s and early 1960s, the Texas Far Right existed as a multi-winged extremist faction, was led by a handful of oil tycoons, raised and spent significant amounts of money, gained widespread visibility, and influenced both major political parties in the state. Yet the Far Right's influence was limited in important ways and should not be mistaken as synonymous with the totality of grassroots efforts and strategic decisions made by the Texas Republican Party during those decades. Assuming a linear progression between the golden age of the postwar Texas Far Right and the Republican ascendancy of later decades grossly oversimplifies the complicated and multifaceted nature of post-1945 conservatism. In fact, as the Texas Republican Party finally began to make its accelerated ascent to eventual dominance, the organized influence of the Texas Far Right, concurrently and not coincidentally, waned. In essence, by passionately animating antiliberalism across the state, the Texas Far Right voiced many of the concerns that conservatives in later decades also shared. However, the often outlandish and conspiratorial style of those animations also stunted the growth of a viable Texas Republican Party. It was not until that extremist style was shed that the Lone Star State finally embraced two-party politics. The Texas Far Right of the 1950s and early 1960s likely would have been pleased with the state's political culture at the dawn of the twenty-first century, but it should not be given too much credit for the GOP's long-term success.

Filmmakers like Oliver Stone have not acted alone in advancing popular perceptions of the Far Right. Academics have also often confused and consolidated the various strands of American conservatism active throughout the twentieth century. The most common of these consolidations is the one that conflates radicalism and conservatism. Yet if the word "radical" implies something marginalized to an ideological fringe, far beyond a middle mainstream, then several aspects of the Texas Far Right's worldview were hardly radical. Informed by a long national tradition that supported the "invisible hand" of the free market, the Texas Far Right opposed "big government"—high taxes, regulations on business, and budget deficits. After World War II, much of the Texas Far Right also prioritized anticommunism and strong national defense. Such attributes were common in the 1950s across party lines, regardless of national geography or ideology. As was true for most conservatives in the South, the postwar Texas Far Right was also fiercely segregationist. Here, the Texas Far Right was on common ground with virtually all Southern Democrats, including some so-called liberals, though Republicans in other parts of the country typically (and irresponsibly) saw race as little more than an unhelpful distraction from larger issues involving labor, economics, and foreign policy. The Texas Far Right also lamented what they and many Americans saw as a decline in Judeo-Christian values and beliefs—concurrently viewed as a rise of modern, secular humanism. At a root level, none of this differentiated the Far Right from the central tenets of mainstream American conservatism.[4]

What broadly differentiated the Far Right from mainstream American conservatism was a fearful and conspiratorial paranoia that found communists and subversives lurking the dark corridors of state and national government, threatening to destroy not only an American way of life but also the very heritage of western civilization. In seeing such plots and fearing a "New World Order," the Far Right further differentiated itself from mainstream conservatism by yelling about communist plots and the "slippery slope of socialism" much more loudly than did most elected Republicans or the conservative Texas Democratic establishment.[5]

Scholars contemporary to the period subsequently conflated the Far Right with modern conservatism. First published in 1955, Daniel Bell's edited study *The New American Right* was among the first significant critical explorations into the origins of modern conservatism. Writing in the wake of Joseph McCarthy's dramatic rise and fall, Bell and the contributing authors advanced a relatively simple thesis: modern American conservatism was shaped by fears and anxieties related to the loss of social status and the onset of modernity. Put differently, the Far Right was having a psychological breakdown. Richard Hofstadter contributed to that volume but also published other works in which he detailed a "paranoid style" upon which populist conservatism was characteristically dependent. Insightful but often misinterpreted and oversimplified by other scholars, the lasting legacy of these and related studies during the 1950s and early 1960s shaped popular and intellectual perceptions for decades to come.[6]

Given the history and state of these popular perceptions, what, specifically, made the postwar Texas Far Right distinct? Where did it come from and how did it operate? The Texas Far Right that experienced its most dramatic ascendancy during the 1950s and early 1960s made that power surge within the context of a national Red Scare. As Americans celebrated the end of World War II, many also feared the outbreak of a third world war, which they assumed would pit the United States against the Soviet Union. Across the nation, all credible political figures—whether Republican or Democrat, conservative or liberal—embraced some brand of responsible anticommunism. But some, including many in Texas, also worried about domestic subversion—the "enemy within." In this worldview, almost anything could be feared as a communist plot. In much of Texas and most of the South, the movement for African American civil rights fell into that category. As was true in most Southern states, Anglo Texans often dismissed civil rights reform as radical social engineering, usually "communist-inspired." Linking race, desegregation, and communism was a common practice among Texans in both parties throughout most of the 1950s, though by the mid-1960s most politicians running for office were tempering their segregationist rhetoric.[7] The Ku Klux Klan made Texas its "banner state" during the 1920s, but during the late 1950s it was the White Citizens Councils that led the charge against integration and "social engineering." Without question, reactionary racism fueled part of a conservative backlash and contributed to a pervasive sense that social tides were turning against established traditions. Virtually all Texans associated with the Far Right held racist views, but not all Texans—or Southerners, for that matter—holding racist views were necessarily "Far Right."[8]

The Texas Far Right was equally concerned with other issues. Well-known defections within the Texas Democratic Party in 1944 and 1948 were caused, in part, by issues of race, but also by a growing opposition to "big government" in general. Such opposition was not simply "code" for racism. In 1944 the president of the University of Texas at Austin, Homer Rainey, was fired by the university's board of regents in a disagreement over how to police the school's economics department, which some claimed had been infested with "homosexuals and communists." National spy cases, including those involving Alger Hiss and the Rosenbergs, made headlines in Texas as they made headlines elsewhere. The House Committee on Un-American Activities (HUAC) was founded by Texas congressman Martin Dies in 1938 and actively worked to root out subversion from all aspects of American life during the late 1940s and early 1950s. At the same time, Joseph McCarthy's popularity in Texas skyrocketed, as it did elsewhere across the country. Overall, Texas political culture in the late 1940s and early 1950s reflected global tensions, the national political discourse, and local resistance to change. For some Texans, this culture contributed to a sense that their social traditions were being jeopardized. It was this "status anxiety" that scholars contemporary to the period saw when they tried to assess the roots of modern conservatism.[9]

To some degree, therefore, popular stereotypes of the Texas Far Right are rooted in a cultural "Texification" of national trends.[10] However, a handful of important, historical actors also lent those stereotypes local grounding. When one thinks of the postwar Texas Far Right, certain well-known names must be considered. These influencers functioned at the heart of the Texas Far Right and helped shape the state's earliest popular response to postwar conservatism.[11]

Sid Richardson is often considered a seminal figure of the Texas Far Right, though that reputation was built as much on the political relationships he maintained as a result of his near-billion-dollar fortune than on public politicking. Rich primarily because of oil, Richardson, though rarely in the public eye, enjoyed close working relationships with both Franklin Roosevelt and Dwight Eisenhower, though he broke with Eisenhower in 1956 over the president's decision to veto a natural gas bill. Richardson's philanthropy was also well known. In 1947 he created the Sid W. Richardson Foundation, which in addition to funding schools, churches, and hospitals also funded several private political operations. One of those included the Foreign Policy Research Institute, which worked with American military bases during the late 1950s in a joint effort to combat the "brainwashing" of troops stationed overseas. These efforts were motivated by fears that, in the wake of the Korean War, American GIs—because of their superficial appreciation for the true "meaning of America"—were susceptible to psychological warfare at the hands of crafty foreign enemies. Such fears were satirized or critiqued in several Hollywood films of the period, perhaps most famously in *The Manchurian Candidate* (1962). With Richardson's help, the Foreign Policy Research Institute also warned of the inevitability of global war with the Soviets and challenged Washington to immediately prepare for that conflict. Though Richardson died in 1959, his foundation still funded the Foreign Policy Research Institute through the mid-1960s as it famously preached to civic groups that Defense Secretary Robert McNamara's plan to shift the basis of the nation's nuclear defense from bombers to missiles was, in fact, a secret strategy for unilateral disarmament.[12]

Richardson, however, was not incapable of rational thought. In 1954, one month after Joseph McCarthy spoke at San Jacinto to commemorate the 118th anniversary of the decisive battle of the Texas Revolution, Richardson spoke to a reporter from *Fortune* magazine and lamented that the nation's most famous anticommunist had lost his luster in the Lone Star State. McCarthy's irresponsible tactics, Richardson suggested, were harming the anticommunist cause. Also quoted in the same article was Clint W. Murchison Sr., who, like Richardson, had been one of McCarthy's most faithful and valuable supporters in Texas. Also like Richardson, Murchison suggested that McCarthy's televised antics in the spring of 1954 were damaging the credibility of the anticommunist Right.[13] Murchison knew a thing or two about anticommunism. Wealthy because of oil and natural gas investments, Murchison made much of his personal fortune available to ultraconservative politicians like McCarthy, though he also contributed to several of Lyndon Johnson's campaigns, beginning in 1941, and was in regular communication with LBJ through at least 1960. Murchison's son, Clint Jr., was also a player in the world of the Texas Far Right. Perhaps most famous as the first owner of the Dallas Cowboys, a franchise he purchased in 1959, Murchison Jr. also financed right-wing politicians and conservative causes until he went bankrupt in 1985. Because of their extravagant wealth and social reputation, the Murchison family became well known as players in the Texas Far Right, though their actual influence in the long-term growth of the state's Republican Party was limited.[14]

Another well-known and exceptionally wealthy figure of the postwar Texas Far Right was Houston's Hugh Roy Cullen. Also rich because of oil, Cullen spent much of his adult life fighting the regulatory legacies of the New Deal. Reactionary and far more public with his opinions than Richardson or Murchison, Cullen—on multiple occasions—decried Harry Truman and Dean Acheson as traitors. He distrusted inherited wealth, championed self-help, was a staunch segregationist, and warned that the internationalism embodied by the United Nations was a frightful step in the direction of "one-world communism." His money helped fund the anti-Truman, segregationist Strom Thurmond's Dixiecrat campaign of 1948, the Eisenhower campaign of 1952, and the gubernatorial campaigns of Price Daniels and Allen Shivers. He was also the nation's single largest contributor to Joseph McCarthy's 1952 reelection in Wisconsin. Like Murchison, Cullen was also among several right-wing Texas millionaires to whom Lyndon Johnson pandered, particularly after 1948. In 1954 Johnson even solicited and received an endorsement from the influential Cullen in an effort to bolster his own anticommunist résumé.[15]

Cullen's bankroll benefited right-wing agendas in other ways as well. In 1949 Cullen used his financial weight to push John T. Flynn's controversial book, *The Road Ahead*, onto several best-seller lists. In that book, Flynn reiterated an earlier charge that FDR had "sold out" America at Yalta. He also offered a doomsday vision of the United States sliding into a totalitarian, communist abyss, greased by the regulatory and welfare legacies of the New Deal. In 1954 Cullen provided government teachers working in the

Houston Independent School District with free copies of another Flynn book, *While You Slept*, hoping for (and achieving) that text's adoption in several classrooms.[16]

In 1951 Flynn's influence over Cullen led to the Houston oil millionaire's investment in the Liberty Broadcasting System, a radio network operated by Gordon McClendon of Dallas. Cullen, with Flynn's help, identified McClendon's network as a potential vehicle for right-wing broadcasting. Temporarily saved by Cullen's investment, the Liberty Broadcasting System provided a forum for antiliberal and anticommunist messages across Texas throughout 1951 and 1952. In 1964 McClendon tried to cash in on his radio celebrity by running for a seat in the US Senate. He challenged one of Texas's most famous liberals, Ralph Yarborough, in the Texas Democratic primary and lost decisively.[17]

Perhaps the most famous name associated with the Texas Far Right was H. L. Hunt. A Dallas-based oil billionaire, Hunt was identified by *Fortune* magazine in 1948 as the wealthiest man in the United States. In 1951 he organized Facts Forum, a tax-exempt foundation best known for its television and radio broadcasting. Its most famous on-air personality was Dan Smoot, a former FBI agent turned ultraconservative political activist. During his broadcasts, Smoot engaged in what Hunt called "public education." For instance, Smoot insisted that the United States was a "republic," not a "democracy." "Democracy," according to Smoot, was "evil." Smoot's views on democracy were rooted firmly in his hagiographic view of the Founding Fathers, and, like Hunt, he advanced the notion that government intervention in any form was a step toward communism. During one particularly memorable broadcast, Smoot claimed to have discovered secret congressional plans to build a "reeducation camp" in Alaska for patriots who dared expose communist subversion within the government. The "camp," he claimed, would be disguised as a community mental health facility. By 1964 Smoot was preaching opposition to America's "invisible government" in his own weekly conservative newsletter, the *Dan Smoot Report*.[18]

With Smoot's help, Facts Forum quickly grew into a significant vehicle for communicating the Far Right's agenda. With Hunt's financial backing, Facts Forum distributed free editions of various ultraconservative pamphlets and books, as well as a regular newsletter called *Facts Forum News*. In 1952 the Minute Women of Houston—a Far Right organization born one year earlier in collaboration with the vociferously anticommunist American Legion—used information gathered from Facts Forum to mobilize resistance to the hiring of George Ebey, an Oregonian educator appointed as the new superintendent of the Houston Independent School District and quickly deemed dangerously liberal by the Texas Far Right. At its peak, Facts Forum was powerful enough to have both Allen Shivers and John Wayne serving on the foundation's board of directors. Facts Forum ceased operations in 1956, but in 1958 Hunt revived the concept under a different name and premise. Known as LIFE LINE, Hunt's new vehicle took a more religious approach to fighting liberalism, socialism, and communist subversion. LIFE LINE broadcast programs via radio and television and distributed a newspaper that by 1962 enjoyed a circulation of over thirty-five thousand.[19]

Hunt's name has long been associated with conspiracy theories surrounding the assassination of John F. Kennedy, but no credible evidence exists to actually connect the Texas oil billionaire to that crime. Critics have speculated that Jack Jones, the fictional archetype portrayed by Larry Hagman in Oliver Stone's *Nixon*, is based on popular perceptions of Hunt. It is true that one of Hunt's sons (Nelson Bunker) purchased the famous full-page advertisement ("Welcome, Mr. Kennedy, to Dallas") that ran in the morning edition of the *Dallas Morning News* on November 22, 1963. That ad reflected the Texas Far Right's highly critical view of Kennedy, but as Chandler Davidson has pointed out, it was no more outrageous than any number of other incidents in Dallas during the early 1960s—and certainly does not make Hunt guilty of murder. However, scholars like Davidson have simultaneously overstated the degree to which Hunt's influence shaped the future course of Texas conservatism, particularly in the narrative that explains the construction of a viable Texas Republican Party. Shortly after Hunt died in 1974, *Texas Monthly* commented that Hunt never became a major power broker in conservative Texas politics because credible conservatives worked hard to distance themselves from Hunt's "lunatic fringe." This was particularly true after the Goldwater debacle of 1964, which Hunt aggressively supported.[20]

Though many of its most prominent spokesmen were oil tycoons and media manipulators, the Texas Far Right was also backed by several advocates external to that rarefied community. The first worth noting is Bruce Alger, a five-term congressman representing the Fifth District of Texas, which covered most of Dallas. First elected in 1954, Alger earned a national reputation in November 1960 when he led a raucous protest near the Adolphus Hotel in downtown Dallas, organized against a Kennedy-Johnson campaign appearance featuring LBJ. At that rally, Alger held a sign that said, "LBJ Sold Out to Yankee Socialists." For this and a legislative record remarkable for its futile obstructionism, Alger contributed to Dallas's reputation as a staging ground for the Far Right.[21]

When elected in 1954, Alger was the first Republican to win a congressional seat from Texas since 1930—clearly an important moment for the Texas GOP. In Dallas, Republican organization around Alger's campaigns established a grassroots culture that benefited John Tower's bids for the US Senate in 1960 and, successfully, in 1961. Alger also used local media to his advantage in ways that Republican candidates had not previously employed. A regular on morning talk shows, Alger courted the local press and used images of his children to present a fatherly persona. At the same time, his weekly newsletters decried liberalism as coded "socialism" and advanced many of the same conspiratorial themes articulated by H. L. Hunt's Facts Forum and LIFE LINE, as well as those proffered by national radio personalities like Billy James Hargis and Clarence Manion, both of whom enjoyed followings in Texas.[22]

Alger's reputation as an ultraconservative was bolstered by his friendship with another famed personality of the Texas Far Right, General Edwin A. Walker. Walker became a darling of the Texas Far Right in 1961 when he moved to Dallas after his military career was cut short because of a controversial program known as "Pro-Blue." Essentially an indoctrination program initiated by Walker while he was stationed in Germany, Pro-Blue was designed to curb the communist "red tide" as it was typically represented on global maps. The program consisted of lectures given by Walker in addition to pamphlets and newsletters published by the John Birch Society. In several lectures, Walker questioned the loyalty of Harry Truman, Eleanor Roosevelt, and Edward R. Murrow, among others. Upon learning of Pro-Blue, John F. Kennedy pressured Walker to resign. Walker then moved to Dallas and prepared for a career in politics. Less than a year removed from the military, Walker ran for the governorship of Texas. His campaign was a disaster and he finished a distant sixth out of six candidates running for the post in the Democratic primary. Walker ran as a Democrat, despite Alger's pleadings that he run as a Republican. A staunch segregationist and believer that the civil rights movement was being directed out of the Kremlin, Walker refused to join the Republican Party, believing that racial egalitarianism could best be fought as a Democrat.[23]

Walker's extremist but very public image polarized conservatives, most of whom actively rejected the retired general's paranoia. In 1964 the conservative and influential student group Young Americans for Freedom dropped Walker from their list of invited speakers to a rally at Madison Square Garden. *National Review* also dismissed much of Walker's conspiratorial viewpoints, choosing to distance itself from the Far Right—as it had already done with the John Birch Society—in the hopes of building a more responsible and ideologically stable conservative movement. By 1965 as Walker continued to warn of domestically organized communist plots, even the John Birch Society questioned the retired general's "touch with reality" and dropped Walker's name from several pieces of organization-produced literature.[24]

Beyond this brief stint in the public eye, Walker is also well known as Lee Harvey Oswald's first target for assassination. On April 10, 1963, Oswald fired a rifle shot at Walker as he sat near a window inside his Dallas home. Oswald's shot was deflected by the windowpane and narrowly missed. These details were released to the public by the Warren Commission in 1964. Walker has also been cited as inspiration for the character "Jack D. Ripper" in Stanley Kubrick's dark Cold War satire *Dr. Strangelove or: How I Learned to Stop Worrying and Love the Bomb* (1964).[25]

J. Evetts Haley also deserves recognition as a seminal figure of the postwar Texas Far Right. Actively oppositional to the New Deal during the 1930s, Haley's vocal but politically impotent Jeffersonian Democrats of Texas reflected an early but isolated brand of Far Right conservatism. During the 1940s his vociferous anticommunism, much of which was directed at the ivory towers of higher education, made him a friend of the countersubversive Far Right. Haley continued to agitate on behalf of the Far Right throughout the early 1950s, which led to a remarkably unsuccessful bid for the governorship of Texas in 1956. Perhaps Haley's most successful political venture came in 1960, when—as head of Texans for America—he led a charge to rid Texas public schools of several textbooks that dared to portray the United Nations, Social Security, and the income tax in a positive light. But Haley's most famous contribution to Texas political culture came four years later when he published *A Texan Looks at Lyndon*, a scathing campaign-year indictment of Lyndon Johnson. Memorable as a tract of the Texas Far Right, Haley's book found its way into many homes, but its message fell on largely deaf ears as Johnson carried his home state by a whopping 27 percent margin.[26]

The Texas Far Right was financed and dominated by these and other personalities, but it would be a mistake to strictly limit one's definition of the Texas Far Right to a handful of colorful individuals. By far the most famous organization of the Texas (and national) Far Right during the early

1960s was the John Birch Society (JBS). Organized in 1958 in Indianapolis by Robert Welch, JBS quickly emerged as a leading organization for the countersubversive Far Right. JBS also developed a reputation for radical, paranoid extremism. For instance, in his 1963 book, *The Politician*, Welch charged that Dwight Eisenhower had been "a dedicated conscious agent of the Communist conspiracy." That paranoid style caused headaches for conservative candidates who were sympathetic to many of JBS's core values but unwilling to embrace the reckless, conspiratorial personality associated with the organization's leadership. William F. Buckley dismissed Welch's paranoia as ridiculous. Conservative intellectuals like Buckley joined a growing list of Republicans who either denounced JBS entirely or at least distanced themselves from Welch.[27]

As it turned out, one of the quickest ways to lose an election during the early 1960s—both nationally and in Texas—was to have an affiliation with the John Birch Society. This was true even in the Texas Panhandle, where JBS successfully recruited, by some estimates, "thousands" of members, though specific numbers remain unknown. In Amarillo, for instance, the leading JBS personalities were Jack Seale, the city's mayor, and Wes Izzard, a local TV pioneer. In 1962 Seale ran for a congressional seat but was overwhelmingly rejected at the polls, his JBS affiliation a major reason why. Despite whatever limited following JBS had among conservative Texans, nothing devastated a political campaign like being labeled a "Bircher"—a lesson Seale learned the hard way in 1962.[28]

Another critically important factor in the history of the postwar Texas Far Right, as well as the history of Texas politics more generally, was the assassination of John F. Kennedy. The nation's fascination with the Kennedy assassination persists well into the twenty-first century. That persistence is due in part to the endurance of conspiracy theories, many of which incorporate players of the Texas Far Right. Dallas's reputation for Far Right antagonism overwhelmed early evidence pointing to Oswald's guilt as JFK's lone killer. Within hours of the assassination, NBC interviewed several random New Yorkers who pointed to Dallas's ultraconservatism as plainly complicit in the president's murder. Those conspiracy theories grossly overestimate the reach of the Texas Far Right into credible circles of power. However, those same theories reflect an anti-extremist backlash that very quickly and severely wounded the Far Right's political influence. In the wake of Kennedy's death, radical, paranoid extremism lost whatever credibility it still had, thereby forcing conservatives, and especially Texas Republicans, to rethink their public associations and strategies for future growth.[29]

This was particularly evident during the elections of 1964. As the nation mourned Kennedy and accused many suspects of his murder, Texas tried to make amends. This was unusually tricky since the new president, Lyndon Johnson, was a Texan. The 1964 presidential campaign centralized a growing backlash against radical extremism. That backlash made it virtually impossible for even responsible conservatives to win elections. Most remember LBJ's anti-extremist campaign against Barry Goldwater, immortalized by the famous "Daisy" advertisement. Fewer remember that it was actually Nelson Rockefeller and the GOP's eastern wing that first catapulted the image of a reckless Goldwater into the nation's consciousness. Due in part to the extremist charge, Goldwater's candidacy in Texas was a disaster—not surprising if one considers how acutely sensitive Texas voters were to such labels after Kennedy's death. Bruce Alger and Gordon McClendon were both overwhelmingly rejected in 1964, a result of the same political climate. In the race for US Senate, George H. W. Bush lost to the liberal Ralph Yarborough, who imprecisely and unfairly portrayed Bush as a "darling of the John Birch Society." Dallas-based political strategist Peter O'Donnell—the brains behind Alger's political career and much of the Goldwater movement—subsequently shifted his focus away from Far Right ideology and toward party building. He grew cautious and surprisingly moderate in the years after Kennedy's death and Goldwater's defeat.[30]

Ultimately, then, what is the legacy of the postwar Texas Far Right? Does the modern Texas Republican Party owe its contemporary dominance to the roots of that legacy? If winning elections counts for anything, then one must conclude that the postwar Texas Far Right described in this chapter was, politically, a miserable failure. After roughly twenty years of fund-raising and growing visibility in the decades following World War II, countersubversive, conspiratorial red-baiting was publicly disavowed, even by a majority of Texans. Organizations like the John Birch Society not only lost membership but also became the coffin nail that conservative, and especially Republican, candidates desperately tried to avoid. Other "extremist" candidates, even of varying stripes, fared little better in Texas during the 1960s and 1970s. For instance, George Wallace's showing in Texas in the 1968 presidential election was by far his worst in any state of the old Confederacy. Relatively liberal Democratic presidential candidates carried Texas in 1964, 1968, and 1976. During that twelve-year stretch, only in 1972, when the Democratic Party nominated the wildly unpopular George McGovern, were Texas's electoral votes carried by the

Republican candidate. Even John Tower, a former Goldwaterite, saw the anti-extremist writing on the wall, making underappreciated inroads with Mexican American voters in his successful reelection campaigns of 1966 and especially 1972. Tower's careful image-management coincided with a broader capitalization on efforts organized from within the state and national GOP to moderate the party's image while selling conservatism as a more responsible alternative to what conservatives increasingly argued was a liberal philosophy shaped by moral relativism and entitlement spending run amok.[31]

Though rapid urbanization, population growth, and economic vitality during the 1960s and 1970s undoubtedly supported the long-term process of partisan realignment, the key factor in the rise of the modern Texas Republican Party was image. After 1963 and 1964, the radical image of the Far Right was a hindrance to partisan realignment among Texas voters, most of whom, according to polls, were more moderate than popular perceptions suggest. The ability of conservative Republican candidates to shed the extremist label and, usually, to replace it with an image of hardworking, plain-folk, populist, cowboy "Americanism"—regardless of whether conservatism actually represented those things—comforted most Texas voters. After roughly 1960, the ability to manufacture a marketable image quickly became the most critical necessity to a successful political campaign in the new TV age. Among other things, the postwar Texas Far Right misunderstood the power of political imagery. Therefore, more than any other figure, Ronald Reagan deserves credit for the success of the modern Texas Republican Party. His regular presence at party fund-raisers and civic organizations in Texas, beginning in 1967 and continuing almost unabated through 1980, coupled with the skilled, crafted charm of a former Hollywood actor, transformed the public's image of conservatism and the Republican Party. Reagan's campaigns in 1976, 1980, and 1984 enabled a younger generation of Texas voters—many of whom had relocated to Texas, along with their parents, from Rust Belt locales in the North—to realign to the GOP, breaking with more than a century of "yellow-dog" traditions. Even if Reagan's conservatism shared much in common with the central tenets of the postwar Texas Far Right's basic worldview, his style did not. Nor was the Far Right the only political faction espousing themes of limited government and strong national defense during the 1950s, 1960s, and 1970s. Reagan did not scare most Texas voters, in part because he typically attacked his opponents as misguided rather than complicit in a global communist conspiracy. His popularity among voters made Republican affiliations respectable in Texas on an unprecedented scale. State leaders who switched parties often did so knowing that Reagan's popularity at the head of the national ticket would provide long coattails.[32]

But none of this happened to any significant degree until the 1980s, which again calls into question the legacy of the postwar Texas Far Right. The wealth and paranoia of the Texas Far Right might very well have contributed to the popular evolution of a conservative worldview that gained resonance after the mid-1960s. Contemporary critics might charge that the paranoid style remains alive and well, thriving in powerful grassroots movements such as the Tea Party. But to see an inevitable, linear continuity between the postwar Far Right and a political culture that would laud Rick Perry for threatening secession is to ignore several decades of partisan contestation—all of which was ultimately contingent on the ability to sell voters on the sanity of an ideological worldview.[33]

Notes

1. *Nixon*, directed by Oliver Stone (Cinergi Pictures Entertainment, Hollywood Pictures, Illusion Entertainment, 1995), DVD.

2. Ibid.; *JFK*, directed by Oliver Stone (Warner Bros., 1991), DVD.

3. See, for example, Kevin Phillips, *American Theocracy: The Peril and Politics of Radical Religion, Oil, and Borrowed Money in the 21st Century* (New York: Viking, 2006).

4. For more on Texas political culture during the 1940s and 1950s, see, for example, Robert Dallek, *Lone Star Rising: Lyndon Johnson and His Times, 1908–1960* (New York: Oxford University Press, 1991); and George Norris Green, *The Establishment in Texas Politics: The Primitive Years, 1938–1957* (Norman: University of Oklahoma Press, 1984). For a particularly accessible overview of the twentieth century's broader conservative movement, see Gregory L. Schneider, *The Conservative Century: From Reaction to Revolution* (New York: Rowman & Littlefield, 2009).

5. For an effective and accessible overview of the life and times of many of Texas' most famous and politically active oil barons, see Bryan Burrough, *The Big Rich: The Rise and Fall of the Greatest Texas Oil Fortunes* (New York: Penguin Press, 2009). See also, for example, Don E. Carleton, *Red Scare!: Right-Wing Hysteria, Fifties Fanaticism, and Their Legacy in Texas* (Austin: Texas Monthly Press, 1985).

6. See, for example, Daniel Bell, ed., *The New American Right* (New York: Criterion Books, 1955). Bell's book was revised and updated in 1963 as *The Radical Right: The New American Right* (Garden City, NY: Anchor Books, 1963). A third edition of the book was released in 2001 by Transaction Publishers. See also Richard Hofstadter, *The Age of Reform* (New York: Vintage Books, 1955); Hofstadter, "The Paranoid Style in American Politics,"

in *The Paranoid Style in American Politics and Other Essays* (Cambridge, MA: Harvard University Press, 1965); Michael Kazin, "The Grass-Roots Right: New Histories of U.S. Conservatism in the Twentieth Century," *American Historical Review* 97, no. 1 (February 1992): 136–55; Christopher Lasch, *The New Radicalism in America, 1889–1963* (New York: W. W. Norton, 1965); and Kendrick Oliver, "'Post-Industrial Society' and the Psychology of the American Far Right, 1950–74," *Journal of Contemporary History* 34, no. 4 (October 1999): 601–18. Oliver's article provides an effective, balanced critique of Bell's thesis. It also mentions a study done by Alan C. Alms, who examined class and social status identifiers for McCarthy supporters in Dallas during the early 1950s, finding that Far Right supporters "were more likely than liberals to be, or to be married to, businessmen or high-income salesmen" (614). See also James Piereson, *Camelot and the Cultural Revolution: How the Assassination of John F. Kennedy Shattered American Liberalism* (New York: Encounter Books, 2007). The study of modern conservatism has enjoyed an academic renaissance since about the mid-1990s. These recent scholars, while not dismissing the Hofstadter-Bell thesis entirely, have certainly complicated the understood origins of the conservative Right. Among contemporary academics, significant debate rages on the origins of modern conservatism, but very few scholars continue to find the origins of a Republican ascendancy in a radical, paranoid, or marginalized Far Right. See, for example, Donald T. Critchlow, *Phyllis Schlafly and Grassroots Conservatism: A Woman's Crusade* (Princeton, NJ: Princeton University Press, 2005); Darren Dochuk, *From Bible Belt to Sunbelt: Plain Folk Religion, Grassroots Politics, and the Rise of Evangelical Conservatism* (New York: W. W. Norton, 2010); Kevin M. Kruse, *White Flight: Atlanta and the Making of Modern Conservatism* (Princeton, NJ: Princeton University Press, 2005); Matthew D. Lassiter, *The Silent Majority: Suburban Politics in the Sunbelt South* (Princeton, NJ: Princeton University Press, 2006); and Lisa McGirr, *Suburban Warriors: The Origins of the New American Right* (Princeton, NJ: Princeton University Press, 2001).

7. Reactionary opposition to the civil rights movement in Texas—including the Far Right's reaction to the passage of the Civil Rights Act of 1964 and the Voting Rights Act of 1965—receives very little attention in this essay. This is not because the Far Right supported these laws. In fact, the Far Right was, predictably, very hostile to the civil rights movement. However, as I contend throughout the chapter, the Far Right's influence waned considerably after 1963 and therefore is less important to the broader political narrative of late-1960s backlash. It is true that most voting Texans opposed the civil rights movement and these two specific acts, particularly the public accommodations provision in the Civil Rights Act of 1964. Yet this backlash was typically less vehement or aggressive in Texas than was the case in several other Southern states, and it did not manifest in immediate partisan realignment. Here, the political impact of Kennedy's assassination cannot be overstated. After Kennedy's death, Johnson used the nation's mourning as a weapon in passing civil rights laws and the Great Society. This tactic was very effective and largely worked in Texas, though it fell on deaf ears across much of Dixie. Put differently, most Texas voters gave Johnson a relative pass on the issue of race and did not hold it against him when he ran for president in 1964. All this is not to say that race was unimportant

to Texas politics. Race was an important factor, but not a decisive one. In short, as the Far Right grew less credible throughout the 1960s, conservative Texans in both parties continued to use race to advance opposition to the Great Society and—particularly by the late 1960s—a civil rights movement increasingly perceived as dangerously militant. Yet the evolution of this opposition is best understood apart from the confines of a study on the rise and fall of a postwar Far Right, which I argue was not synonymous with the more influential and mainstream brand of populist American conservatism. For a more detailed discussion of how race contributed to the rise of modern conservatism in Texas, see Sean P. Cunningham, *Cowboy Conservatism: Texas and the Rise of the Modern Right* (Lexington: University Press of Kentucky, 2010), 97–126.

8. Green, *Establishment in Texas Politics*; Jeff Woods, *Black Struggle, Red Scare: Segregation and Anti-Communism in the South, 1948–1968* (Baton Rouge: Louisiana State University Press, 2004).

9. Bell, *New American Right*; Randolph Campbell, *Gone to Texas: A History of the Lone Star State* (New York: Oxford University Press, 2003), 410–29; Carleton, *Red Scare!*; Green, *Establishment in Texas Politics.*

10. The term "Texification" is borrowed from Phillips, *American Theocracy.*

11. For example, see again Burrough, *Big Rich.*

12. Rick Perlstein, *Before the Storm: Barry Goldwater and the Unmaking of the American Consensus* (New York: Hill and Wang, 2001), 146; Ben H. Procter, "Richardson, Sid Williams," in *Handbook of Texas*, Texas State Historical Association, http://www.tshaonline.org; *The Manchurian Candidate*, directed by John Frankenheimer (MC Productions, 1962), DVD.

13. For example, see again Burrough, *Big Rich*; and Charles J. V. Murphy, "Texas Business and McCarthy," *Fortune* 49 (May 1954): 100–101, 208.

14. Ibid.; Dallek, *Lone Star Rising*, 201, 365, 399, 420, 457; Chandler Davidson, *Race and Class in Texas Politics* (Princeton, NJ: Princeton University Press, 1990), 68, 145, 264.

15. Carleton, *Red Scare!*, 89–93, 117–18, 166; Dallek, *Lone Star Rising*, 366, 450.

16. Ibid.; for example, see again Burrough, *Big Rich.*

17. Ibid.; Patrick Cox, *Ralph W. Yarborough: The People's Senator* (Austin: University of Texas Press, 2001), 207–9; Davidson, *Race and Class in Texas Politics*, 137–38.

18. Burrough, *Big Rich*; Carleton, *Red Scare!*, 93, 119–20, 180–82; Davidson, *Race and Class in Texas Politics*, 209–10; Perlstein, *Before the Storm*, 152.

19. Ibid.

20. Davidson, *Race and Class in Texas Politics*, 209–10.

21. David Pietrusza, *1960—LBJ vs. JFK vs. Nixon: The Epic Campaign That Forged Three Presidencies* (New York: Union Square Press, 2008), 386–87.

22. Cunningham, *Cowboy Conservatism*, 41–51. For much more on Clarence Manion, see Perlstein, *Before the Storm.*

23. Cunningham, *Cowboy Conservatism*, 41–51; John A. Andrew, *The Other Side of the Sixties: Young Americans for Freedom and the Rise of Conservative Politics* (New Brunswick, NJ: Rutgers University Press, 1997), 142–57; Schneider, *Conservative Century.* The best

treatment of Edwin Walker and his legacy as part of the rise of modern conservatism can be found in Jonathan M. Schoenwald, *A Time for Choosing: The Rise of Modern American Conservatism* (New York: Oxford University Press, 2001), 100–123.

24. Cunningham, *Cowboy Conservatism*, 41–51.

25. Cunningham, *Cowboy Conservatism*, 41–51; *Dr. Strangelove or: How I Learned to Stop Worrying and Love the Bomb*, directed by Stanley Kubrick (Columbia Pictures Corporation, Hawk Films, 1964), DVD.

26. Perlstein, *Before the Storm*, 150–51; For an excellent overview of American anticommunism, including an effective delineation between responsible and countersubversive anticommunism, see Richard Gid Powers, *Not Without Honor: The History of American Anticommunism* (New Haven, CT: Yale University Press, 1995).

27. Schoenwald, *Time for Choosing*, 62–99.

28. Ibid.; Lawrence Wright, *In the New World: Growing Up with America from the Sixties to the Eighties* (New York: Vintage Books, 1989). Wright reflects on his youth in Texas, including observations on the political culture of the Far Right, particularly in Dallas.

29. Cunningham, *Cowboy Conservatism*, 66; Davidson, *Race and Class in Texas Politics*, 206.

30. Bush's association with JBS was largely unfounded; Cunningham, *Cowboy Conservatism*, 54–56; Piereson, *Camelot and the Cultural Revolution*, 58–60.

31. Cunningham, *Cowboy Conservatism*, 1–11, 141–48, 218–19, 243–42.

32. Ibid.

33. Ibid., 90–91, 159–62.

Focus on the Family

Twentieth-Century Conservative Texas Women and the Lone Star Right

NANCY E. BAKER

Not long ago, the online magazine *Salon* heralded the revival of old-fashioned grassroots political tactics as a hopeful sign that big money and the mass media have not subverted American democracy. As increasingly expensive mass media political campaigns have become the norm, the use of mass media to reach the public is actually decreasing in effectiveness. Instead, the resurgence of "fieldwork" involving "personal networks, volunteers and door-knocking" is once again being seen as valuable.[1] The use of social networks and personal interactions to build a grassroots political movement has been seen before in this country, and perhaps there is no better example of the effectiveness of such politicking than in the growth of the conservative movement in the latter half of the twentieth century.

In recent years, historians of twentieth-century American history have paid greater attention to conservatives and conservative movements.[2] Whereas older studies had pathologized conservatives, some recent works have sought to examine conservatives without passing moral judgments or engaging in amateur psychiatric assessments.[3] Over the last two decades, historians of Texas have begun to explore the question of when and how Texas modernized; a recurring theme in the newer Texas historiography is "the conservative ascendancy."[4] At the same time, historians of women's history have broadened the definition of political activism to include women's activities that previously were not considered political in nature; other historians of women's history have sought to expand the field to include Southern women, as well as conservative or right-wing women.[5] Finally, twentieth-century Texas women's history is emerging as a topic in its own right, though this is a development in its earliest stages.[6]

At the crossroads of all of these developments stand a handful of historians whose work brings greater attention to conservative women's political activism, previously overlooked by both women's historians and political historians. Currently, no monograph exists on conservative women in twentieth-century Texas; what little research has been done tends to focus on women in Dallas and Houston, women leaning to the Far Right (rather than more moderate conservatives), and white, married, middle-class women. Often, a brief mention of conservative women can be found embedded within larger studies of politics. This chapter seeks to synthesize existing scholarship and add to the state of our knowledge on conservative women and the Right in twentieth-century Texas, beginning with the antisuffrage campaign of the 1910s and ending with the antibusing, antifeminist, and pro-family campaigns of the 1970s and 1980s.[7]

In the twentieth century, the first organized right-wing movement to attract conservative women in Texas was the antisuffrage movement of the 1910s. The Texas antisuffrage movement formed late compared to other states, as there was no sustained woman suffrage movement in the state requiring a response. The woman suffrage movement in Texas had had a particularly difficult time in taking root from the 1890s to the 1910s, but it had revived in 1913, and by 1915 was finally flourishing under the leadership of Minnie Fisher Cunningham.[8] The burgeoning woman suffrage movement alarmed Pauline Wells, who would become the founder of the Texas Association Opposed to Woman Suffrage (TAOWS). Married to James B. Wells of Brownsville, "a wealthy rancher and political boss," Pauline Wells was a lifelong conservative Catholic and, through her husband, able to gain access to the political elite. When the Texas Legislature first voted on woman suffrage in early 1915, Pauline Wells addressed the Texas state senate on the subject. Wells personally linked suffragism to "socialism" in remarks she made to the Texas Senate that day; thanks to Wells, Texas had the dubious distinction of being the only Southern state in which antisuffragists employed anticommunist rhetoric in their attacks on woman suffrage.[9] Possibly Wells's interest in the communist threat was spurred by living in a borderlands area (Brownsville is on the border of Mexico), where immigration and a vibrant socialist movement were more visible than in other Southern locales.[10] Less unusual was Wells's use of race as a theme in her antisuffrage arguments, in which she "united the 'red menace' with the 'black menace.'"[11]

In March 1915 Pauline Wells founded TAOWS and was elected its president. Hewing to traditional ideas about respectable female deportment, antisuffragists avoided parades, public demonstrations, and the like in favor of producing and disseminating antisuffragist propaganda.

The political pamphlets produced by Wells's TAOWS tended to focus on a few arguments that antisuffragists believed would be compelling: women involved in politics neglected their homes and children. Women had all the rights they needed, and the vote would not yield any necessary, additional benefits. Woman suffrage was inherently a radical measure, "hand in hand" with socialism. Finally, woman suffrage would mean "Negro rule" because in some areas black women outnumbered white women, and because, as Wells commented once, black women were extremely likely to vote "because they enjoy it."[12] Though Wells was a traditional woman focused on her home, she can be credited for helping another conservative Texas woman, Ida M. Darden, get her start in a right-wing political career through involvement in TAOWS.

Ida M. Darden is arguably the woman who most deserves to be thought of as the "grandmother of twentieth-century Texas right-wing women." Darden was a journalist and activist whose vigor was undiminished by the apparent contradiction her forty-year career posed to her traditional position on women's role. First famous as an antisuffragist, Darden provides a bridge from that conservative movement to the conservative movement of the next generation, anticommunism.[13]

Widowed at the age of twenty-three, Darden found herself forced to work full-time outside the home to support her one-year-old daughter. Working for James A. Arnold at the Texas Businessmen's Association, Darden received an education in lobbying for "big business" and soon had established her own network, complete with an influential political mentor, Senator Joseph Weldon Bailey.[14] Bailey inculcated Darden with his own love of "states' rights" and belief that any threat to states' rights meant "racial equality and miscegenation."[15]

In 1916 Darden's conservative views and friendship with Pauline Wells landed her the position of publicity directory for TAOWS.[16] The antisuffrage propaganda that Darden produced in her role showcased her developing political views, including an emerging misogyny and elitism. Darden subscribed to the nineteenth-century ideology of separate spheres, in which men were charged with duties in the public realm (such as business and politics) while women were to devote themselves to the private realm (home, family, and religion). On the basis of the belief that politics would be outside women's natural abilities, Darden argued that women were "hysterical" and not able to handle the responsibility of voting. However, women were not the only ones who ought to be barred from the political arena, according to Darden. She declared, "[T]he great majority of American people are incapable of governing themselves. . . . Instead of increasing the number of unintelligent voters, I would favor taking away the right of suffrage from most of the men who exercise it now."[17]

Despite the efforts of Wells, Darden, and the antisuffragists, the Texas Legislature in 1918 granted Texas women the right to vote in primaries.[18] The Democratic Party dominated Texas politics; therefore, voting in primaries was equivalent to being able to vote in elections.[19] In 1919 the legislature unanimously passed a state constitutional amendment allowing women to vote; voters were to have the final say on the issue at the polls in May 1919. Legislators had included in the proposed amendment that aliens would no longer have the right to vote, and this posed a potential complication; voters would be forced either to approve both sections of the amendment (giving women the vote while taking the vote away from aliens) or neither section. Creating a further challenge for woman suffrage supporters, aliens would have the right to vote on this proposed amendment, while women would not.[20]

Pauline Wells and Ida Darden rallied their antisuffragists for one more battle, to oppose the amendment. (Given Wells's and Darden's shared antiradicalism, one cannot help but wonder if they had any misgivings about fighting to defeat an amendment that would disfranchise aliens, a group often linked to radicalism.) As before, the antisuffragists' main strategy was to spread their campaign literature and personally lobby those they knew. Antisuffragists' arguments also were identical to their prior campaign.[21] Wells and Darden must have felt tremendous satisfaction when the state woman suffrage amendment was defeated at the polls by a margin of twenty-five votes. Analysis of the election returns, however, revealed that voters had voted against depriving aliens of their right to vote, rather than voting against women gaining the right to vote.[22]

Almost immediately, the issue of woman suffrage was back in play. On June 4, 1919, Congress passed the federal constitutional amendment for woman suffrage and sent it to the states for ratification. On June 28, Texas became the first Southern state to ratify this amendment.[23] This turn of events effectively ended the suffrage and antisuffrage movements, but it certainly did not end the career of Ida Darden.

Despite having lost the antisuffrage struggle, "Darden emerged from the suffrage fight as a heroine among Texas conservatives."[24] Darden turned her energies toward fighting communism. In the end, this shift in Darden's focus may have still contributed to her meeting the goal of her original activism, which was to suppress feminism. Recent scholarship has argued that "anticommunist attacks on women in government and policy circles curbed both feminism and the social democratic potential of the New Deal."[25]

Building upon her experience as an antisuffrage activist and fully exploiting her political contacts, Darden joined the "inner circle of Texas politics" as a protégé of Senator Bailey within the Democratic Party. In time, Darden and her brother, Vance Muse, "became important lobbyists and fund-raisers for [ultraconservative] . . . efforts." Darden's work as a lobbyist "may have been motivated by financial rewards as well as by loyalty to conservative causes."[26] Doing financially well enough to buy herself a farm, Darden remarried in 1920, to Walter Frank Myrick, who soon joined Muse and Darden in their lobbying work.

While Ida Darden held right-wing political views, she was an implacable foe of the reborn Ku Klux Klan (KKK) in the 1920s, which had added a nativist dimension to its traditionally racist agenda. Darden objected to the new KKK not because of its racism, but on the grounds that its persecution of Catholics was at odds with the US Constitution's promise of freedom of religion.[27] Other right-wing Texan women, however, found the KKK to be congenial with their own organizations. Founded in 1922, the Grand League of Protestant Women was "[o]ne of the most prominent right-wing women's societies of the 1920s . . . headquartered in Houston." The Grand League espoused "'white supremacy, protection of womanhood, defense of the flag' and social service work." The women of the Grand League sought to take under their wing young, unskilled, rural women migrating to Houston in search of jobs. While helping these young women improve their marketable skills, the Grand League also sought to cultivate future members of their organization.[28] Other organizations with explicitly anti-immigration agendas included the Order of American Women in Texas, as well as the Order of Protestant Women in Texas and Oklahoma.[29]

Women in such right-wing Protestant nativist groups joined the newly created Women's Ku Klux Klan beginning in 1923. The national leader of the WKKK was Lulu Markwell, an Arkansas woman who had previously been active in championing the causes of Prohibition and woman suffrage.[30] Indeed, the WKKK differed with the KKK in urging women's independent political participation, the better to protect one's family, home, community, and country.[31] Emphasizing this point, "the WKKK declared itself an organization 'by women, for women, and of women [that] no man is exploiting for his individual gain.'"[32] Conflict arose over gender and money, two entangled issues. The KKK chafed at the WKKK's independent attitude and inaccessible coffers, and the WKKK members were determined to maintain their organization's autonomy. In 1925 three powerful Dallas WKKK members (Alice Cloud, D. B. George, and Flora Alexander) filed multiple suits against the new national WKKK leader, Mrs. Robbie Gill Comer, and her husband, Judge James Comer, for a variety of gross financial improprieties. While money was an issue, however, the suits may also have been prompted by the Comers' marriage and Mrs. Comer's subsequent surprising rise to WKKK power, developments which spawned "rumors that a small group of Klansmen led by Judge Comer controlled the affairs of the allegedly autonomous WKKK." Ultimately, the various suits were dropped and Mrs. Gill Comer drummed the Dallas women out of the organization.[33]

In Texas, the appeal of the new KKK crossed class lines, drawing in white Protestant members from all walks of life. The new KKK "transcended the limits of a nativist and racist organization and became a device for the ruthless dictation of community morals and ethics."[34] The Texas KKK focused on "moral and political reform," which to Klan members "meant preserving or restoring the status quo . . . [as well as] direct, often violent attempts to force conformity . . . and to rid state and local governments of dishonest politicians."[35]

Dissatisfaction with politicians was something the Klan and Ida Darden shared. During the 1920s, Darden began to evince a new mistrust of the federal government and a general distaste for all government.[36] Darden's disgust with government led her to run for the US House of Representatives in 1932, an interesting decision on the part of a once staunch anti-suffragist. Despite political and financial support from powerful friends and a platform focused on the single issue of repealing Prohibition, she lost the Democratic primary.[37]

During the Great Depression, Darden and Muse became increasingly concerned with the direction in which the federal government and the country were headed. Spurred on by her brother's ceaseless political lobbying and activism for right-wing causes, Darden took on the New Deal, along with labor union growth, socialism, and civil rights, as threats to the American way of life and system of government. In their opposition to Roosevelt's policies, Muse and Darden had plenty of company.

Texas became "a hotbed of business anti-New Deal sentiment."[38] Opposition to the New Deal in Texas centered on the idea that the new policies being proposed or enacted by the federal government were dangerously close to socialism. For example, US representative George B. Terrell (a Democrat from Alto, Texas) claimed that adopting a compulsory federal tax on cotton was akin to "adopt[ing a] . . . Soviet system of government and [would] Russianize this country."[39] In 1936 an anti–New Deal faction of the Democratic Party emerged, calling itself "the Jeffersonian Democrats" and seeking to prevent Roosevelt's reelection. The Jeffersonian Democrats included among them US representative Joseph Weldon Bailey Jr. (the son of Ida Darden's political mentor).[40] By the 1940s the division in the Texas Democratic Party over the New Deal had created "the most bitter intra-Democratic [Party] fight . . . in the South."[41] In addition to hostility toward federal control over the economy, anti–New Deal sentiment now also explicitly included opposition to racial equality.[42] The anti–New Deal Democrats created their own third party in 1944, the Texas Regulars; their platform broadly repudiated Roosevelt's policies while championing white supremacy and states' rights. The Texas Regulars were composed largely of the elite connected to oil and business concerns, with Oveta Culp Hobby as the most prominent female member.[43] Although the Texas Regulars ended in 1945, many went on either to join the Dixiecrats in 1948 or to become Democrats-for-Eisenhower.[44]

Ida Darden spent the height of the Cold War era working as a right-wing journalist.[45] From 1949 to 1961, Darden published the newspaper *Southern Conservative*. Due to a conservative benefactor's largesse, Darden had a platform for her right-wing political views, a platform that she alone controlled. She made the most of it.[46]

Championing right-wing causes that allowed her to blend her elitism, racism, and anticommunism, Darden was outspoken in her opposition to Hawaiian statehood. Darden rejected Hawaiian statehood, as many Southern whites did who favored segregation, on the grounds that a "polyglot race" should not have equal rights to whites. Grimly giving voice to a view shared by segregationists throughout the South, Darden declared, "[A]n integrated society encouraged the lust of nonwhite men for white women and invariably resulted in 'race mixing.'"[47] Furthermore, segregationist whites opposed to Hawaiian statehood were convinced that nonwhites were incapable of self-government and also that "nonwhites were more susceptible to manipulation by communist agitators."[48] Believing that race, culture, and politics were somehow linked at a level impervious to education or charity, Darden and her ilk could not imagine nonwhites having the innate ability for democracy and freedom that whites had.

The other issues that Darden chose to attack were a veritable smorgasbord of "every reform movement of the day."[49] In the pages of her newspaper, Darden advocated "economic conservatism, social conservatism, and constitutional conservatism with the rhetoric of anti-Communism and Christian fundamentalism."[50] In inflammatory language tinged with violence, Darden attacked the very concept of racial equality, and she argued that the alleged ignorance of recent immigrants had allowed the federal government to erode states' rights. Women, too, were at fault for the inexcusable leftward tilt of government, Darden claimed, as indicated by the growth of the welfare state. Darden insisted socialism or communism was behind every development or movement she disliked, which included racial equality and feminism.[51]

Darden's disgust with politically active, liberal-leaning women boiled over in the 1950s, as she blamed "left-wing females . . . for ushering in Socialistic practices in government" and instead lavishly praised what she saw as a new breed of conservative woman who might prove to be a valuable counterforce. In 1954 Darden singled out two conservative women's groups, the National Association of Pro America and the Minute Women of America, for special commendation as the women who would right the wrongs feminists and their fellow travelers had perpetrated.[52] These groups, particularly the Minute Women, and Ida Darden's *Southern Conservative* would together instigate and sustain one of the country's most vicious Red Scares of the 1950s.

In the postwar era of the 1940s and 1950s, Houston was a city in transition. During and after World War II, Houston underwent booming economic growth, a dramatic influx of newcomers, and a shift in identity from small town to metropolis. Enormous change, resultant uncertainty and anxiety, and tensions between the existing population and the newcomers with different ideas, values, and politics all created a situation ripe for conflict. Owing to the local "power elite" and a small number of would-be crusaders, Houston was convulsed by a particularly ugly, energetic Red Scare.[53] The Minute Women of Houston were largely responsible.[54]

The Minute Women of Houston were a local chapter of a national organization, the Minute Women of America, begun by Suzanne Stevenson in 1949 in Connecticut.[55] The Minute Women had a "purposefully vague and nonspecific . . . platform concocted to chase phantoms." The lack of a list of major objectives, political goals, or desired legislation gave the organization tremendous flexibility.[56] One exception to this vagueness was when Helen Darden Thomas, Ida Darden's daughter, requested that the Houston Minute Women have permission to include in their statement of beliefs a "states' rights clause," which Stevenson allowed; this suggests a regionally specific principle.[57] Founded in 1951, the Houston chapter attracted white, affluent Republican women in their midthirties to fifties. The women who took the lead in organizing the Houston Minute Women were Eleanor Watt and Helen Darden Thomas. To generate interest in the organization, they held "[s]mall gatherings of women at teas, country clubs, and at a meeting of physicians' wives . . . in the winter of 1950–51."[58] The Minute Women had a streamlined, extremely hierarchical organizational approach to decision making; national leader Stevenson appointed all leaders, made all major decisions, and vested in local leaders all power for deciding agendas and controlling meetings. If a local leader displeased her, Stevenson summarily removed and replaced her. Ostensibly, the Minute Women's undemocratic ways were to "prevent Communist infiltration."[59]

By 1952 the Houston Minute Women counted five hundred members, possibly more; the organization had made a name for itself as "the most militant Red Scare group in Houston."[60] Seven of the Houston Minute Women performed the bulk of leadership activities that led the rest of the membership: Mrs. Virginia (Ross) Biggers, the appointed chairwoman of the group; Mrs. Virginia (Willard O.) Hedrick; Mrs. Eleanor (James) Watt; Mrs. Faye (J. C.) Weitinger; Mrs. Helen (Rosser) Thomas; Mrs. Dallas (Frank) Dyer; and Mrs. Bertie (Earl) Maughmer.[61] A group of no more than thirty women were the "hardcore of active followers" who would reliably carry out the mundane work that needed doing, whether helping with a mass mailing, writing letters to newspapers or politicians, or attending meetings.[62] Another seventy-five to one hundred members who were very affluent doctors' wives disdained the group's usual protests and more extreme right-wing issues, instead preferring to write letters and to focus on economic conservatism (such as preventing socialized medicine, attacking the income tax, etc.).[63] Ida Darden assisted her daughter's organization by using her newspaper, the *Southern Conservative*, to print anticommunist attacks against selected targets and to shower praise upon the Minute Women.[64] Suzanne Stevenson was a fan of Ida Darden's, declaring that her newspaper "should be required reading for all Minute Women" and that Darden herself was "brilliant."[65]

Stevenson had admonished her Minute Women not to act as a unit; instead, she preferred their activities appear to be the "spontaneous and unorganized" actions of various independent citizens.[66] The Houston Minute Women's standard operating procedure was to pounce on announcements of special events or speakers, do enough background research (if needed) to determine whether the event or person could be claimed to be "controversial," and then exert all manner of pressure tactics to prevent that event from occurring or that speaker from speaking.[67]

In 1952–53 the Minute Women turned their attention to the Houston Independent School District, determined to root out any and all subversive influences in public schools that might pollute their children. Among other school-related efforts, in 1952 the Minute Women attempted unsuccessfully to take over the local school board, and they successfully persecuted the new deputy superintendent of Houston's schools, George Ebey. The "Ebey affair" blew up into such a controversy that it was the leading news story in the entire city for all of 1953.[68] Despite sterling credentials and an impressive record of experience, Ebey was deemed by the Minute Women to be unacceptably radical. Ebey was forced out after only one year because he "provided a single target for those in the community who wanted to attack many different enemies." In this case, anticommunism was revealed to be a "symbolic issue" that allowed room for attacks on racial integration, New Deal liberalism, progressive education, outsiders, and intellectuals. A local power struggle over control of the schools was an additional factor.[69]

The Houston Minute Women began to marginalize themselves when they attacked one they might have formerly considered an ally: Oveta Culp Hobby.[70] Despite her brief involvement with the anti–New Deal Texas Regulars, Hobby had been chosen by President Roosevelt to lead the Women's Army Auxiliary Corps during World War II; then, during the Eisenhower administration, she became the first secretary of the newly created Health, Education, and Welfare Department (HEW). Hobby and her husband, Will, owned the *Houston Post* newspaper and were extremely powerful, not just at the city or state level but on a national level. The Hobbys were conservative Democrats in Texas "because of the realities of a one-party state. In national politics, however, they worked vigorously for moderate Republicans."[71] Oveta and Will Hobby coaxed Texas Republicans to support Eisenhower rather than Senator Robert Taft in 1952; many of the Minute Women had been Taft supporters and never forgave the Hobbys for this betrayal.[72] As one Republican Party faithful later commented, "In the 1952 national primary between Taft and Eisenhower, a rift developed in the Republican ranks. . . . Eisenhower had spoken out against the red-baiting of Sen. Joseph McCarthy and was generally considered by Taft supporters to be a liberal."[73]

The Minute Women and Oveta Culp Hobby had vastly differing perspectives on the Red Scare. "True believers" in the Red Scare, the Minute Women were disturbed that President Eisenhower did not dismantle the New Deal bureaucracy and root out all the communist sympathizers that the women believed had infiltrated the government. Worse yet, when Hobby became HEW secretary, one of her first duties was to develop a national health insurance plan, which quickly led the Minute Women to attack her for her "communist sympathies."[74] Hobby implemented her own ideological purge of academics identified as "security risks" from the pool of those receiving federal money to conduct medical research and those who held federal positions under her purview; some of her decisions in this were later reversed by the Supreme Court. Hence, Hobby was hardly soft on communism but was simply more moderate than the Minute Women.[75] Like Eisenhower, Hobby considered red-baiting a useful tactic to win elections; once Republicans were in power, red-baiting lost its utility. As the Minute Women increasingly criticized Hobby, as well as President Eisenhower and HEW, Hobby took steps to silence them.[76] The Hobbys' newspaper, the *Houston Post*, began to distance itself from the right wing in Houston over the summer of 1953, and in October published an extremely well-researched, eleven-part expose of the Minute Women.[77] The change in editorial tone, followed by the searing exposé, marked "the power elite's withdrawal of the sanction of legitimacy for the extreme right-wing's accusations."[78]

Although the *Post*'s exposé gained a national audience, the Houston Minute Women continued to wreak havoc in the Houston Independent School District.[79] In late 1953 and early 1954, they broadened their activist horizons and became involved in state-level and national-level politics, supporting Texas governor Shivers's reelection campaign and the federal Bricker Amendment, for which they combined forces with Minute Women in other states.[80] The Minute Women successfully lobbied to have Wisconsin senator Joseph McCarthy appear in Houston on San Jacinto Day on April 21, 1954; enthusiastically hosting McCarthy at precisely the moment he was becoming politically radioactive "would play a role in their decline."[81] During Governor Shivers's 1954 reelection campaign, his opponent, Judge Ralph Yarborough, seized upon the Minute Women's support of Shivers as a liability.[82] The Houston Independent School District school board elections of 1954 also signaled a change: voters elected a new liberal majority running on a platform promising to end the Minute Women's influence over the board.[83] The election of a liberal majority to the school board was singular in Houston's history: conservatives had always dominated the board.[84]

However, the new, liberal direction of the school board was cut short, likely due to the Supreme Court's historic *Brown v. Board of Education* decision in 1954; suddenly, racial integration was a more compelling fear than communism. Only two years later, in the 1956 election, the Minute Women's candidates returned to dominate the board based on their new, overtly pro-segregation platform.[85] From 1957 to 1959 the Minute Women and their allies on the school board focused on reviving their witch hunt for subversives within the schools while also promoting racial segregation. While the Minute Women were "pariahs" in some circles, they exercised tight control over the city's educational system.[86] As a result, the school board "strove to derail all efforts to integrate the city's public schools, including a federal judge's order to proceed 'with all deliberate speed.'"[87] Now that the right wing dominated the school board, they began to quarrel among themselves. Inglorious departures of right-wing school board members and their allies from 1958 to 1961, along with bitter infighting among the group, heralded the end of the Houston Red Scare by 1961. By the time Houston's Red Scare had ended, the Houston Minute Women had helped to "force some individuals out of their jobs, severely restrict freedom of speech, create contention in the churches, [and] disrupt the public school system."[88] Despite these deplorable achievements, however, the Red Scare in Houston lacked grassroots support, and instead at its most powerful was "a phenomenon of the press and community elite."[89]

One remnant of the red-baiting right wing's former power and far-reaching influence may have been the passage in the spring of 1957 of House Bill 523, which gave the state of Texas the right to draft women for service in the state militia. With all but one member voting in support of HB 523, the Texas Legislature suspended the usual procedures in order to pass the bill as quickly as possible, because there was "an emergency and imperative public necessity" to do so.[90]

In the 1960s, as anticommunism waned, the right wing identified new crusades. In 1964 the Sexual Information and Education Council of the United States (SIECUS) made publicly available "the nation's first comprehensive sex education program." Within four years about half the schools in the country were offering such classes. To conservative parents, this was an appalling overreach of the school system (and by extension the government) into one of the most private realms of parents' moral influence on their children. The Association of Volunteers for Educational

Responsibility in Texas (AVERT) formed to fight the threat. The John Birch Society, which was decreasing in numbers, sponsored a new offshoot organization known as the Movement to Restore Decency (Motorede), aimed at preventing sex education in schools.[91] Some conservatives scrutinized public schools not only for their sex education curricula but also for their curricula more generally. In Texas, possibly the best-known "textbook watchdogs" were the husband-and-wife team of Mel and Norma Gabler of Longview.[92] "[D]evout Southern Baptists and ranchers . . . [the Gablers] held conservative views in politics and religion" and were horrified to discover in 1961 that their son's high school textbooks lauded the New Deal, Keynesian economics, the expansion of federal power, and Darwin's theory of evolution, among other disturbing ideas. The Gablers devoted themselves to assessing textbooks and sharing their assessments with the Texas State Board of Education; the Gablers' kitchen-table critiques began to exert influence over which textbooks were chosen for use throughout the state, and textbook companies sat up and took notice. The Gablers were so successful in their surveillance efforts that "[b]y 1981, their home-based organization had become a nationally known conservative pressure group with a mailing list of twelve thousand members."[93]

During the Cold War era, many conservative women were finding new, effective and sustainable ways to channel their concerns for their homes, families, education, and the nation's moral compass. In certain parts of the nation, conservative women blossomed into enthusiastic participants in grassroots party politics.[94] In Texas, conservative women were largely responsible for the successful development of a two-party system in the latter half of the twentieth century.[95]

Texas was predominantly a conservative state, with most Texans adhering to a belief in "self-reliance" and individualism, which brought with it opposition to labor unions, welfare, and government intervention. The expansion of federal power during the New Deal, as well as government support for labor and racial minorities, alienated many conservative Texans from the Democratic Party and prompted some to look to the Republican Party as an option.[96] Beginning in 1938, conservative Texas women joined the new National Federation of Republican Women (NFRW), and by 1955 their numbers in the state had grown to such an extent that they formed the Texas Federation of Republican Women (TFRW).[97] Due to changes in leadership, the state's Republican Party was ready after 1950 to "wage . . . serious campaigns for elected offices for the first time." Not considered suitable potential political leaders, Republican women worked "to support the new leadership and rising candidates" through their clubs.[98] Republican women's clubs flourished in this era, attracting "white, middle-class, civic-minded, patriotic, Protestant women."[99] When a neighborhood lacked any formal Republican Party apparatus, "the local Republican Women's Club was the de facto party organization (and often the impetus for establishing a county party)."[100]

During Eisenhower's 1952 presidential campaign and Bruce Alger's 1954 run for Congress, Republican women "showed their ability to do the 'shoe leather politicking' that was necessary for victory."[101] Unlike their husbands' structured work schedule, women could adjust their domestic responsibilities to meet their political needs.[102] Housewives were also "motivated by Cold War anti-Communism and the conviction that women should be on the front lines in defending their communities."[103]

The NFRW emphasized the threat of communism, which, in effect, elevated members' mundane political work to participation in "a moral crusade" to protect God and country.[104] Seen in this light, "menial labor" and tedious tasks such as "compil[ing] . . . voter lists, . . . precinct surveys, telephoning, and door-to-door canvassing" were imbued with great meaning and urgency.[105] The sociability inherent in recruiting and working with one's neighbors and friends toward a political goal added to the sense of fulfillment and meaning that Republican women derived from their involvement.[106]

Key political contests established that Republican women were essential to a successful campaign. In 1954 the Dallas Women's Republican Clubs did everything they could think of to support Bruce Alger's campaign for the US House of Representatives. The women hosted "Coffee with Bruce Alger" gatherings and circulated tirelessly throughout their neighborhoods to distribute pamphlets, bumper stickers, and signs door to door. Their unpaid labor helped staff Alger's campaign office and answer his phones. Alger won in 1954, "the first Texas Republican sent to Washington since the 1920s," and he credited his success in large part to "Republican clubwomen [whom he thought of as] his most effective workers."[107]

Apparently, some of Alger's female supporters were loyal to a fault. Four days before the 1960 presidential election, Alger led a group that included Junior League women and was later nicknamed the "Mink Coat Mob" in an alarming attack on Democratic vice presidential candidate Lyndon Johnson and his wife, Lady Bird, in the lobby of Dallas's Adolphus Hotel. Alger's supporters held signs "denouncing Johnson as a Carpetbagger controlled by Yankee Socialists" and swarmed the couple, "verbally and physically assault[ing] the Johnsons, hitting Lady Bird on the head with a picket sign and spitting at them."[108] Alger's confrontational method of protest with women in the vanguard would be repeated in October 1963, when US ambassador to the UN Adlai Stevenson visited Dallas to give a public address praising the United Nations. During his speech, Stevenson was heckled; as he exited the building, an angry crowd met him. One irate protestor, Mrs. Cora Lacy Fredrickson, hit Stevenson on the head with her placard reading "Down with the UN." When an astonished Stevenson asked his assailant, "What is wrong? What do you want?" Frederickson responded vehemently, "Why are you like you are? Why don't you understand? If you don't know what's wrong, I don't know why. Everybody else does."[109]

John Tower borrowed Alger's formula for success in 1961, when Tower ran for US Senate in a special election. Tower won, but only just barely, by ten thousand votes. His election was an enormous accomplishment for the state's Republicans, as Tower was the first Texas Republican in the Senate since the end of Reconstruction. Tower "credited women's work as crucial to his victory." In addition to their usual duties of hosting political coffee klatches, staffing campaign offices, and distributing political literature, Republican women in this contest engaged in an exhaustive, face-to-face effort to bring voters to the polls on election night. Tower institutionalized women's support by creating a "Womanpower for Tower" organization during his 1966 reelection campaign. From that time on, Republican candidates understood "women did the grassroots electioneering; candidates needed them to win."[110] Ray Barnhart, campaign manager for Republican Ronald Reagan's Texas primary race in 1976, once said, "[F]rankly, women do all the work in political campaigns. The men are the big deals and talk big, but it's the women who do the work."[111]

The story of one woman's journey from housewife to Republican political activist to candidate, and then party insider, offers a view into conservative women's experiences of this era. Raised from birth to be a conservative by her father, Marjorie Meyer Arsht would one day become a major force in Republican Party politics in Texas. Arsht described her father as passionately dedicated to the US Constitution and fond of "polemics" and dinner table debates; her father's "conservative Democrat philosophy had become the Republican Party platform" by late 1950s.[112] Arsht recalled being the lone Republican and outspoken anti-Zionist in her Houston temple's women's organization, the Congregation Beth Israel Sisterhood; as a Jew, her anti-Zionism was an extremely unpopular position to maintain, but she did so based on her belief in the separation of religion and the state.[113] At a monthly meeting in 1960, the Sisterhood hosted a debate between Republican candidate Bob Overstreet and Democratic candidate Wally Miller. Impressed by Overstreet, Arsht wrote him a five-dollar personal check, and "that one check put me on what few lists existed at that time. I knew a lot about national and foreign policy, not much about state structure, and nothing at all about precinct-level politics. But I soon learned."[114] Overstreet lost, which was no surprise to Arsht; as she explains, "Texans had become accustomed to voting for Republicans nationally, but they remained Democrats at the state level. They contended that a two-party state wasn't needed because Texas actually had two parties, one liberal and one conservative, all within the Democrat Party, of course. . . . Victory [in Democratic primaries] . . . was tantamount to election because seldom, if ever, did a Republican oppose the Democrat nominee in November."[115]

Arsht was not satisfied with this de facto one-party state system, arguing instead that "Liberty thrives on competition."[116] Soon after having donated money to Overstreet, Arsht found herself in demand: "I received call after call to help with one project or another. I became a very busy Republican activist at the local level."[117]

Arsht became such a powerful resource to John Tower's 1961 US Senate campaign that she herself was asked by the Harris County Republican Party to run as a Republican for the Texas Legislature in November 1962. When she agreed, the local Democratic Party tried unsuccessfully to woo her to be their candidate, a testament to her talents as a political asset.[118]

Arsht's run for office was essentially learning on the job how to be a candidate, not just a supporter. She held informal fund-raising gatherings at friends' homes and relied on her friend Oveta Culp Hobby for an unprecedented editorial endorsement in the *Houston Post*.[119] Arsht then personally made the rounds to other newspapers to argue that the press owed it to voters to offer state-level politics more coverage. She won an endorsement in the *Houston Chronicle* (which had previously endorsed her opponent, Wally Miller); the *Houston Press*; the leading African American newspaper in Houston, the *Informer*; and after public jousting with liberal Jews who attacked her candidacy, the right-wing *Human Events*.[120] Despite an energetic campaign, Arsht lost; however, the 48.9 percent of the vote she received "was amazing" and "losing didn't dampen [her] . . . enthusiasm" for party politics.[121] In particular, Arsht was now keenly interested "in building the party, not in running again for public office."[122]

Arsht would "help . . . launch [future US president] George H. W.

Bush's political career during a 1963 gathering in her Houston home," becoming instrumental in his election to Harris County Republican Party chairman that year.[123] In 1964 Bush ran for a seat in the US Senate and lost; however, his campaign for the House of Representatives in 1966 was a success. In both races, women became a key group of his supporters, nicknamed the "Bush Belles." The Bush Belles, like the women who had helped John Tower in 1962, were "suburban housewives who worked day and night for George Bush [and] . . . staffed his headquarters."[124] Arsht would spend the next forty years working tirelessly "to build the Texas Republican Party" and was active as a "GOP speechwriter and high-level assistant in the Department of Housing and Urban Development during the Reagan era."[125]

Arsht is an example of conservative women's involvement in nurturing the Texas Republican Party from its infancy to maturity; while in certain respects her story is unique, in other ways it represents what many Republican women experienced. For the most part, Arsht played a supporting role, facilitating the political successes of others. Generally, conservative women remained in the background, "[d]oing the Republican Party's mundane 'housekeeping' chores [that] earned women male praise but not authority in the party hierarchy."[126]

Barry Goldwater's presidential campaign in 1964 may have been an exception to the rule, as Goldwater selected certain leading Republican women in Texas to whom he delegated national responsibilities. Barbara Man, southern regional director of Goldwater's campaign, had come to his attention as a leader of the Texas "Draft Goldwater" movement and had been president of the TFRW during the first Tower campaign. Rita Bass (Clements) was the Republican National Committee's door-to-door canvas chairman in 1964, "encouraging the state organizations to adopt the plan that the Texas Federation of Republican Women had developed for the Tower campaign."[127] She had been chosen the previous year to be the NFRW's National Chairman of Campaign Activities, and she had cochaired the Texas Goldwater for President Committee in 1964. She had gotten her start knocking on doors to urge Texas voters to choose Eisenhower in 1952, and she would go on to hold various committee positions within the state and national Republican Party structures.[128]

Although Goldwater's campaign relied on "Goldwater Girls" and a grassroots volunteer army of housewives in California, Texas proved much less hospitable territory to the Arizona senator and presidential candidate.[129] To an extent, Goldwater was a victim of bad timing. In

October 1963 Goldwater was viewed favorably in Texas as a "responsible conservative," but after the tragic, violent assassination of President John F. Kennedy during a Dallas visit, most Texans recoiled from anything or anyone who had ties to extremists, particularly right-wing extremists.[130] Unfortunately for Goldwater, his most prominent supporters in Texas were widely considered right-wing extremists by their fellow Texans: J. Evetts Haley, H. L. Hunt, and Dan Smoot; their backing of Goldwater "contributed to the perception that his campaign was the arm of the Republican Party's lunatic fringe."[131] After a bitter fight within the Republican Party over the 1964 nomination, followed by President Johnson's attack ads during the campaign, Goldwater's image deteriorated quickly from "responsible conservative" to "dangerous extremist."[132] And, as historian Sean Cunningham has succinctly described the situation in Texas: "To be an extremist in 1964 was almost as bad as being a communist in 1952."[133] Texans' revulsion of all extremism led to Johnson trouncing Goldwater in that state, with a return of 63 percent versus 37 percent.[134] Although the Republican Party had made great strides in a short time, grappling with charges of right-wing extremism proved a distraction and an obstacle, delaying a political realignment of Texan conservatives to the Republican Party until the early 1970s.[135]

During the 1970s, previously apolitical conservative women across the country were shocked into political activism as a response to several issues they found extremely threatening, issues that have come to be called "social issues," such as school busing, abortion rights, gay rights, and women's rights. In forming various countermovements to oppose what they saw as federally supported and mandated change in several areas, conservative women thought of themselves as protecting the sanctity of marriage, home, family, and community, while also defending religion and the traditional American way of life. In Texas, two examples of conservative women taking action to protect from change all that they held dear occurred in the antibusing movement and the anti–Equal Rights Amendment (anti-ERA) movement. Movements such as these contributed by the late 1980s to a preoccupation within the national Republican Party with "family values" and a "pro-family agenda."

School busing was an incendiary issue of the early 1970s due to a number of Supreme Court decisions intended to increase racial desegregation of schools by mandating busing. In Dallas, Rose Renfroe established herself as a leading antibusing activist. Like Ida Darden long ago, Renfroe first became aware of politics and deal making on the job, working as a secretary. Unlike Darden, Renfroe worked for a labor union, the local AFL-CIO. As she later recalled, "I used to watch those politicians come in asking for favors, and I learned they are normal people like me." While working for the AFL-CIO, Renfroe challenged her employers on issues of sexual discrimination, and she won; later, she would vehemently reject the label of "feminist."[136] Renfroe put herself through college as an adult, finally earning a degree from Dallas Baptist College in 1974. Renfroe's confidence in asserting herself in the face of perceived injustice and her determination to succeed would come in handy in 1971, when a court order determined that busing would facilitate the desegregation of Dallas public schools.

Since the Supreme Court's *Brown v. Board of Education* (1954) decision, school desegregation had proceeded at a glacial pace. In 1968 the *Green v. County School Board* decision changed what desegregation meant; legally ending segregated schools was no longer enough and must now be followed with "desegregation plans that specifically ensured race mixing." *Swann v. Charlotte-Mecklenburg Board of Education* (1971) explicitly stated that school busing was mandatory in order to end racially segregated schools.[137] The era of school busing had begun; Dallas officials scrambled in the summer of 1971 to come up with a plan to satisfy Judge William Taylor, who presided over *Tasby v. Estes*, a lawsuit charging Dallas schools were segregated.[138]

The plan settled upon by school officials and Judge Taylor called for the "busing of almost 9,000 students from three high schools in South Oak Cliff" plus busing another 5,000 high school students (more African Americans than whites) from elsewhere in Dallas. Renfroe and her neighbors felt that their neighborhood, Oak Cliff, "[bore] the brunt of the . . . busing order." In addition, the middle-class white residents of Oak Cliff were seething with "a pervasive resentment" toward the power elites in the city, feeling that their interests had been ignored for a long while.[139] Renfroe spearheaded an antibusing campaign. Over one thousand parents and children attended an antibusing demonstration at City Hall on July 13, 1972, holding homemade signs that read "I'M FUS'IN ABOUT BUS'IN," "MY KIDS WILL NOT BE BUSSED," and "I WILL NOT BUS!"[140] On August 4, 1971, a crowd of unprecedented size showed up at the Dallas school board meeting to protest the "discriminati[on]" against Oak Cliff. The neighborhood had "only 16 percent of the total high school population [of Dallas, but] . . . would provide 64 percent of the transported students."[141] The antibusing activists from Oak Cliff were able to persuade Judge Taylor to stay his busing order for their neighborhood, which at first he did for five months, and then "[i]n January 1972 he made the stay permanent."[142] The busing plan Judge Taylor enforced would end up being "one-way busing of blacks as usual."[143] Renfroe and her antibusing group had had their way, and Renfroe had established a name for herself in the process.

Renfroe wanted to make the transition from activist to politician, much as Arsht had done, though in Renfroe's case, she had not started out as a political party activist. Renfroe ran for the Texas Legislature in 1972 unsuccessfully. In 1974 she was approached about being a volunteer in a women-staffed office in Oak Cliff for a Democratic mayoral candidate, clearly an adaptation of the "Womanpower for Tower" strategy; instead, after receiving her husband's approval, Renfroe decided to run for an office herself. She marshaled her resources—neighborhood children bribed with pizza—to go out and get signatures so she could put her name on the ballot.[144] In February 1975 a federal district judge changed the way Dallas elected its city council, replacing the "at-large method" with a "single-member district" approach; in other words, a candidate could focus on campaigning in one district or neighborhood of the city, rather than trying to drum up citywide support. This played to Renfroe's strengths; a thirty-two-year-old housewife herself at the time, she had a fingertip feel for her neighbors' concerns, and she was willing to put in "tireless door-knocking, phone calling, letter mailing, all harping on the day-to-day concerns of Oak Cliffians."[145] Running as a Democrat, Renfroe was "tough-talking . . . with a fierce anti-busing campaign and a call for 'a new Oak Cliff chauvinism.'" Her victory over the incumbent "rocked the city's political establishment."[146] Renfroe seemed to attract as much media attention for her feminine attributes (or perceived lack thereof) as for being "one of the most vocal members on the Dallas City Council." In 1976 *Texas Monthly* snidely commented on Renfroe's recent efforts to make herself more attractive, while others referred to her as "tacky."[147] Belittling Renfroe may have been an attempt to play down the threat she seemed to represent to the city's traditional power elite. Renfroe was an "uncompromising populist" determined to represent the people the elite had previously thought of as those "who should neither be seen nor heard when it came to city politics." Her antibusing crusade became extremely controversial "as the city's civic establishment was trying to implement a desegregation order quietly and without incident."[148] One pundit saw in Renfroe "the first visible manifestation in Dallas of the socio-political arousal of the white, blue collar, middle class begun by George Wallace 10 years ago." Furthermore, he credited Renfroe, and mayor Adlene Harrison, as "two middle class women [who have] ... force[d] a demonstrable change in the political life of this city."[149] Unfortunately for Renfroe, the politics of resentment she had so ably built upon crumbled, as school busing was extended to the entire city and Oak Cliff began to attract new residents and evince a renewed "optimism."[150] The changing times, as well as an unprecedented coalition of Renfroe's many political enemies, unseated her in 1977.[151]

Renfroe's defeat would not be the end of her political career; in 2002 and again in 2006, she ran as a Democratic candidate for Dallas County commissioner, and her campaign was noted for being controversial. In the Democratic primary, Renfroe outrageously accused a competitor of condoning pedophilia. Oddly, Rose Renfroe implied she was a Latina, putting "Rosita Renfroe" on the ballot and claiming it was a nickname her husband called her. Critics charged that she did this to win the Hispanic vote, as Dallas had "becom[e] ... more Hispanic, more ethnic and less white."[152] Despite the disgust of the press, in 2006 Renfroe won her party's nomination by thirty-eight votes.[153] With little support from the local Democratic establishment and little money in her coffers, Renfroe ran a tight race, ultimately losing to the Republican incumbent, Kenneth Mayfield.[154] In 2010 Renfroe once again packaged herself as "Rosita" Renfroe in her party's primary but was defeated by Elba Garcia, a former city council member.[155] Renfroe's brash, populist, controversial style that had worked well in 1975 was wearing thin in 2010; she was seen as ill-informed on issues and preoccupied with casting doubt on her competitors' credentials.[156]

At the same time as Renfroe's political debut in the 1970s, another example of Texan conservative women's activism emerged in the countermovement against the federal Equal Rights Amendment (ERA).[157] The text of the ERA stated:

> "Section 1. Equality of rights under the law shall not be denied or abridged by the United States or by any state on account of sex.
>
> Section 2. The Congress shall have the power to enforce, by appropriate legislation, the provisions of this article.
>
> Section 3. This amendment shall take effect two years after the date of ratification."

The ERA was first introduced into Congress in 1923, and Congress passed it in 1972. In order for the amendment to become part of the Constitution, thirty-eight states needed to ratify the ERA by 1979 (this deadline was later extended to 1982). Initially, the ERA was tremendously successful in garnering ratifications, but within a year of its congressional passage, anti-ERA activists had begun to mobilize and campaigned effectively against the amendment. In states where the legislatures had acted quickly and had already ratified the amendment in 1972, anti-ERA activists determined to be heard demanded rescission of their state's ratification. This is what occurred in Texas.

Unlike the majority of states that ratified the federal ERA, Texas had had a pro-ERA movement dating back to the late 1950s. In 1958 feminist lawyer Hermine Tobolowsky and the Texas Federation of Business and Professional Women (TX-BPW) began lobbying for a state Equal Legal Rights Amendment (ELRA).

The Texas Legislature finally passed the state ELRA in 1971. As mentioned above, in March 1972, Congress passed the federal ERA. The Texas Legislature quickly ratified the federal amendment only eight days later. In November 1972 Texas voters approved the state ELRA by an overwhelming majority of four to one.[158]

In 1973 conservative Texas women mobilized a grassroots anti-ERA movement. According to one study, conservative women in Texas who supported rescission were middle-aged, white, and middle- to upper-middle-class Republicans. Half of them were college educated, and 70 percent were housewives. Nearly all these women were church members, with a disproportionate representation of fundamentalist Christians; in fact, "a strong commitment to religion would seem to be the major source of their political beliefs."[159] According to these demographics, anti-ERA women as a group illustrate the emergence of evangelical Christians on the political scene in the 1970s in Texas, drawn into politics by their outrage over abortion, which had been legalized by the Supreme Court decision *Roe v. Wade* (1973), a case that originated in Dallas.[160] However, the conservative Texan women who engaged in anti-ERA activism do not all neatly fit the profile described in this one study; the women, their network, and their arguments are too complicated to be reduced to a single group: affluent, Republican, Christian fundamentalist housewives.

Dianne Edmondson was one of the key anti-ERA activists in Texas. Edmondson was initially a supporter of the ERA. After studying the amendment closely, however, she turned against it and became, in her own words, "one of its most ardent opponents."[161] In San Antonio in 1973, she founded the anti-ERA organization the Committee to Restore Women's Rights. Defying the stereotype of anti-ERA activists, Edmondson had worked as a teacher, journalist, and public relations director before becoming a full-time homemaker, wife, and mother of three.[162] Her activism showcased her professional skills in television appearances, a statewide seminar on the ERA, and speaking engagements.[163] By November 1974, the Committee to Restore Women's Rights had forty chapters in Texas, with another twenty to thirty more anticipated.[164] A self-described "'proud' member of the John Birch Society" (JBS), Edmondson insisted that the JBS had not provided any funds for her organization; perhaps more valuable than funding, though, would have been the guidance in how to organize a grassroots political campaign.[165]

Disproving the common perception of anti-ERA activists as being entirely dependent upon conservative Phyllis Schlafly's national anti-ERA leadership, Dianne Edmondson took the initiative in developing her own political network. She contacted Ann Daniels, a leader of the successful rescission movement in Tennessee, and sought her assistance as a resource in the Texas rescission movement. Edmondson asked Ann Daniels to persuade Tennessee state representative Larry Bates, the legislator who had led the rescission fight in Tennessee, to attend the public hearings in Texas in April 1975.[166]

Ann Daniels was also contacted by Women Who Want to be Women (WWWW), one of the most vigorous anti-ERA groups in Texas. There were reported to be chapters of WWWW in several cities throughout Texas. Headquartered in Fort Worth, WWWW received support from the Parker Chiropractic Research Foundation, also located in that city. The Parker Foundation was a leader in the relatively new technique of practice-building seminars aimed at helping chiropractors increase profits while also legitimizing their marginal status within the field of medicine. The Parker seminars relied heavily on Protestant evangelicalism and stressed the importance of a supportive traditional wife to a chiropractor's success in the world.[167] WWWW had strong ties to the Church of Christ, a Christian fundamentalist denomination; Mrs. Becky Tilotta and Lottie Beth Hobbs, WWWW founders, were prominent female members of the denomination.[168] WWWW saw themselves as part of a national rescission movement, seeking to spread their cause far beyond the confines of Texas.[169] By 1975 Hobbs claimed that WWWW had members in forty-six states in the nation; Hobbs hoped rescission in Texas would send an anti-ERA message to the federal government.[170]

While WWWW fit into stereotypes about religious conservatives being anti-ERA, one WWWW ally stunned reporters: the Mary Kay Cosmetics Company. There were reports that legislators were being flooded with anti-ERA mail prompted by chairman of the board Mary Kay Ash's use of her mailing list for the anti-ERA cause. The *Texas Observer* reported that an infamous piece of WWWW propaganda (a pink anti-ERA flyer decorated with clip art of women telephoning each other and sporting the title "Ladies, have you heard?") was discovered to have been included in a director's memo sent to Ash's mailing list. Furthermore, a WWWW newsletter explicitly acknowledged Mary Kay Ash for her support. Ash issued denials at first. Only when Texans for ERA contacted Ash to threaten a boycott of Mary Kay products did Ash officially distance herself from involvement in the ERA battle in Texas.[171]

Aside from the Church of Christ and the Mary Kay Cosmetics Company, there were a handful of other national organizations that were involved in the Texas rescission fight. The Texas group Women Activated to Rescind was a branch of the national organization Motorede, the JBS affiliate that crusaded against sex education in the schools.[172] By 1975, WWWW and Edmondson's Committee to Restore Women's Rights had joined in a coalition with Stop ERA, Phyllis Schlafly's national anti-ERA organization. In addition, there were a few Texas organizations that remained independent of this coalition, such as the Committee to Rescind the ERA, the Texas Farm Bureau, and Daughters Already Well Endowed.[173]

In 1975 the Texas State House of Representatives responded to the anti-ERA activism and considered a rescission bill, HCR 57. The House Committee on Constitutional Revision held a public hearing on April 14 to discuss whether to rescind ratification of the federal ERA, and over seventy witnesses testified. The arguments that anti-ERA witnesses made varied, but can be boiled down to a few key themes: that the ERA was "unnecessary, undesirable, and uncertain."[174]

The ERA was allegedly unnecessary because piecemeal legal reforms could be more precise and more flexible than a broadly stated constitutional amendment; witnesses pointed to recent laws as proof that this approach worked. As national anti-ERA leader Schlafly testified, "All the machinery is there to help any woman who has been discriminated against."[175] The claim that women already had all the rights they needed echoed antisuffrage arguments of old.

According to anti-ERA witnesses, the ERA was undesirable because a majority of women did not want it—only a vocal minority of radical feminists who wanted to compete with men favored the ERA. Flown in just for the occasion, Tennessee state representative Larry Bates denounced supporters of ERA as "women's libbers," extremists who "don't need men and are quick to boast about it." Bates claimed that such radicals admired "bastions of collectivity" such as China, the USSR, and Cuba. Dianne Edmondson declared, "It is apparent to anyone researching the [feminist] movement that certain radical elements who hold most of the decision-making positions are seeking a change in our society's structure and morals. . . . [T]he ERA is the primary legislative goal of these radical feminists." In portraying the ERA as undesirable, opponents' implication that communism had inspired women's rights activists hearkened back to the antisuffrage days of Pauline Wells and Ida Darden. Finally, anti-ERA witnesses believed the ERA was uncertain because neither the Supreme Court nor the federal government could be trusted. Given decisions regarding other issues such as school busing and abortion, conservatives had lost faith in the reasonableness of the Supreme Court.[176]

According to the conservative witnesses, dire consequences to women, the family, and society would be risked for an amendment without a single compelling benefit worth the cost. For that reason, rescission of the ERA ratification was necessary. As Edmondson concluded, "If you believe, as we do, that women are indeed the heart of the home, and that the family is the heart of our country, then you in good conscience must vote in favor of HCR 57."[177] However, HCR 57 remained buried in committee, and the rescission effort failed. Undeterred, the anti-ERA activists sought an alternative way to defeat the ERA and focused on a variant of rescission, a recall. Introduced into the Texas Legislature in 1977, the recall bill was also unsuccessful.[178]

Meanwhile, some of the anti-ERA activists decided to broaden their agenda. In the summer of 1975, WWWW was renamed the National Association of the Ws, out of deference to the large number of men who had joined the organization.[179] The Ws created a new charter and sought new, paying members, indicating their desire to be more than a temporary, single-issue organization. According to the *Dallas Morning News*, "The group is antifeminist, antipornography, and antiabortion. It supports parent monitoring of textbooks."[180] According to the Ws, their organization's activism would now address "all issues that involve the family."[181] The Ws' goal in general was "to see if we can turn this country around."[182] One member, Jo Ann McAuley, continued her crusade to monitor textbooks in the schools well into the 1980s.[183] Edmondson, founder of the Committee to Restore Women's Rights, became more deeply involved in politics, pursuing a career as a political insider; she is currently the Denton County Republican Party chairwoman.[184]

Perhaps the most symbolic event to highlight what conservative women in Texas (and nationally) had accomplished with their anti-ERA movement was the 1977 Pro-Family Rally, organized by Phyllis Schlafly and held in Houston at the same time as the International Women's Year (IWY) Conference. Schlafly intended the rally to prove to the nation that the IWY Conference, and feminism more generally, did not speak for all women. What the twenty thousand conservatives in attendance at the rally did was to codify what would come to be thought of as the "family values" agenda.[185] Conservatives were beginning to realize that there was enormous potential power in the kinds of social issues that had mobilized right-leaning women for decades.[186]

From the antisuffrage movement of Wells and Darden eschewing female political participation, to the WKKK's determination that women engage in politics free of male control, to the rabid anticommunism of the Houston Minute Women, to the hardworking housewives who built a two-party system in Texas, to the mothers monitoring textbooks, sex education, and school busing, to the anti-ERA women, the variations in the beliefs and goals of women on the right in Texas is astonishing in its complexity. Indeed, if any one theme unites the disparate women this essay has attempted to survey, that theme would be the way in which a focus on the family gave many different kinds of conservative women the motivation, and justification, for women's political involvement. Positioning themselves as protectresses of homes, families, and communities in their maternalist politics did not require conservative women to be traditional mothers, or even mothers at all. The very variety of the women on the right in Texas, and their different political agendas, suggests how flexible a concept "protecting the family" can be. Fertile ground for further research would be why some women have more successfully employed this maternalist "pro-family" rhetoric than others.

Notes

1. David Sirota, "The Rebirth of Grass-Roots Politics," *Salon*, June 7, 2011, http://www.salon.com/news/david_sirota/2011/06/06/grassroots_politics_reborn/index.html (accessed June 10, 2011).

2. For a recent review of the literature on the history of conservatism and ensuing discussion by many leading scholars in the field, see "Conservatism: A Round Table," *Journal of American History* 98, no. 3 (December 2011): 723–73.

3. See Donald Critchlow, *Phyllis Schlafly and Grassroots Conservatism: A Woman's Crusade* (Princeton, NJ: Princeton University Press, 2005); Michelle Nickerson, "Women, Domesticity, and Postwar Conservatism," *OAH Magazine of History* 17, no. 2 (January 2003): 17–21; and Lisa McGirr, *Suburban Warriors: The Origins of the New American Right* (Princeton, NJ: Princeton University Press, 2002).

4. Nancy Beck Young, "Beyond Parochialism: Modernization and Texas Historiography," in *Beyond Texas through Time: Breaking Away from Past Interpretations*, ed. Walter L. Buenger and Arnoldo De León (College Station: Texas A&M University Press, 2011), 221–69. Ty Cashion contends, "In order to understand Texas as it is emerging in the 21st century, a new meta-narrative is needed that seizes the intellectual center of gravity from the revolution and 19th-century frontier, and repositions it in the emergence of modern Texas, with a focus on the rise of multiculturalism and the conservative ascendancy." Ty Cashion, e-mail correspondence with author, October 4, 2011. According to Nancy Beck Young, Texas scholars are divided on when the state entered the modern era, although most would agree that the period's start can be situated somewhere between the New Deal and the civil rights era. For an alternative perspective, see Walter Buenger, *The Path to the Modern South: Northeast Texas between Reconstruction and the Great Depression* (College Station: Texas A&M University Press, 1997); Buenger argues that modernization of Texas began two decades before the New Deal era.

5. See Catherine Allgor, *Parlor Politics: In Which the Ladies of Washington Help Build a City and a Government* (Charlottesville: University of Virginia Press, 2000), for one example of a historian expanding the definition of "politics" to include women's traditional social networking role as political in nature. Another example is Danielle L. McGuire, *At the Dark End of the Street: Black Women, Rape, and Resistance—A New History of the Civil Rights Movement from Rosa Parks to the Rise of Black Power* (New York: Alfred A. Knopf, 2010), in which McGuire reframes African American women's resistance to rape (including testifying in court) as political activism that made a major (and previously ignored) contribution to the civil rights movement. Jean Gould Bryant has written a helpful review essay on the development of Southern women's history as a subfield; see Jean Gould Bryant, "From the Margins to the Center: Southern Women's Activism, 1820–1970," *Florida Historical Quarterly* 77, no. 4 (Spring 1999): 405–28. Recent works on right-wing women (or that include right-wing women) are Michelle M. Nickerson, *Mothers of Conservatism: Women and the Postwar Right* (Princeton, NJ: Princeton University Press, 2012); Kathleen M. Blee, *Women of the Klan: Racism and Gender in the 1920s, with a New Preface* (Berkeley: University of California Press, 2008); Catherine E. Rymph, *Republican Women: Feminism and Conservatism from Suffrage through the Rise of the New Right* (Chapel Hill: University of North Caroline Press, 2006); Kathleen M. Blee, *Inside Organized Racism: Women in the Hate Movement* (Berkeley: University of California Press, 2003); Paola Bacchetta and Margaret Power, eds., *Right-Wing Women: From Conservatives to Extremists around the*

World (New York: Routledge, 2002); Rebecca E. Klatch, *A Generation Divided: The New Left, the New Right, and the 1960s* (Berkeley: University of California Press, 1999); Susan E. Marshall, *Splintered Sisterhood: Gender and Class in the Campaign against Woman Suffrage* (Madison: University of Wisconsin Press, 1997); Donald G. Mathews and Jane Sherron DeHart, *Sex, Gender, and the Politics of the ERA: A State and the Nation* (New York: Oxford University Press, 1992); and Rebecca E. Klatch, *Women of the New Right* (Philadelphia: Temple University Press, 1987).

6. For example, see the following: Judith N. McArthur and Harold L. Smith, *Texas through Women's Eyes: The Twentieth-Century Experience* (Austin: University of Texas Press, 2010); Judith N. McArthur and Harold L. Smith, "Not Whistling Dixie: Women's Movements and Feminist Politics," in *The Texas Left: The Radical Roots of Lone Star Liberalism*, ed. David O'Donald Cullen and Kyle G. Wilkison (College Station: Texas A&M University Press, 2010); and Rebecca Sharpless, *Fertile Ground, Narrow Choices: Women on Texas Cotton Farms, 1900–1940* (Chapel Hill: University of North Carolina Press, 1999). There are also forthcoming works that will continue to focus on Texas women's history; see, for example, Stephanie Cole, Rebecca Sharpless, and Elizabeth Turner, eds., *Texas Women/American Women: Their Lives and Times* (Athens: University of Georgia Press, in press). Including Texas in his research, Kyle Goyette examines "the grassroots conservative backlash against the Equal Rights Amendment in the South and how that contributed to the rise of modern conservatism." (Goyette is completing his doctoral dissertation at the University of Houston.) E-mail correspondence with author, June 22, 2011.

7. In this essay, the terms "conservative" and "Right" are broadly construed.

8. In the 1890s the woman suffrage movement in Texas was a failure. Founded in 1903, the Texas Woman Suffrage Association died two years later. Women involved in a variety of Progressive-Era reform efforts in the 1910s began to develop an interest in woman suffrage at that time, and the growing mass support for woman suffrage led to a revival of the Texas Woman Suffrage Association (TWSA) in 1913. Minnie Fisher Cunningham was elected president of the TWSA in 1915. Judith N. MacArthur and Harold L. Smith, *Texas through Women's Eyes: The Twentieth-Century Experience* (Austin: University of Texas, 2010), 25.

9. Elna C. Green, "From Antisuffragism to Anti-Communism: The Conservative Career of Ida M. Darden," *Journal of Southern History* 65, no. 2 (May 1999): 292, 295. As Elna Green observes, linking suffrage to communism or socialism was not a rhetorical strategy used in the South, aside from in Texas. For an examination of socialism in Texas, see Kyle Wilkison, *Yeomen, Sharecroppers, and Socialists: Plain Folk Protest in Texas, 1870–1914* (College Station: Texas A&M University Press, 2008).

10. E. Green, "From Antisuffragism to Anti-Communism," 296.

11. Ibid.

12. Ibid.

13. Ibid., 287–316.

14. Ibid., 291. Indeed, Darden's "education" in politics may have skirted the edges of legality. See Kevin C. Moti, "Under the Influence: The Texas Business Men's Association

and the Campaign against Reform, 1906–1915," *Southwestern Historical Quarterly* 109, no. 4 (April 2006): 494–529.

15. E. Green, "From Antisuffragism to Anti-Communism," 292.

16. Ibid.

17. Ibid., 293–94.

18. A. Elizabeth Taylor, "The Woman Suffrage Movement in Texas," *Journal of Southern History* 17, no. 2 (May 1951): 194–215; see 210.

19. Ibid., 211.

20. Ibid., 212.

21. Ibid., 214.

22. Ibid., 214–15.

23. Ibid., 215.

24. E. Green, "From Antisuffragism to Anti-Communism," 296.

25. Landon R. Y. Storrs, "Red Scare Politics and the Suppression of Popular Front Feminism: The Loyalty Investigation of Mary Dublin Keyserling," *Journal of American History* 90, no. 2 (September 2003): 491–524; 496 (direct quotation).

26. E. Green, "From Antisuffragism to Anti-Communism," 298, 299.

27. Ibid., 297. See also Blee, *Inside Organized Racism*, 17.

28. Blee, *Inside Organized Racism*, 25.

29. Ibid., 189n46.

30. Ibid., 28–29.

31. Ibid., 31–33. The KKK emphasized the supportive, submissive, traditional role of the WKKK.

32. Ibid., 28.

33. Ibid., 60–61, 64.

34. Charles C. Alexander, *The Ku Klux Klan in the Southwest* (Lexington: University Press of Kentucky, 1965; Norman: University of Oklahoma Press, 1995), 19.

35. Ibid. For the focus on moral and political reform, see 25; for the meaning of reform, see 21.

36. E. Green, "From Antisuffragism to Anti-Communism," 299–300.

37. Ibid., 301. E. Green explains, "Conservative women could justify their involvement in politics by claiming that they had the 'right' politics."

38. Anthony J. Badger, *FDR: The First Hundred Days* (New York: Hill and Wang, 2008), 125.

39. Keith J. Volanto, *Texas, Cotton, and the New Deal* (College Station: Texas A&M University Press, 2005), 72.

40. For direct quotation, see George Norris Green, *The Establishment in Texas Politics: The Primitive Years, 1938–1957* (Norman: University of Oklahoma Press, 1984), 25. For Joseph Weldon Bailey Jr.'s membership in the Jeffersonian Democrats, see Lionel V. Patenaude, "Jeffersonian Democrats," in *Handbook of Texas Online*, Texas State Historical Association, http://www.tshaonline.org/handbook/online/articles/waj01 (accessed November 20, 2011).

41. G. Green, *Establishment in Texas Politics*, 6. Original quotation is from V. O. Key, *Southern Politics* (New York: Alfred A. Knopf, 1949) 254, 259, 269–70.

42. G. Green, *Establishment in Texas Politics*, 47.

43. Ibid., 49–50.

44. Numan V. Bartley, *The Rise of Massive Resistance: Race and Politics in the South during the 1950s* (Baton Rouge: Louisiana State University Press, 1999), 51; G. Green, *Establishment in Texas Politics*, 197–98. Bartley says that these same conservatives eventually became Republicans in the 1960s and 1970s.

45. E. Green, "From Antisuffragism to Anti-Communism," 302–8. Before launching her career as a journalist, Darden had survived a divorce, the death of her mother, and relocation to Houston to be near her married daughter.

46. Ibid., 303–8. See Nickerson, *Mothers of Conservatism*, 37, for the national readership of Darden's *Southern Conservative.*

47. Ann K. Ziker, "Segregationists Confront American Empire: The Conservative White South and the Question of Hawaiian Statehood, 1947–1959," *Pacific Historical Review* 76, no. 3 (August 2007): 439–66. See 451 for fears of "race mixing" and the direct quotation.

48. Ibid., 454n29, for belief that nonwhites lacked the ability to self-govern; see 455 for nonwhites' vulnerability to communism.

49. E. Green, "From Antisuffragism to Anti-Communism," 309–10.

50. Ibid.

51. Ibid., 309–10.

52. Ibid., 311.

53. Don E. Carleton, *Red Scare!: Right-Wing Hysteria and Fifties Fanaticism and Their Legacy in Texas* (Austin: Texas Monthly Press, 1985), 5 and throughout.

54. Ibid., 122.

55. Ibid., 111.

56. Ibid., 113.

57. Ibid., 122.

58. Ibid., 101, 111, 113. Carleton says that a second Houston chapter was started by Adria Allen at the same time, until she became aware of Watt and Thomas's chapter, at which point the two merged to become one. See Carleton, *Red Scare!*, 122.

59. Ibid., 114–15.

60. Ibid., 124–25. There were reported to be about fifty thousand members nationwide; Stevenson ended her role in the organization in 1952 to pursue other political opportunities. See Carleton, *Red Scare!*, 116, 121.

61. Ibid., 125–26. Carleton lists these women with their husbands' names first and their own first names in parentheses; I have chosen to reverse this order. The women's first names appear first, followed by their husbands' first names in parentheses.

62. Ibid., 131.

63. Ibid., 132.

64. Ibid., 142.

65. Ibid., 130.

66. Ibid., 115.

67. Ibid.

68. Ibid., 220; this was according to the *Houston Post.*

69. Ibid., 221–22.

70. Ibid., 237.

71. Ibid., 228.

72. Ibid., 228–30.

73. Marjorie Meyer Arsht, *All the Way from Yoakum: The Personal Journey of a Political Insider* (College Station: Texas A&M University Press, 2005), 134.

74. Carleton, *Red Scare!*, 230–31.

75. Ibid., 231.

76. Ibid., 233.

77. Ibid., 233–37.

78. Ibid., 234.

79. Ibid., 244–54.

80. Ibid., 255–56, for Bricker Amendment. The Bricker Amendment was an attempt to protect the primacy of the US Constitution over international treaties and presidential agreements with foreign governments. The amendment was a response to President Truman's use of American troops in the Korean War without first seeking a congressional declaration of war.

81. Ibid., 267–72; direct quotation, 272.

82. Ibid., 275–76.

83. Ibid., 276–82.

84. William Henry Kellar, *Make Haste Slowly: Moderates, Conservatives, and School Desegregation in Houston* (College Station: Texas A&M University Press, 1999), 134. Kellar claims that 1954–56 was the "one interruption" in conservative control over the Houston Independent School District school board.

85. Carleton, *Red Scare!*, 285–87.

86. Ibid., 287–90.

87. Kellar, *Make Haste Slowly*, 93.

88. Ibid., 134.

89. Ibid., 176.

90. The direct quotation is from the enrolled version of HB 523, section 2. HB 523 amended Article 5766 of the *Revised Civil Statutes of Texas* (1925). The only difference between males and females subject to the draft was that males age eighteen to forty-five could be drafted, while females needed to be age twenty-one to forty-five. Further research on the circumstances around passage of this bill in 1957 is a future project of mine.

91. Daniel Williams, *God's Own Party: The Making of the Christian Right* (Oxford: Oxford University Press, 2010), 82–83.

92. Ibid., 135, for the phrase "textbook watchdogs."

93. Ibid., 83–84.

94. Michelle Nickerson has written in detail about the important role conservative

women played in California politics in the 1950s and 1960s. See Nickerson, *Mothers of Conservatism*, and "Moral Mothers and Goldwater Girls," in *The Conservative Sixties*, ed. David Farber and Jeff Roche (New York: Peter Lang, 2003), 51–62.

95. McArthur and Smith, "Not Whistling Dixie," 162–64.

96. Kristi Throne Strickland, "The Significance and Impact of Women on the Rise of the Republican Party in Twentieth Century Texas" (PhD diss., University of North Texas, 2000), 4–6; McArthur and Smith, "Not Whistling Dixie," 162.

97. Strickland, "Significance and Impact of Women on the Rise of the Republican Party," see dissertation abstract; see also 4. There must be at least one Republican women's club in 75 percent of the state's congressional districts to qualify for that state to create a state-level federation; see McArthur and Smith, "Not Whistling Dixie," 163.

98. Strickland, "Significance and Impact of Women on the Rise of the Republican Party," 6.

99. McArthur and Smith, "Not Whistling Dixie," 162; originally from Rymph, *Republican Women*, 112.

100. McArthur and Smith, "Not Whistling Dixie," 163.

101. Strickland, "Significance and Impact of Women on the Rise of the Republican Party," 7.

102. Nickerson, "Moral Mothers and Goldwater Girls," passim.

103. McArthur and Smith, "Not Whistling Dixie," 162.

104. Ibid.

105. Ibid., 163.

106. Ibid.

107. Ibid.

108. Robert Dallek, *Lyndon B. Johnson: Portrait of a President* (New York: Oxford University Press, 2004), 120.

109. "Texas: A City Disgraced," *Time*, November 1, 1963, http://www.time.com/time/magazine/article/0,9171,875296,00.html (accessed September 17, 2011). See also "Stevenson Buffeted in Texas," *Capital Times*, October 25, 1963, 2.

110. McArthur and Smith, "Not Whistling Dixie," 164.

111. Gilbert Garcia, *Reagan's Comeback: Four Weeks in Texas That Changed American Politics Forever* (San Antonio: Trinity University Press, 2012), 40.

112. Marjorie Meyer Arsht, *All the Way from Yoakum: The Personal Journey of a Political Insider* (College Station: Texas A&M University Press, 2006), 133.

113. Arsht believed that "Judaism is a religion, not a nationality," and that "when religion and the state are intertwined, religion inevitably suffers." She held fast to this position (and her membership in the American Council for Judaism, the only American Jewish anti-Zionist organization to exist) even after the Holocaust and the creation of the state of Israel made this a fringe, right-wing stance. See Arsht, *All the Way from Yoakum*, 130–34.

114. Ibid., 133.

115. Ibid., 133–34.

116. Ibid., 134.

117. Ibid.

118. Ibid., 136–38.

119. Ibid., 142–43.

120. Ibid., 143–45.

121. Ibid., 150–51, 155.

122. Ibid., 155.

123. Hollace Ava Weiner and Kenneth D. Roseman, eds., *Lone Stars of David: The Jews of Texas* (Waltham, MA: Brandeis University Press, 2007), 214.

124. Arsht, *All the Way from Yoakum*, 166.

125. Weiner and Roseman, *Lone Stars of David*, 214.

126. McArthur and Smith, "Not Whistling Dixie," 164.

127. Ibid.

128. A short biography of Rita Bass Clements is available at the following Texas A&M University website: http://libraryasp.tamu.edu/Cushing/collectn/modpol/rcc/bio.htm (accessed July 28, 2011). Clements would also go on to marry William P. Clements Jr., who would become governor of Texas.

129. For details on women's involvement in California, see Nickerson, "Moral Mothers and Goldwater Girls."

130. Sean P. Cunningham, *Cowboy Conservatism: Texas and the Rise of the Modern Right* (Lexington: University Press of Kentucky, 2010), 58.

131. Ibid., 58–59. These men were linked to the ferociously anticommunist John Birch Society, which by 1964 was seen as radically right wing by many Americans.

132. Ibid., 62–63.

133. Ibid., 57.

134. Ibid., 66.

135. Ibid., 39.

136. Jim Atkinson, "Rose Renfroe and the Political Awakening of White Oak Cliff," *D Magazine*, July 1, 1975, http://www.dmagazine.com/Home/1975/07/01/Rose_Renfroe_and_the_Political_Awakening_of_White_Oak_Cliff.aspx (accessed July 29, 2011).

137. Gerald S. McCorkle, "Busing Comes to Dallas Schools," *Southwestern Historical Quarterly* 111, no. 3 (January 2008): 304–33; see 312.

138. Ibid., 310–18.

139. Jim Atkinson, "Texas Monthly Reporter," *Texas Monthly*, June 1977, 72.

140. McCorkle, "Busing Comes to Dallas Schools," 304 (illustration and caption).

141. Ibid., 318.

142. Ibid., 318–19.

143. Ibid., 319.

144. Atkinson, "Rose Renfroe."

145. Richard West, "Texas Monthly Reporter," *Texas Monthly*, June 1975, 14. West refers to Renfroe as a housewife and an antibusing activist. For direct quotation, see Atkinson, "Rose Renfroe."

146. Atkinson, "Texas Monthly Reporter," *Texas Monthly*, June 1977, 70.

147. Richard West, "Texas Monthly Reporter," *Texas Monthly*, November 1976, 83. For the "tacky" comment, see Atkinson, "Rose Renfroe."

148. Atkinson, "Texas Monthly Reporter," 70.

149. Atkinson, "Rose Renfroe."

150. Atkinson, "Texas Monthly Reporter," 72.

151. Ibid. According to Atkinson, one political observer commented that other than Rose Renfroe, "The only other thing I can think of that could bring those folks together would be to stop a city resolution to bomb Oak Cliff."

152. Matt Pulle, "Party Poop: With Dems Like These, Who Needs the GOP?" *Dallas Observer News*, August 31, 2006).

153. Ibid.

154. Kevin Krause, "Dallas County Commissioners Court Candidates Kenneth Mayfield, Elba Garcia Are a Study in Contrasts," *Dallas Morning News*, October 29, 2010, http://www.dallasnews.com/news/politics/local-politics/20101028-Dallas-County-Commissioners-Court-candidates-Kenneth-836.ece (accessed July 29, 2011).

155. Steve Blow, "Some Campaigns Offered a Laugh, Not Much Else," *Dallas Morning News*, March 4, 2010, http://www.dallasnews.com/news/columnists/steve-blow/20100304-Some-campaigns-offered-a-laugh-6745.ece (accessed July 29, 2011).

156. "Editorial: We Recommend Garcia in Commissioner Primary," *Dallas Morning News*, February 18, 2010, http://www.dallasnews.com/opinion/editorials/20100218-Editorial-We-recommend-Garcia-in-775.ece (accessed July 29, 2011).

157. For more information on the history of the ERA battle in Texas, see Nancy E. Baker, "Texas Feminist Hermine Tobolowsky, Conservative Women, and the Texas Fight over Equal Rights, 1972–1982," in *Texas Women/American Women: Their Lives and Times*, ed. Stephanie Cole, Rebecca Sharpless, and Elizabeth Turner (Athens: University of Georgia Press, in press).

158. Jane Ulrich, "Battle Lines on ERA Drawn," *Dallas Morning News*, December 6, 1974, 4C.

159. David W. Brady and Kent L. Tedin, "Ladies in Pink: Religion and Political Ideology in the Anti-ERA Movement," *Social Science Quarterly* 56, no. 4 (March 1976): 564–75, direct quote from 574. Brady and Tedin interviewed 154 women out of an estimated 2,500 pro-rescission women attending a hearing at the Texas Legislature on April 14, 1975.

160. Cunningham, *Cowboy Conservatism*, 156–57.

161. Texas Legislature, House of Representatives, Committee on Constitutional Revision, public hearing, HCR 57, Sixty-Fourth Legislature, April 14, 1975, audiocassettes. (No publicly available transcript exists.) Hereafter referred to as public hearing on HCR 57.

162. Ibid.

163. Kaye Northcott, "Fighting the ERA: The Ladies Mobilize," *Texas Observer*, November 15, 1974, 5. For mention of the television appearances, see public hearing on HCR 57.

164. Northcott, "Fighting the ERA," 5.

165. "Political Intelligence," *Texas Observer*, March 28, 1975, 8. The *Texas Observer* constantly implied in its coverage that the anti-ERA groups were linked to the JBS, never

offering substantive proof but commenting on how similar anti-ERA arguments of the two were.

166. Public hearing, HCR 57.

167. Kaye Northcott, "'Dirty, Mean and Vicious,'" *Texas Observer*, December 13, 1974, 7; Hans Baer, "Practice-Building Seminars in Chiropractic: A Petit Bourgeois Response to Biomedical Domination," *Medical Anthropology Quarterly*, new series, 10, no. 1 (March 1996): 29–44; see especially 37–38.

168. Northcott, "Fighting the ERA," 3 (for Tilotta), 3 (for Hobbs). See also "Miss X Revealed," *Texas Observer*, December 13, 1974, 14.

169. Sharon Cobler, "ERA Has Its Good, Bad Days," *Dallas Morning News*, January 29, 1975, C1.

170. Public hearing, HCR 57.

171. For the full story, see "Political Intelligence: Mary Kay and the ERA," *Texas Observer*, March 28, 1975, 8.

172. Ibid.

173. This is drawn from the written records of the Texas House of Representatives Video/Audio Services for HCR 57, which includes a list of proponents and opponents of HCR 57 who were prepared to testify at the hearing in April 1975. Daughters Already Well Endowed lobbied legislators in January 1975 to rescind but did not testify at the hearing. For more on this, see Lea Donosky, "ERA Ratification: Legislators Told to Stand Firm," *Dallas Morning News*, January 9, 1975, A24.

174. Tennessee state representative Larry Bates says this, and other witnesses echo him. Public hearing, HCR 57.

175. Ibid.

176. Ibid.

177. All these arguments are drawn from the public hearing, HCR 57.

178. Norma Cude, "Sniping at ERA," *Texas Observer*, March 11, 1977, 5.

179. Nene Foxhall, "W's Probe Moral Decay," *Dallas Morning News*, August 29, 1975, C2.

180. Sharon Cobler, "Anti-ERA Movement Goes National," *Dallas Morning News*, November 27, 1975, C1.

181. Nene Foxhall, "Faction Broadens Attack," *Dallas Morning News*, July 3, 1975, C3. The quotation is given in the article without indication of who said it, though it is clearly from one of the Ws or their written material.

182. "Ideals Forum Topic," *Dallas Morning News*, August 22, 1975, C3. The reporter was quoting an unnamed spokeswoman.

183. McAuley's involvement in monitoring textbooks is first described in Foxhall, "W's Probe Moral Decay." Her continued work on this issue is documented in Marlin Maddoux, *Public Education Against America: The Hidden Agenda* (New Kensington, PA: Whitaker House, 2006). An excerpt from this book detailing McAuley's activism can be accessed at http://www.churchbusiness.com/hotnews/63h3142419.html# (accessed March 12, 2007). Maddoux was a Dallas-area conservative Christian leader in radio broadcast

and print. A brief biography is on his radio program's website, http://www.pointofview.net/partner/Article_Display_Page/0,,PTID320166|CHID685254|CIID1689098,00.html (accessed March 12, 2007).

184. Dianne Edmondson's website, http://gopgal.com/index.cfm (accessed March 12, 2007), makes no mention of her former anti-ERA activities or her membership in the John Birch Society in 1975.

185. Donald Critchlow, *The Conservative Ascendancy: How the GOP Right Made Political History* (Cambridge, MA: Harvard University Press, 2007), 161.

186. Tanya Melich, *The Republican War against Women: An Insider's Report from behind the Lines* (New York: Bantam Books, 1998), passim. Melich is a formerly staunch Republican who documents the rightward shift in the party, including the reliance on a "family values" agenda.

Texas Traditions and the Right

Continuity and Change

MICHAEL LIND

As political coordinates, "left" and "right" derive from the seating arrangements in the French National Assembly at the time of the French Revolution. Their application to the politics of Texas and the United States may obscure more than it illuminates. One problem is that the meaning of left and right, liberal and conservative, have changed dramatically in relatively short periods of time. Conservatism, identified with isolationism and protectionism in the mid-twentieth century, became identified with military hawkishness and free trade by the century's end.

Partisan identities have been even more fluid and confusing than political compass points. During the century between the Civil War and the civil rights revolution, the Republican Party was still the party of Abraham Lincoln, based in the Northeast, Midwest, and Pacific Coast, while the Democrats, based in the South, were the party of Andrew Jackson if not necessarily of Jefferson Davis. The New Deal brought great numbers of former Republican progressives into Franklin Roosevelt's coalition, while alienating white Southern conservative Democrats. The process of partisan realignment accelerated during the turmoil caused by the civil rights revolution and the cultural revolutions of the 1950s and 1960s. By the end of the twentieth century, the two coalitions had swapped their labels, but the old North-South division remained the same. In presidential races in 2000 and 2004, Republican candidates did best in southern and western states that had been Democratic a century earlier, while the new Democratic Party heartland was the former heartland of McKinley Republicans and Theodore Roosevelt's Progressives.

These changes were striking but superficial. At the level of political culture, American politics was characterized by strong continuities. Nowhere was this truer than in Texas. The majority culture in the Lone Star State, in 1900 and 2000 alike, has been shaped by evangelical Protestantism, suspicion of government, and the style if seldom the substance of populism. Equally important has been a strong, even tribal, sense of identity derived from the ethnic culture of the white Southern majority that dominated Texas from its secession from Mexico through the end of the twentieth century.

Attempts by scholars to explain the American Right can be divided into three schools: the economic determinist theory, the status anxiety theory, and the ethnocultural theory. Theories that reduce conservatism to the self-interest of business elites in general, or particular industries, have produced little serious scholarship but have been popular among progressives, populists, and Marxists. But while all major political movements reflect the economic interests of important constituents, reductionist explanations of conservatism as nothing more than a rationalization of economic interests do not work. If conservatism serves only the narrow class interest of an elite minority, then it is necessary to posit that working-class voters are suffering from "false consciousness" and fail to apprehend their own interests—in some cases, generation after generation. Approaches that focus on the political agendas of particular economic sectors—finance, industry, agriculture—provide a better explanation of the persistent regional divisions in American politics, because particular industries tend to be concentrated in particular areas. But they cannot explain why small farmers in Massachusetts would vote differently than small farmers in Texas.

The most influential explanation of American conservatism by American social scientists has been the status anxiety theory, developed by the historian Richard Hofstadter and the sociologists Daniel Bell and Seymour Martin Lipset, among others.[1] They were influenced by German socialist émigrés of the Frankfurt School like Theodore Adorno, who conflated European fascism with American conservatism and tried to attribute support for both to working-class voters with "authoritarian personalities."[2] The similar status anxiety theory similarly explained McCarthyism and the Goldwater movement in terms of the personal defects of maladjusted individuals, including small business owners threatened by economic modernization. Recent work on the social background of postwar American conservatives has refuted the idea that opponents of postwar liberalism were motivated by emotional or social maladjustment. The ideas of the authoritarian personality and status anxiety have been convincingly criticized, in the cases both of European fascism and postwar American conservatism.[3] But the status anxiety theory remains popular among liberal journalists and academics who believe that there literally must be something wrong with people who do not share their convictions.

A far more plausible account of conservatism and other American political traditions was developed in the 1960s, a little later than the still-influential status anxiety theory. This is the ethnocultural theory or political culture theory of Daniel J. Elazar, D. W. Meinig, and David Hackett Fischer, among others.[4] According to this school, partisan and regional differences in political orientation in the United States have always been shaped chiefly by ethnic and religious subcultures. Perceptions of economic self-interest play a role, but they are filtered through inherited ethnic and regional values, which are not the same among all American groups. The ethnocultural theory provides the best guide to understanding politics in Texas, as in the United States in general.

The fundamental fact about Texas politics is that Texas is a Southern state with a Southern political culture.[5] The political culture of the South is a blend of two distinct cultures—the aristocratic "Cavalier" culture of the coastal plantation regions dominated by Anglo-American gentry, and the populist culture of Scots-Irish "Borderers," whose ancestors lived in northern Britain and Ulster in northern Ireland and migrated to Texas from Appalachia and the Ozarks. While both Southern cultures have shaped Texas, the Cavalier culture has been weak and the Scots-Irish influence strong. The archetypical Texan—violent and given to braggadocio but also plain-spoken and honorable—is a cousin of the stereotypical Scots-Irish "hillbilly" of Appalachia and the Ozarks.

In *Albion's Seed: Four British Folkways in America* (1989), David Hackett Fischer describes the Scots-Irish conception of freedom as "natural liberty."[6] But it is a mistake to identify Scots-Irish political culture with libertarian individualism. In fact this tradition has always been highly communitarian, combining a high degree of conformity within the community with a suspicion of outsiders and a determination to preserve local control over the behavior and beliefs of the community's members. While the Cavalier culture of the South, modeled on that of early modern

British elites, valued Greco-Roman classicism and humanism, the culture of the Borderers of the Appalachia-to-Texas "Bible Belt" has always been centered on the Bible, as interpreted by evangelical Protestant pastors whose learning is often more limited than their zeal.

The unattractiveness of the impoverished South to European immigrants in the nineteenth and early twentieth centuries meant that, until significant domestic migration from other regions began after World War II, Texas like other Southern states had a majority white population that descended from white Southerners. Other white ethnic groups were either isolated, like the Germans of the Hill Country, or assimilated to the Anglo-Celtic Southern norm. Blacks were excluded socially and exploited economically, as were Latinos.

While racism existed in North and South alike, the white South, notwithstanding encapsulated white minorities like Texas Germans and Louisiana Cajuns, had nothing like the experience of white ethnic pluralism that shaped the North in cities and regions where large numbers of Irish Catholic and continental European immigrants shared the ballot with old-stock Anglo-American Protestants from the early nineteenth century onward. Instead of white ethnic pluralist politics, conceived of as bargaining among numerous groups, Texas and other Southern states were characterized by "ethnarchy," with a dominant tribe subordinating or excluding other races and other ethnic groups of the same race. Anthropologists call such a system *Herrenvolk* (master race) democracy.[7] In the Southern version of Herrenvolk democracy, a considerable degree of populism and egalitarianism among members of the Anglo-Celtic Protestant Herrenvolk was compatible with xenophobia toward and oppression of racial and religious outsiders. Ethnocentrism was often most intense among non-elite white Southerners, whose identity as white, Christian, and Southern gave them claims to better treatment than that allotted to outsiders to the community.

The disfranchisement of black Texans and the marginalization of Tejanos until the civil rights revolution meant that Texas politics was more or less the politics of the Anglo-Celtic Protestant majority. The need to defend the identity of the Herrenvolk from real or imaginary threats was shared by all significant political factions—for example, most New Dealers and anti–New Dealers alike defended white supremacy and evangelical Protestant morality. But within the white Texan majority, there have been three major traditions of political economy, which have interacted in shifting, kaleidoscopic combinations. These three traditions are populism, traditionalism, and modernism.[8] These three major traditions have been joined by a fourth, largely ineffectual tradition of Texan progressivism.

Populism derives from Jeffersonian and Jacksonian ideology, with its motto of "Equal rights for all [white men], exclusive privileges for none." Originating in the labor theory of value shared by John Locke, Adam Smith, and Thomas Jefferson, the economic theory of populism was producerism, which identified the virtue of the community and the strength of the democratic republic with the yeoman farmer or self-employed proprietor. The ideal of the yeoman republic was never remotely approximated in Texas and other Southern states, which were always characterized by grotesque extremes of inequality and large numbers of landless laborers and tenant farmers among native whites, to say nothing of exploited blacks and Latinos. Nevertheless, populist producerism provided a powerful language that could be drawn on to denounce plutocracy and oligarchy as well as to demonize the allegedly parasitic and welfare-dependent poor.

Unlike populism, the schools of traditionalism and modernism tended to be limited to elites in Texas and similar Southern states. Traditionalism in Texas was the legacy of the plantation South. Traditionalists believed in a hierarchical society with a rentier economy in which a disfranchised and poorly paid workforce engaged in agriculture or low-skilled manufacturing. The poor, unfree workforce could consist of slaves, sharecroppers, or illegal immigrants; it could be white, Latino, or black. From the point of view of traditionalists, attempts to organize the labor force and mobilize it in politics represented a threat to economic prosperity as well as the power and status of the oligarchic families.

Within the elite of the Anglo-Celtic Herrenvolk community, traditionalism coexisted with modernism. Sometimes called "business progressivism," this school of political economy included supporters of the New South after the Civil War and many New Dealers, as well as otherwise conservative "boosters" focused on economic development in big cities and small towns alike.

The two elite schools differed in their view of the proper relation of Texas to the northeastern-midwestern industrial core of the United States. The traditionalists were content for Texas to complement the industrial core of the Northeast and Midwest, by specializing as a resource colony, supplying raw materials like cotton to core factories and food from farms and ranches to core consumers, and later, oil and gas. The modernists wanted Texas to compete with the Northern industrial core, by industrializing itself and joining the other metropolitan cores in the national and world economies. While they shared ambitious visions of economic development with boosters in other parts of the American periphery such as the rural Midwest and Far West, Texan modernists usually shared the values and prejudices of other members of the Anglo-Celtic Protestant majority. Their commitment to technological and commercial modernity did not necessarily make them liberal in matters of race, religion, or lifestyle.

To the populists, traditionalists, and modernists, a fourth tradition in Texan politics might be added, that of progressives (who like their allies elsewhere preferred the term liberal from the 1930s to the late twentieth century).[9] As in other Southern states, the progressive tradition in Texas was weak, isolated, and usually ineffectual.

Progressive leaders throughout the twentieth century tended to be independently wealthy, like the Houston reformer Frankie Randolph, or lawyers or other members of metropolitan establishments.[10] Their affluence and status protected them when they expressed opinions and supported causes like civil rights and unionization that would have brought economic punishment and social ostracism to less secure Texans. Well educated and well traveled, many Texan progressives tended to identify with national liberal political movements. A number played roles behind the scenes in national politics, such as Edward Mandell House, the Texan power broker who became an adviser to Woodrow Wilson and Franklin Delano Roosevelt, and Creekmore Fath, the liberal Austin attorney who worked for Roosevelt as an aide.[11]

These progressives of the upper class and upper middle class, in Texas as in other Southern states, have had a tense and often disappointing relationship with working-class and rural white populists, struggling to bridge the distance imposed by class, education, and racial and religious attitudes. Belonging to an enclave that looked to Washington, DC, in politics and to New York in culture, progressive Texans were more successful in allying themselves with other encapsulated minorities who were frozen out of the Texan *Gemeinschaft*: organized labor, black Texans, and Tejanos.

The progressive Texans preferred Ralph Yarborough to Lyndon Johnson, whom many viewed as a treacherous opportunist. As Johnson recognized, their politics of principle tended to be both self-righteous and self-defeating. Some Texan progressives welcomed the election of John Tower, hoping that the collapse of one-party Democratic rule in Texas might eliminate corrupt centrists and produce a thoroughly liberal Democratic Party. They greatly overestimated the strength of progressivism among Texan voters. Many of their black and Latino allies were conservatives, not progressives, with respect to social issues like abortion and homosexuality—issues that tended to inspire upper-middle-class liberals in Texas, as elsewhere, more than the distributional politics of the old New Deal liberalism. What the historian Clinton Rossiter said of conservatism in the 1950s might be said of progressivism in Texas in the twentieth and early twenty-first centuries—most of the time it has been a "thankless persuasion."[12]

As many historians have observed, the modern period of Texas politics begins in the 1930s, with bitter debates within the dominant Democratic Party over Franklin Roosevelt's New Deal. One familiar interpretation holds that the modern division between Democrats and Republicans in Texas can be dated back to the split within the midcentury Democratic Party between liberal supporters of the New Deal and conservative opponents. This division of Texas politics along left-right lines is too simple, compared to a more nuanced view of politics in the state as a kaleidoscopic combination of the four traditions I have identified: populist, traditionalist, modernist, and progressive.

The Texan politicians who succeeded while championing the New Deal in the 1930s and 1940s, like Lyndon Johnson and Governor James Allred, did so because they appealed to populists and probusiness modernists as well as the much weaker Texan progressives. New Deal relief and economic security programs offered something to populists, while business boosters reaped benefits from infrastructural modernization programs in Texas like hydroelectric dams, paid for in part by the federal government, and from the aid to Great Depression–stricken businesses and banks ladled out by the Reconstruction Finance Corporation, headed by the Houston banker Jesse Jones, whose conservatism was that of a modernist of the right.[13]

But the formula of a populist-modernist-progressive alliance against Old South traditionalism has seldom been successful in Texas. Far more common has been the winning political formula developed in the late 1930s by Governor W. Lee "Pappy" O'Daniel and used in different versions by conservative Democrats and Republicans alike, including Allan Shivers, George W. Bush, and Rick Perry. This formula unites folksy cultural populism and support for public investments sought by business in infrastructure and education with support for nonunion, low-wage labor in the traditionalist sectors of agriculture and menial services. Excluded from the coalition are white progressives, racial minorities, and organized labor. The populist-modernist-traditionalist alliance has been united against these supposed political enemies within, and the alleged enemy without, the federal government, which is portrayed as a threat to the cultural autonomy of the Herrenvolk majority and to the political sovereignty of the state of Texas, even by politicians who do not scruple to supplement state and local taxes with federal spending.

The oil and gas industry, which rose to importance in the Texan economy by the 1920s, does not fit easily into either the traditionalist or modernist camps within the Texan elite. Seen from one perspective, fossil fuels were commodities exported to Northern core manufacturers and consumers, no different in kind from cotton or cattle or lumber. From another angle, the energy industry was a technologically advanced and capital-intensive industry that did not rely on a large low-wage workforce. While individual oilmen were often reactionaries, a high-road, high-wage economy did not threaten the oil and gas industry the way that high wages and political power for farmworkers and tenant farmers threatened the rich farmers and rich ranchers of the traditional agricultural sector in Texas.

Unlike wealth gained by individuals who rose slowly through corporate or financial hierarchies, wealth obtained from the oil fields was not the result of years of socialization into a particular elite subculture. As a result, the values of oil tycoons were generally the values that they had grown up with before they struck it rich. Most first-generation Texas oilmen were conservatives because most Texans were conservatives, by national standards.

Among the "big rich" who made fortunes in the twentieth-century Texan oil business, there were many traditionalists like H. L. Hunt. Hunt was a classic reactionary in the Southern cavalier tradition, from his obsession with communist and Catholic conspiracies (he funded anti-Catholic propaganda used against John F. Kennedy) to the childhood dream he realized of living in a big white mansion like a Southern plantation house. Along with other reactionary oilmen, Hunt funded Senator Joseph McCarthy, who succeeded the Texan Martin Dies as the chief red-baiter in Congress. McCarthy came to be known as "the third Senator from Texas."

But there were modernists or business progressives in the Texan oil sector as well, including Sid Richardson, who kept a low profile and maintained good relations with New Deal liberals like Franklin Roosevelt and Lyndon Johnson. In the late twentieth century, the use of hydraulic fracturing or "fracking" to liberate previously unrecoverable amounts of natural gas from shale was pioneered by George P. Mitchell, the Galveston-born son of a Greek immigrant who promoted ecological sustainability and used the Woodlands development in Houston to embody the conservationist ideals of the visionary Ian McHarg.[14]

A case can be made that oil served to reduce what otherwise would have been much sharper conflicts among Texas modernists, traditionalists, and populists. The initial abundance of the resource created a highly modern economic sector more or less out of thin air, paid for largely by investment from outside the state and staffed to a large degree by immigrants from other parts of the country and the world. Severance taxes on oil and gas, and the funding of much of the University of Texas system from oil and gas revenues, reduced the need for other taxes. This spared the business modernists the need to battle against traditionalists for higher taxes to pay for a public infrastructure capable of attracting other industries. It also gave the modernists less of a stake in creating a well-educated citizenry, a goal that would have brought them into conflict with the parochial populists and fundamentalists who exercised disproportionate influence on Texas school boards and over the adoption of textbooks.

In effect the oil economy was a First World enclave within a Third World economy. So was the Texan information technology industry, which from the early days of Texas Instruments was fostered directly and indirectly by the Defense Department. Beginning during World War II, Texan politicians in Washington like Lyndon Johnson steered federal military investment to Texas, and later used their patronage power to put NASA facilities like the Johnson Space Center in Texas during the space race. Like the oil industry, the tech industry in Texas was disproportionately staffed and funded by nonnative Texans, and worked closely with Texan universities in industry-related research.

Without outside investment in oil and federal investment in the military and the military-related tech industry, the state of Texas would have been much more agrarian, with a relatively more powerful traditionalist elite based in the low-wage commodity sector. The fact that Texas was able to host two important modern economic sectors on the basis of accidental resource location and federal largesse arguably retarded the social and economic development of the state. Without these unearned advantages, the modernists of Texas might have been forced to challenge the traditionalist culture of minimal government and the populist culture for which the purpose of education was communal socialization. The probusiness modernists would have had no choice but to promote higher levels of taxation so that adequate infrastructure and good public education could attract investment by national and global businesses that were not based on resources or cheap, unskilled labor. Because they permitted modernization of the economy without prior modernization of the society, oil and gas and military-driven tech investment have had retarding effects on Texan politics and society similar to those found in kleptocratic societies afflicted by "the resource curse."

Texas has long been deeply involved in the modern Middle East. The oil industry brought Texan business and financial elites into close relationships with the elites and governments of Saudi Arabia, the shah's Iran, and many other oil-exporting countries in the Middle East and North Africa. At the same time, Christian Zionism became increasingly central to the worldview of Protestant fundamentalists in Texas. For a time in the 1970s, Texas had some of the most pro-Muslim and pro-Israel groups in the United States.

The Texan oil industry's close ties with Middle Eastern regimes gave its members a stake in good relations between them and the United States. The most notorious example came in 1980, when a PBS documentary on the beheading of a Saudi princess who had married a commoner, "Death of a Princess," was not shown by the PBS affiliate in Houston, after Mobil Oil and other businesses with Middle Eastern interests had denounced it.[15]

During his campaign for the Republican presidential nomination in 1980, John Connally was opposed by conservatives who claimed that he was insufficiently "pro-Israel." Similarly, when President George H. W. Bush pressured Israel to return occupied territory, he and Secretary of State James Baker were harshly criticized by neoconservatives and fundamentalists allied with the right wing in Israel.

The Texan business elite were also deeply involved with the regime of the shah of Iran. Sedco, the company owned by Texas governor Bill Clements, worked with the Iranian government. Following the Iranian revolution, Ross Perot sent a private mercenary team headed by a retired Green Beret on a successful mission to rescue two of his EDS employees who had been taken hostage by the Iranian government.

While Texans in the modernist business sector were cultivating good relations with the autocratic elites of Middle Eastern petrostates, many Texan fundamentalist pastors and their congregations were busy identifying some of the same rulers with Gog and Magog and other figures in the book of Revelation. Christian Zionism was part of the evangelical Protestant heritage that the Scots-Irish had brought with them to the Southern backcountry and Texas. Lyndon Johnson's grandfather told him, "Take care of the Jews, God's chosen people." His aunt explained: "If Israel is destroyed, the world will end."[16]

Inspired by a nineteenth-century British evangelical named John Nelson Darby, Cyrus Scofield, a Michigan-born evangelist who settled in Dallas, used his influential annotated Bible, the Scofield Reference Bible, to popularize dispensationalism, an elaborate interpretation of history leading up to the events foretold in the book of Revelation such as the rapture, the battle of Armageddon, and the Second Coming of Christ. Guided by Scofield's Bible and similar literature, generations of evangelicals in the Bible Belt from Texas to Virginia have sought to connect "prophecy" with current events, particularly those that occurred in the Middle East. The creation of Israel was seen as a fulfillment of biblical prophecy, while the wars between Israel and its Arab neighbors were interpreted as the signs that the last days were approaching.[17]

The Israeli political right cultivated Texan and American fundamentalists as allies. What began as a political alliance deepened into a kind of cultural and religious hybridization, with Southern fundamentalists subsidizing Jewish settlements in the occupied territories, and fundamentalist Protestant pilgrims hungry to learn more about Judaism making frequent trips to the Holy Land. Texas became a center not only for a brand of Israel-centered Christianity that incorporated ever more elements of Judaism, but also for Messianic Judaism, which identifies Jesus with the Jewish messiah but otherwise retains many Jewish traditions.

The elite "Arabists" in the Texas establishment lost power rapidly to the Christian Zionists, following the nationalization of US oil company properties by the Arab states and the Arab oil embargo in the 1970s, and the rise to power of a militant, anti-American theocracy in Iran. Unlike his father, who as president had sought a degree of neutrality between Israel and its neighbors, George W. Bush, who had dabbled in the oil business in his youth, and whose company, Harken, had received an important early contract from Bahrain, sided with Israel more closely than any other US president, partly because of the strength of Christian Zionism in Texas and the national Republican Party, but partly, perhaps, because of his own convictions as a born-again Protestant.

While the values of white Southerners have been characterized by continuity, despite their changing party allegiances, their increasing importance in the national Republican electorate and leadership has dramatically altered the definition of conservatism at the national level. Beginning in the mid-twentieth century, conservative Texan oilmen played both direct and indirect roles in the southernization of the national right.[18]

Until the 1950s, both the North and the South had their own distinctive versions of conservatism. The Old Right of Ohio senator Robert A. Taft, known as "Mr. Conservative," shared the Southern Right's antipathy to communism and liberal statism. But there the resemblance ended. Based in the Midwest, the Old Right was the heir to Greater New England political culture and Lincoln-to-Hoover Republicanism. It was isolationist in foreign policy and protectionist in trade policy. The foreign policy values of Southerners were precisely the opposite. The Southern culture of honor encouraged support for the military and hawkish foreign policy attitudes. And the traditional reliance of Southern commodity exporters on foreign export markets, along with the absence in the South of industries threatened by foreign competition, produced the South's commitment to free trade.

The shift away from the isolationist, protectionist Old Right to the "movement conservatism" of Barry Goldwater and Ronald Reagan was centered on *National Review*. Its editor, William F. Buckley Jr., was the son of William Frank Buckley Sr., a Texan who grew rich from oil leases in Mexico and Central America.[19] The senior Buckley had the typical Texan oilman's dread of communism and statism of any kind, reinforced by a devout Catholic's horror at the persecution of the church in the Soviet Union and revolutionary Mexico, where he helped to finance the conservative Catholic *Cristero* rebellion.

The younger Buckley, a supporter of McCarthy who wrote a book entitled *McCarthy and His Enemies* (1954), was schooled abroad and raised in the East, where he criticized his alma mater for allowing the teaching of Keynesianism in *God and Man at Yale* (1951). He failed to interest the right-wing Texas tycoon H. L. Hunt in funding his magazine, and most of the intellectuals and writers associated with *National Review* were Northerners or European émigrés, many of them ex-radicals.

Notwithstanding all this, it can be argued that a distinctively Texan and Southern version of conservatism informed the Buckley circle's combination of anticommunist militancy, Christianity, and economic libertarianism. Buckley and his allies purged Old Right isolationists who opposed the Cold War from the developing conservative movement. They rejected the libertarian philosopher Ayn Rand because of her hostility to Christianity. Beginning in the 1960s, libertarians who opposed the Cold War broke with the movement Right and formed their own movement, with its own institutions like the Cato Institute and its own flagship journal, *Reason*. The fact that the postwar right at a national level might have gone in a different direction is suggested by the example of the conservative polemicist Patrick Buchanan, who combines conservative social views with support for isolationism and protectionism reminiscent of the Old Right.[20]

In light of the influence of Texan political culture through Buckley on movement conservatism, it was only natural that the movement would appeal to white Southern conservatives, once it found standard-bearers first in Barry Goldwater and then Ronald Reagan. Increasingly the peculiar obsessions of the Anglo-Celtic South, like Christian Zionist support for hard-liners in Israel and opposition to gun control, came to define national conservatism.

The libertarian strain of the American Right has had limited appeal to the Populist Right in Texas. The antiwar and antimilitary views of Representative Ron Paul made him a hero to national libertarians but are shared by few of his fellow Texans. Significantly, Paul was an immigrant from the Midwest who moved to Texas as an adult. Another individual who moved to Texas as an adult, the wealthy James Leininger of San Antonio, became a player in Texan conservative politics as a donor, not as a politician. But while Leininger's crusade against abortion resonated with conservative Texan Protestants and some Tejano Catholics, his campaign for school vouchers for poor children failed, as did a similar campaign by another rich Republican, Theodore Forstmann, in New Jersey. Leininger, a midwestern Lutheran who had grown up in Florida, failed to understand that a program that combined the alleged interests of inner-city blacks with the utilitarian logic of libertarianism was alien to the communitarian culture of Texan Herrenvolk populists.[21]

Since World War II, Texas has experienced rapid growth as a result of both domestic and international migration. Between the end of World War II and the resumption of mass immigration that followed federal immigration reform in 1965, most immigrants were whites from other parts of the United States, drawn to the Texan version of the post-1945 Sun Belt lifestyle characterized by suburbs and warm weather. Many of the domestic migrants were employed by businesses like IBM that transferred some factories or operations to Texas or were members of the military who chose to remain after serving on the many military bases established in Texas with the help of the Texas delegation in Congress. In the early twenty-first century, thanks to a new wave of domestic migration from other parts of the United States, some of the fastest-growing cities in the nation have been in Texas, including Austin, Dallas, and Houston.

In recent decades, immigration from Mexico and Central America has been even more important than domestic migration as a driver of demographic change in Texas. Texas is already a majority minority state, if the self-description of about half of Latinos as "white" is ignored. Because the black population of Texas is expected to remain more or less stable, the future of Texas politics will be shaped by the relationship between numerically declining "Anglos" and the expanding population of Latinos and their descendants.

Will demographic change, as a result of both international and domestic migration, erode or eliminate the distinctive political culture of Texas? In California, the growth in Latino numbers disempowered the conservative whites, many of them Scots-Irish "Okies" and their descendants, who had supported Nixon and Reagan.[22] The result was a new majority coalition of Latinos, blacks, and white progressives. Could something similar happen in Texas? If it did, then politics in Texas would change radically, from traditional Herrenvolk populism to brokered pluralism, of the kind familiar among "white ethnics" in the Northeast and Midwest and among races in postconservative California.

But predictions of the "Californication" of Texan politics may be misguided. The term "the founder effect" is used by historians for the tendency of latter settlers in an area to adopt the folkways of the first pioneers.[23] This phenomenon can occur even if the initial founders were numerically insignificant in relation to the later population. Unless there is a sudden, abrupt displacement of one population by another, demographic change takes the form of relocations by many individuals. If they seek to join the majority in their new home, they may adopt the folkways, dialects, and political values of the majority in order to belong.

In the case of Texan conservatism, the founder effect has been supplemented by the hostility of many white migrants from the North to the more liberal, statist political cultures of the states and regions they have left. Former Northeasterners and Midwesterners who moved to Texas in order to enjoy lower taxes than those of their former homes have probably reinforced the antistatist strain in Texan political culture.

For the most part, these northeastern and midwestern white migrants were changed more by Texan political culture than they changed it. One example, if not the most typical, was George Herbert Walker Bush, the Yale-educated son of a liberal Republican senator from Connecticut, who went into the Texas oil business after World War II before a career in national politics that culminated in the presidency. While he remained a cultural outsider in many ways, Bush's politics were those of his adopted home, rather than of his ancestral Northeast. His sons, who spent their childhoods in the state, were conservative Texans in culture as well as politics.

Nor will the increase in Latino numbers necessarily turn Texas into a progressive state like contemporary California. From John Tower to George W. Bush and Rick Perry, Texan Republicans have worked to court Latino voters, to counteract the alliance between white liberals and blacks. Anti-immigrant attitudes among conservatives have hurt these efforts in recent elections. But if they can retain a majority in statewide politics, Texan Republicans may be helped in their effort to maintain their majority by the choices confronting politicians in a one-party state. Ambitious Latinos, particularly those in majority-minority districts, may prefer to have influence by working within the dominant party rather than to belong to the Democrats, if the latter remain as marginalized as the Republican Party was for a century after the Civil War in Texas.

Perhaps the most important factor that can prolong a majoritarian Herrenvolk politics in Texas is residual racism. As George Yancey and I have argued, the binary American caste system is not white-nonwhite but black-nonblack.[24] Even today, nearly half a century after the civil rights revolution, intermarriage—the ultimate measure of integration—is far higher among whites, Latinos, and Asian Americans than among blacks and other groups, although that is increasing. By the third generation, Latinos are more likely to marry outside their ethnic group than within it. Native-born Latinos are also much more likely than immigrants to belong to evangelical Protestant churches, which are growing overall even as mainline Protestantism and Catholicism decline. The assimilation of Latinos and their amalgamation through intermarriage with non-Hispanic whites, instead of producing a politics of ethnic pluralism based on black, Latino, and white blocs, might replace the old white ethnocultural majority with a "beige" majority, accompanied by a new kind of majoritarian identity politics in Texas.

Social and demographic change have eroded or altered many of the political traditions of Texas. But trends like modernity and globalization are not irresistible, homogenizing forces. Communities can adopt some innovations, reject others, and modify still others to make them more compatible with their inherited traditions. Similarly, communities can assimilate immigrants from different backgrounds into preexisting traditions. For these reasons, it would be a mistake to assume that immigration-driven demographic change in Texas will necessarily lead to the disappearance, rather than the modification, of the Lone Star state's distinctive political culture.

Notes

1. Richard Hofstadter, *The Paranoid Style in American Politics and Other Essays* (New York: Alfred A. Knopf, 1966); Daniel Bell, ed., *The New American Right* (New York: Criterion Books, 1955); Seymour Martin Lipset, "Democracy and Working-Class Authoritarianism," *American Sociological Review* 24, no. 4 (1959): 482–501; Lipset, "'Working-Class Authoritarianism': A Reply to Miller and Reisman," *British Journal of Sociology* 12, no. 3 (1961): 277–81.

2. T. W. Adorno, E. Frenkel-Brunswick, D. J. Levinson, and R. N. Sanford, *The Authoritarian Personality* (New York: W. W. Norton, 1950).

3. Michael Mann, *Fascists* (Cambridge: Cambridge University Press, 2004); Lisa McGirr, *Suburban Warriors: The Origins of the New American Right* (Princeton, NJ: Princeton University Press, 2002).

4. Daniel J. Elazar, *American Federalism: A View from the States* (New York: Thomas W. Crowell, 1966); D. W. Meinig, *Imperial Texas: An Interpretive Essay in Cultural Geography* (Austin: University of Texas Press, 1969); David Hackett Fischer, *Albion's Seed: Four British Folkways in America* (New York: Oxford University Press, 1989); Paul Kleppner, *Continuity and Change in Electoral Politics, 1893–1928* (Westport, CT: Greenwood Press, 1987); Kleppner, *The Third Electoral System, 1853–1892: Politics, Voters, and Political Culture* (Chapel Hill: University of North Carolina Press, 2010).

5. Meinig, *Imperial Texas.*

6. Fischer, *Albion's Seed.* See also James Webb, *Born Fighting: How the Scots-Irish Shaped America* (New York: Broadway Books, 2004).

7. Pierre L. van den Berghe, *Race and Racism* (New York: Wiley, 1967); van den Berghe, *The Ethnic Phenomenon* (New York: Elsevier, 1981).

8. This classification draws on, and modifies, my argument in *Made in Texas: George W. Bush and the Southern Takeover of American Politics* (New York: Basic Books, 2003).

9. See Patrick Cox, "A Modern Liberal Tradition in Texas?" in *The Texas Left: The Radical Roots of Lone Star Liberalism*, ed. David O'Donald Cullen and Kyle G. Wilkison (College Station: Texas A&M University Press, 2010), 209–24.

10. Ann Fears Crawford, *Frankie: Mrs. R. D. Randolph and Texas Liberal Politics* (Austin: Eakin Press, 2000).

11. Godfrey Hodgson, *Woodrow Wilson's Right Hand: The Life of Colonel Edward M. House* (New York: Yale University Press, 2006); Davie Richards, "So Long to the 'Communist

Threat': Creekmore Fath, Last of a Generation of Progressive Activists," *Texas Observer*, August 21, 2009.

12. Clinton Rossiter, *Conservatism in America: The Thankless Persuasion* (New York: Alfred A. Knopf, 1966).

13. Jordan Schwartz, *The New Dealers: Power Politics in the Age of Roosevelt* (New York: Alfred A. Knopf, 1993).

14. Tom Fowler, "Stubborn in His Vision: Mitchell's Persistence Laid Groundwork for Shale Gas Surge," *Houston Chronicle*, November 14, 2009; Frederick Steiner, "Design for a Vulnerable Planet: An Excerpt from the Introduction," *Texas Monthly*, May 2011.

15. Thomas White and Gladys Ganley, "The 'Death of a Princess' Controversy," Program on Information Resource Policy (PIRP), Harvard University, 1983.

16. Michael Oren, *Power, Faith, and Fantasy* (New York: W. W. Norton, 2007), 523.

17. Lind, *Made in Texas.*

18. Sean P. Cunningham, *Cowboy Conservatism: Texas and the Rise of the Modern Right* (Lexington: University Press of Kentucky, 2010); Bryan Burrough, *The Big Rich: The Rise and Fall of the Greatest Texas Oil Fortunes* (New York: Penguin, 2009); Robert Bryce, *Cronies: How Texas Business Became American Policy—and Brought Bush to Power* (New York: Public Affairs, 2004).

19. John B. Judis, *William F. Buckley, Jr.: Patron Saint of the Conservatives* (New York: Simon and Schuster, 2001).

20. See, for example, Patrick J. Buchanan, *A Republic, Not an Empire: Reclaiming America's Destiny* (Washington, DC: Regnery Publishing, 1999).

21. For Leininger's school voucher crusade, see Mitzi Mahoney, "When Powers Collide: School Voucher Politics in Texas," in *Texas Politics Today*, ed. William Earl Maxwell and Ernest Crain, with Edwin S. Davis, Elizabeth N. Flores, Joseph Ignani, Cynthia Opheim and Christopher Wlezien, 13th ed. (Boston: Thompson Wadsworth, 2008), 163–67.

22. Darren Dochuk, *From the Bible Belt to the Sun Belt: Plain Folk Religion, Grassroots Politics, and the Rise of Evangelical Conservatism* (New York: W. W. Norton, 2011).

23. The founder effect, a concept that originated in population biology, has been applied by students of American regional dialects, which track closely with regional American political cultures. See, for example, Walt Wolfram and Natalie Schilling-Estes, *American English: Dialects and Variation* (New York: Wiley-Blackwell, 2005): "The durable imprint of language structures brought to an area by the earliest groups of people forming a new society in the region is referred to as the FOUNDER EFFECT" (capital letters in the original).

24. Michael Lind, "The Beige and the Black," *New York Times Magazine*, August 16, 1998; George Yancey, *Who Is White? Latinos, Asians, and the New Black/Nonblack Divide* (Boulder, CO: Lynne Riener, 2003).

About the Contributors

Nancy E. Baker (PhD, Harvard University) is Assistant Professor of History, Sam Houston State University. She is currently completing a manuscript for Baylor University Press entitled "'Too Much to Lose, Too Little to Gain': The Role of Rescission Movements in the Equal Rights Amendment Battle, 1972–1982" and has contributed "Texas Feminist Hermine Tobolowsky: Conservative Women and the Texas Fight over Equal Rights, 1972–1982" to the forthcoming *Texas Women/American Women: Their Lives and Times.*

David O'Donald Cullen (PhD, University of North Texas) is Professor of History, Collin College. He is coeditor of *The Texas Left: The Radical Roots of Lone Star Liberalism*, coauthor of "The Communist Party of the United States and African American Political Candidates" in *African Americans and the Presidency: The Road to the White House* and the author of numerous other publications including "Back to the Future: Eugenics, a Bibliographic Essay" in *The Public Historian: A Journal of Public Policy.*

Sean P. Cunningham (PhD, University of Florida) is Assistant Professor of History, Texas Tech University. He is the author of *Cowboy Conservatism: Texas and the Rise of the Modern Right* and currently is under contract with Oxford University Press for *The Contested Ascendancy: Sunbelt Politics since 1945*, a monograph examining American politics since 1945.

George N. Green (PhD, Florida State University) is retired as Professor of History, University of Texas at Arlington. He is the author of *The Establishment in Texas Politics: The Primitive Years, 1938–1957*, and "Unions in Texas from the Time of the Republic through the Great War," and coauthor of "Looking for Lefty: Liberal/Left Activism and Texas Labor, 1920s–1960s," in *The Texas Left: The Radical Roots of Lone Star Liberalism.* He is currently working on an overview of Texas labor history.

MICHAEL LIND (JD, University of Texas at Austin) cofounded the New America Foundation where he is Policy Director of the Economic Growth Program. He is the author of numerous publications including *Made in Texas: George W. Bush and the Southern Takeover of American Politics*; *Up from Conservatism: Why the Right Is Wrong for America*; and most recently, *Land of Promise: An Economic History of the United States.*

MICHAEL PHILLIPS (PhD, University of Texas at Austin) is Professor of History, Collin College. He is the author of the award-winning *White Metropolis: Race, Ethnicity, and Religion in Dallas, 1841–2001*, and coauthor of *The House Will Come to Order: How the Texas Speaker Became a Power in State and National Politics* as well as other publications.

SAMUEL K. TULLOCK (PhD, University of Texas at Dallas) is Professor of History, Collin College. He is the author of "Benjamin Miller" and "John Hart: Signer of the Declaration of Independence and Friend to the Baptists" in *A Noble Company: Biographical Essays on Notable Particular-Regular Baptists in America* and is currently at work on "The Transformation of American Fundamentalism: The Life and Career of John Franklyn Norris."

KEITH VOLANTO (PhD, Texas A&M University) is Professor of History, Collin College. He is the author of *Texas, Cotton, and the New Deal*; "James E. Youngblood: Race, Family, Farm Ownership in Jim Crow Texas" in *Beyond Forty Acres and a Mule: African American Farmers since Reconstruction*; "The Life and Work of Dr. Beadie Eugene Conner: An African American Physician in Jim Crow Texas," *Southwestern Historical Quarterly*; "Strange Brew: Recent Texas Political, Economic, and Military History," in *Beyond Texas through Time*; and coauthor of *Beyond Myths and Legends: A Narrative History of Texas.*

KYLE G. WILKISON (PhD, Vanderbilt University) is Professor of History, Collin College. He is the author of *Yeomen, Sharecroppers, and Socialists: Plain Folk Protest in Texas, 1870–1914* and coeditor of *The Texas Left: The Radical Roots of Lone Star Liberalism.*

Index

AAA. *See* Agricultural Adjustment Administration (AAA)
academic freedom, 78, 80, 81, 91, 92
Acheson, Dean, 107
Adams, John, 21
Adorno, Theodore, 156
AFL-CIO, 137. *See also* Congress of Industrial Organization (CIO)
Agricultural Adjustment Administration (AAA), 69, 70
Albion's Seed (Fischer), 157
Alexander, Flora, 124
Alger, Bruce, 97; and the use of female campaign workers, 132–33; and the Texas Far Right, 109–110, 113
Allen, Adria, 148n58
Allende regime (Chile), 102
Alliance Movement, 5
Allred, James (Jimmie) V., 61, 90, 161
Alms, Alan C., 116n6
American Association of University Professors, 81
American Communist Party, 82. *See also* communism
American Council for Judaism, 150n113
American GI Forum, 17
American Legion, 108
American Liberty League, 6, 70–71, 73; oil wealth support, 71
American Right, 26, 47, 156; economic determinist theory, 156; ethnocultural theory, 6, 156, 157, 169; status anxiety theory, 3, 6, 105, 156–57 (*see also under* status anxiety theory)
American War for Independence, 35–36
Anderson, Clayton and Company, 70, 74, 76
anticommunist movement, 103–105; and desegregation, 105, 128; as women's moral crusade, 132 (*see also* Minute Women of Houston); and the Texas Far Right, 111. *See also* communism; Darden, Ida; Dies, Martin, Jr.; New Deal
Arnold, James A., 121
Arsht, Marjorie Meyer, 133–35, 138; and Judaism, 150n113
Ash, Mary Kay, 142.
Association of Volunteers for Educational Responsibility in Texas (AVERT), 130–31
At the Dark End of the Street (McGuire), 145n4

Bailey, Joseph Weldon, 121, 123
Bailey, Joseph Weldon, Jr., 74, 125, 85n3
Baker, James, 164
Baker, Nancy, 6
Baptist General Convention of Texas, 53, 65n9
Baptist Standard (*The Standard*), 37, 39–40, 52, 64n4
Baptists, 37, 41, 42, 52, 59; Northern, 58; Southern, 63, 131
Barnhart, Ray, 133
Barrett, J. R., 37–39
Bartley, Numan V., 148n44
Bass (Clements), Rita, 135; marriage of 151n28

Bates, Larry, 141, 143, 153n174
Baylor University, 52, 55, 63, 65n4. *See also* Norris, J. Frank: at Baylor
Bell Curve, The 26–27
Bell, Daniel, 156; *The New American Right,* 104; and Hofstadter-Bell thesis, 116n6. See also *The Radical Right*
Bennett, William, 4
Bible Baptist Seminary, 60, 61
Bible Baptists Union of America, 52–53
Bible Conference Movement, 51
Biddle, Francis, 81
*Big Rich, The (*Burrough), 73
Biggers, Virginia, 127
Black, Hugo, 74
Bolshevik, 16, 55, 71. *See also* communism
Bonomi, Patricia, 36
Bonzano (cardinal), 54
Bradford, M. E., 4
Brady, David W., and Kent L. Tedin, "Ladies in Pink," 152n159
Bricker Amendment, 149n80
Browder, Earl, 82
Brown and Root Construction Company, 90
Brown v. Board of Education, 97, 130, 137
Buchanan, Patrick, 167
Buckley, William F., Jr., 47, 112, 167; *God and Man at Yale,* 166; *McCarthy and His Enemies,* 166
Buckley, William F., Sr., 166
Bullington, Orville, 80, 91, 92, 99n11
Burrough, Bryan: *The Big Rich,* 73
"Bush Belles," 135
Bush, George H. W., 134–35, 164, 168–69; and John Birch Society, 113, 118n30
Bush, George W., 1, 102, 161, 165, 169
Butler, T. B., 64n4
Byrd, Harry, 93

Campbell, Alexander, 41
"Campbellite" movement, 41
captialism: and class, 20; laissez-faire doctrine of, 83; Lemmon's views on, 43–45; undermining of, 62, 71; and unequal distribution of wealth, 11
Carpenter, Lewis, 24–25
Carrigan, William, 18
Carroll, George W., 39
Cashion, Ty, 145n4
Catholics (Catholicism): as allies of the right, 51, 62, 120, 167; anti-Catholic sentiment, 25, 51, 53, 56, 75; and charges of conspiracies, 162; in decline, 169; and identification cards, 17; and Irish immigrants, 158; as pawn of Rome, 53–54; persecution of, 123, 166; prejudice toward, 75–76; and the Postal Service, 76
Cato Institute, 167
Census Bureau. *See* US Bureau of the Census
Cheney, Dick, 102
Chipps, D. E., 53, 59, 64, 65n8
Christian Americans (organization), 3
Christian Coalition, 3
Christian Zionism, 164–65, 167
Church(es) of Christ (denomination), 141, 142; and conflicts over socialism, 42, 44; and defense of cultural and political status quo, 34; and the ERA rescission fight, 142; and *Firm Foundation,* 42; racist views of, 44; and rejection of the world, 41–42, 44–45; and the "Restorationist" movement, 41; and the WWWW, 141 (*see also* Women Who Want to be Women)
CIO. *See* Congress of Industrial Organizations
Civil Rights Act (1964), 116n7
civil rights movement, 3, 5, 17; as communist inspired, 105, 110; and racism, 116–17n7
Clark, George, 2; career of, 7–8n3
Clayton, Will, 70, 74, 76
Clements, Rita Bass, 135; marriage of 151n28

Clements, William (Bill) P., Jr., 1, 151n28, 164
Cloud, Alice, 124
Cold War, 111, 125; and grassroots political activities of conservative women, 131–32; opposition to, 166
Collins, Carr P., 90
Comer, James, 124
Comer, Robbie Gill, 124
Committee to Rescind the ERA, 142
Committee to Restore Women's Rights, 141–44; and the JBS, 152n165
communism, 5, 71, 87, 130, 166; and the ERA, 143 (*see also* Equal Rights Amendment); growth of, 61–62, 87, 96; and labor unions, 6, 60, 88 (*see also* unions); and the Red Scare, 6, 10, 104–105, 110, 126, 129 (*see also* Red Scare); and subversion of democracy and capitalism, 68–69, 71, 75, 94, 96, 105, 108; and the suffrage movement, 120, 146n9; and the United Nations, 107; on university campuses, 76, 80. S*ee also* American Communist Party; anticommunist movement; Communist Party
Communist Party, 75, 91; American Communist (party), 82; law prohibiting membership in, 97. *See also* anticommunist movement; communism
Congregation Beth Israel Sisterhood, 133—34
Congregation Emanu-El (Dallas). *See* Temple (Congregation) Emanu-El (Dallas)
Congress of Industrial Organization (CIO), 60, 77; and accusations of being communist, 78; and labor unions, 91. *See also* AFL-CIO
Connally, John, 164
Connally, Tom, 60, 77
conservatism (in Texas), vii, 2, 6, 116–17nn6, 7; beginnings of, 9n9, 47–48, 104; defined, 18, 103–104, 155–57, 161, 165–68; economic, 127; and fear, 104, 111 (*see also under* status anxiety theory); and grassroots politics, 119, 146n6; and influence of H. L. Hunt, 108–109; issues, 2, 55–56, 88 (*see also* New Deal); and loss of social status, 104, 105; public image of, 103, 114; as reactionary, 2, 4–6, 8n5 (*see also* progressive movement); religion's role in, 34–35 (*see also* religion); and the southernization of the national right, 166; transformation of, 55–56; and women in the conservative movement, 99n16, 119, 121, 126–27. *See also* Texas Far Right
Constitutional Democrats of Texas, 74
Cooper, Samuel Bronson, 72
Coxey, Jacob, 42
Cranfill, J. B., 39; and Prohibition, 48n8
Creager, Rentfro Barton, 55
Cristero rebellion, 166
Criswell, W. A., 3, 63, 67n45
Cullen, Hugh Roy: education of, 71–72, 84; and formation of the Texas GOP, 96; and opposition to the New Deal, 5–6, 72–74, 107; and support of the right wing, 79, 107–108; and the Texas Regulars, 82, 83, 94
Cunningham, Minnie Fisher, 120, 148n8
Cunningham, Sean, 6, 136

Dabney, Lewis, 20
Dallas Baptist College, 137
Dallas City Council, 138
Dallas Cowboys, 107
Dallas Critic Club, 20
Dallas Morning News: denunciation of UT economics professors, 92; and Kennedy advertisement, 109; stand on unions, 16, 90, 91; support of O'Daniel, 90, 94; and the National Association of Ws, 143
Dallas Women's Republican Clubs, 132
Dallas: Department of Public Health, 16; as right-wing haven, 8n4

Dan Smoot Report, 108. *See also* Smoot, Dan
Daniels, Ann, 141
Daniels, Price, 107
Darby, John Nelson, 165
Darden, Ida M., 136; as active member of TAOWS, 121–22; as antisuffrage activist, 123, 143, 144; and feminism, 123; as foe of communism, 122–23; as foe of the KKK, 123–24; as lobbyist for right-wing causes, 123–25; personal life of, 121, 123, 126, 148n45; as publisher of *Southern Conservative,* 125–27
Darwin, Charles, 43, 45; and theory of evolution, 131
Daughters Already Well Endowed (organization), 142; and anti-ERA activism, 153n173
Davidson, Chandler: *Race and Class in Texas Politics,* 1, 109
Davis, Jefferson, 155
Davis, John W., 71
Dawson, Joseph M., 64n4
Democracy and Populism (Lukacs), 3
Democratic Party (national), 6
Democratic Party (Texas). *See* Texas Democratic Party
Democrats-for-Eisenhower, 125
Denton County Republican Party, 144
desegregation (of schools), 26, and busing, 136–38, See also *Brown v. Board of Education;* race (racial): integration
Detroit Baptist Union, 58
Devil and Socialism, The (Lemmons), 44–46
Dewey, Thomas, 82, 83, 93, 94
Dies, Martin, Jr.: and the delima of the New Deal, 78, 94; and denunciation of labor strikes, 78, 88, 89; and domestic subversion, 78, 89; and the HUAC, 78, 97, 105; and support for McCarthy, 78, 96, 97, 162; and the Texas Regulars, 83 (*see also* Texas Regular movement)
Dies, Martin, Sr., 78
Disciples of Christ (denomination), 40, 41
dispensationalism, 25, 165
Dixiecrat Party, 2, 77, 107, 125
Dochuk, Darren, 47, 9n6
Dolph Briscoe Center for American History, 22
Dos Passos, John: *U. S. A.,* 81, 92
Du Pont family, 71, 73
Dyer, Dallas, 127

Ebey, George, 109, 128
Edmondson, Dianne, 140–43, 154n184. *See also* Committee to Restore Women's Rights
EDS (Electronics Data Systems), 164
Eisenhower, Dwight: and charges of being a communist, 112; presidential campaign, 107, 132; and red-baiting, 128, 129; support of, 62, 84, 96, 135; and Texas Republicans, 97–98, 106
Elazar, Daniel J., 157
Ellis, A. Caswell, 21–22
End of Racism, The, 26
Entzminger, Louis: *Inside the Cup,* 65n5; as official of Fort Worth First Baptist Church, 60, 67n42
Environmental Protection Agency, 102
Equal Legal Rights Amendment (ELRA), 140
Equal Rights Amendment (ERA): and anti-ERA movement, 136, 140–44; and backlash, 146n6; history of, 140; organized opposition to, 153n173; provisions of, 139; support for, 140, 153n173
Establishment in Texas Politics, The (Green), 1
ethnocentrism, 158
ethnocultural theory of political identity, 6, 156, 157–58; and the majority, 169
eugenics, 21, 26; and assumptions of white supremacy, 22–23; legislation, 24–25

European Recovery Program, 96
evangelicalism: and the American right, 156, 158–59; and conservatism, 47; and dispensationalism, 165; and fear of communism, 87; and immigrants, 169; and Messianic Judaism, 165; and political involvement, 89, 140, 141
Evans, Hiram Wesley, 20, 27
*Evils of Socialism, The (*Lemmons), 43–44
Ewing, J. R. (fictional character), 102

Facts Forum (foundation), 108–109, 110
Facts Forum News, 108
Fair Deal, 88
Fair Employment Practices Committee, 95
Farmers Branch, Texas, 27
Fath, Creekmore, 160
Faust, Drew Gilpin, 36
Fed Up! (Perry), 2
federal government: and the ERA, 141, 143; growth of, 87; mistrust of, 124–25, 143, 162; and the New Deal, 161; opposition to, 2, 71, 73, 126. *See also* states' rights
Feldman, Glenn, 8n5
feminism, 7; opposition to, 123, 126, 137, 144. *See also* Equal Rights Amendment
Firm Foundation (newspaper), 42
First Baptist Church (Dallas), 63
First Baptist Church (Fort Worth), 51, 52, 55, 59; and the Baptist General Convention, 65n9; financial burdens of, 56, 60, 67n41; and the Klan, 66n39; and the leadership of Entzminger, 67n42; and the needs of the poor, 56–57, 60; and Tarrant Baptist Association, 65n9. *See also under* Norris, J. Frank
Fischer, David Hackett: *Albion's Seed,* 157
Fleming, Lamar, Jr., 74, 76, 94
Flynn, John T.: *The Road Ahead,* 107; *While You Slept,* 108
Ford, Henry, 58
Foreign Policy Research Institute, 106
Forstmann, Theodore, 167
Fort Worth Star-Telegram, 90
Fortune, 4, 106, 108
founder effect, 168, 171n23
Frankfurt School, 156
Fredrickson, Cora Lacy, 133
freedom of speech, 91, 130
fundamentalism (Christian), 51, 61, 78, 126; and Catholics (Catholicism), 53–54, 62; and communism, 61, 87; emergence of, 51–53, 59; and the Middle East policies, 164–65; and political activism, 55–56, 63, 140, 141, 153; political influence of, 163; in the South, 61. *See also under* Norris, J. Frank
Fundamentalist (newspaper), 56, 60

Gabler, Mel, 131
Gabler, Norma, 131
Gaddy, J. M., 64n3
Gambrell, J. B., 40
Garcia, Elba, 139
Garner, John Nance, 77, 93
Garrison, Homer, 88
General Motors, 58
George, D. B., 124
Germany, E. B., 80, 90
Giles, Bascom, 95
Glazer, Nathan, 3, 8n4. See also *The Radical Right*
Goldwater movement, 135, 156
Goldwater, Barry, 47; as extremist, 109, 136; and the "Goldwater Girls," 135; and LBJ, 113; and "movement conservatism," 166–67; and women in responsible roles, 135
Goyette, Kyle, 146n6
Grand League of Protestant Women, 123
Great Depression, 5, 56, 60, 68, 72; and the role of the federal government, 93, 124, 161. *See also* federal government
Great Society programs, 3, 26; race-based opposition to, 116–17n7

Green, Elna C., 146n9, 147n37
Green, George N., 6; *The Establishment in Texas Politics,* 1; and the Radical Right, 78
Green v. County School Board, 137
Grovey v. Townsend, 14

Hagman, Larry, 101, 109
Haley, J. Evetts, 61; attacks on university faculty by, 76; and the Jeffersonian Democrats, 74–76; *A Texan Looks at Lyndon,* 111; viewed as extremist, 136
Hankins, Barry, 58
Hargis, Billy James, 110
Harken (oil), 165
Harris County Republican Party, 134, 135
Harrison, Adlene, 139
Harrison, Dan, 80, 91, 99n11
Hatch Act, 90
Head Start, 26
Health, Education, and Welfare Department (HEW), 128, 129
Hedrick, Virginia, 127
Herrenvolk democracy, 159, 162, 167–68; and racism 169 (*see also* race (racial): and racism); and xenophobia, 158
Herrnstein, Richard J. and Murray Charles: *The Bell Curve,* 26, 27
Hillbilly Boys, 79
"Hillbilly Flour," (radio program) 79
Hillman, Sidney, 82
Hine, Darlene Clark, 29n15
Hiss, Alger, 96, 105
Hitler, Adolf, 94
Hobbs, Lottie Beth, 141
Hobby, Oveta Culp, 125; and editorial endorsement of Arsht, 134; and the Minute Women of Houston, 128–29; in Republican politics, 128–29
Hobby, Will, 128
Hoblitzelle, Karl, 91, 94
Hofstadter, Richard, 3; and Hofstadter-Bell thesis, 116n6; and paranoia of the Far Right, 104; and preachers in "right-wing movement," 48–49n8; and status anxiety theory, 156. See also *The Radical Right;* status anxiety theory
Hogg, James S. 2
Holbrook, T. J., 74
Hoover, Herbert, 53, 55, 62; defeat of, 69; support of, 56
Hopkins, Anthony, 101
House Un-American Activities Committee (HUAC), *See* US House of Representatives: Un-American Activities Committee (HUAC)
House, Edward Mandell, 160
Houston Chronicle, 134
Houston Independent School District, 108; and appointment of superintendent Ebey, 109, 128 (*see also* Ebey, George); and the Minute Women, 128–29 (*see also* Minute Women of Houston); School Board, 129–30, 149n84
Houston Oil Company, 72
Houston Post, 128, 129, 134
Houston Press, 134
Houston Public Library, 71–72
Howard University, 73
HUAC. House Un-American Activities Committee. *See* US House of Representatives: Un-American Activities Committee (HUAC)
Human Events (newspaper), 134
Humble Oil (Baytown refinery), 91
Hunt, H. L., 136, 166; influence of, 96, 109; tax-exempt foundations, 108–109, 110; and the Texas Far Right, 108, 136, 162
Hunt, Nelson Bunker, 109

Immigration Act (1917), 24
immigrants (immigration), 14–15, 78, 121; and anti-immigration policies, 27, 123, 169; assimilation of, 15, 17, 169–70; disenfranchisement of, 5, 10, 18, 27–28, 158–59; domestic, 167–68;

economic impact of, 25, 163; and Quota Act (1921), 24; and reform laws of 1965, 167; restrictions and quotas on, 21, 23–25, 87; status of, 17; as threat to white status quo, 14–15, 20, 24, 27 (*see also* Judaism [Jews]; white supremacy). *See also* Johnson-Reed Act; voting rights
In the New World (Wright), 118n28
Informer (newpaper), 134
Inside the Cup (Entzminger), 65n5
International Ladies' Garment Workers Union (ILGWU), 16
International Women's Year (IWY) Conference, 144
Iran, 165; shah of, 164
Izzard, Wes, 112

Jackson, Andrew, 155
Jackson, F. E., 24
JBS. *See* John Birch Society
Jefferson, Thomas, 21, 35, 36, 37, 159; on clerical political power, 48n5
Jeffersonian Democrat (newspaper), 75, 76
Jeffersonian Democrats, 2, 74, 80; and ultraconservatives, 77, 84; and opposition to FDR, 6, 61, 75–77, 93, 111, 125; paranoia of, 76
Jester, Beauford, 95
Jim Crowism, 15; in housing, 18–19; laws, 16, 47
John Birch Society (JBS), 2, 3, 6, 110, 111; and anti-ERA groups, 152n165; and Edmondson, 141; and Movement to Restore Decency (Motorede), 131, 142; oil wealth support of, 88; paranoia of, 112, support for, 3, 112–13, 151n131; and the Texas Far Right, 112
Johnson Space Center, 163
Johnson, Lady Bird, 132–33
Johnson, Lyndon B., 107, 132, 160, 164; as candidate for US senate, 90, 95–96; defeat of Goldwater, 136; far right opposition to, 109–110, 111; and federal investment in Texas, 163; and Great Society, 116–17n7; and New Deal, 161–62; as president, 113; and right-wing financial support, 107
Johnson-Reed Act, 25
Jones, Jack (fictional character), 101–102, 109
Jones, Jesse, 161
Jones, Marvin, 69
Judaism (Jews), 15, 134, 150n113; and advocacy of deportation of, 88; and conditional whiteness, 16–17; as economic threat, 24; and fundamentalists, 25, 45, 47, 165; and the undermining of white supremacy, 23, 94

Kellar, William Henry: and Houston School Board, 149n84
Kennedy, John F., 67n45; assassination, 109, 112–13, 116n7, 136; and far right opposition, 162; fictional portrayal of, 101; and the Pro-Blue program, 110
Kimball, Justin, 20
Kirby Lumber Company, 6, 72
Kirby, John Henry, 5–6, 61, 82; Constitutional Democrats of Texas, 74; and the Jeffersonian Democrats, 61, 74, 77 (*see also* Jeffersonian Democrats); and opposition to the New Deal, 71, 77, 78; and personal life, 72, 82; and Southern Committee to Uphold the Constitution (SCUC), 73–74
Kissinger, Henry, 102
KKK. *See* Ku Klux Klan
Korean War, 106, 149n80
Ku Klux Klan (KKK): and Evans, 20; in pinstripes, 73; racist positions of, 10–11; and relationship with the WKKK, 123–24, 147n31 (*see also* Women's Ku Klux Klan [WKKK]); and segregationist rhetoric, 105; and vigilantism, 5
Kubrick, Stanley: *Dr. Strangelove,* 111

labor unions. *See* unions
Landon, Alf, 74, 75, 77
Lanham, Fritz D., 85n3
League of United Latin American Citizens (LULAC), 17
Lefkowitz, David, 16–17
Leininger, James, 167
Lemmons, William F., 3; as advocate of the status quo, 34, 47; *The Devil and Socialism,* 44–46; *The Evils of Socialism,* 43–44, 50n32; and influence of the pulpit, 34, 48; personal life of, 41; racist attitudes of, 43–44, 46–47; on railroad interests, 49n21; and the role of women, 43, 44, 46; and the use of disputation, 42; and white supremacy, 44–45, 46
Lewis, John L., 60, 62
liberalism, 6, 53, 101; futility of, 26; in higher education, 80; as New Deal liberalism, 128, 161; and opposition by the Far Right, 103, 109–110, 157
libertarian(s): break with "movement conservatism," 166; economic and free market, 6, 166; individualism, 157; limited appeal of, 167; and the take over of the national GOP, 96; and Texas populists, 167
Liberty Broadcasting System, 108
LIFE LINE (foundation), 109, 110
Life, 4
Lincoln, Abraham, 155
Lind, Michael, 6
Lipscomb, David, 41–42, 45
Lipset, Seymour Martin, 3, 156. See also *The Radical Right*
Locke, John, 159
Locke, Joseph, 48n8
Long, Huey, 73
Love, Thomas B., 13
Lukacs, John: Democracy and Populism, 3

Maddoux, Marlin, 153–54n183
Man, Barbara, 135
Manchurian Candidate (film), 106
Manion, Clarence, 110
Marcus, Stanley, 16
Marsden, George, 56, 64
Marshall, John, 68
Marx, Karl, 43, 45
Mary Kay Cosmetics Company, 142
Maughmer, Bertie, 127
Mayfield, Kenneth, 139
McAuley, Jo Ann, 143, 153n183
McCarthy, Joe: appearances in Texas, 97, 129; declining credibility of, 104, 106–107; paranoia of, 78; and red-baiting, 128, 162; rise of, 96–97, 105; support for, 3, 6, 162, 166. *See also* McCarthyism
McCarthyism, 96, 97, 156
McClendon, Gordon, 108, 113
McGovern, George, 113
McGuire, Danielle L.: *At the Dark End of the Street,* 145n4
McHarg, Ian, 163
McKinley, William, 87, 156
McKinney Avenue Baptist Church (Dallas), 52
McNamara, Robert, 106
Meacham, H. C., 65n8
Measures, Royce, 60, 67n41
Medrano, Pancho, 17
megachurches, 5, 60, 63
Meinig, D. W., 157
Melich, Tanya, 154n186
Methodist (denomination), 37, 41
Miller, Nathan, 71
Miller, Wally, 134
Minute Women of America, 126, 148n60
Minute Women of Houston, 108, 144, 148n58; and the Red Scare, 126–30; tactics of, 127–30
Mitchell, George P., 162
Mobil Oil, 164
modernism, 159–61, 169; effect on business, 162–64; attacks on, 51, 58–59; and the elite, 159, 162; and the fundamentalist-modernist controversy, 59, 62; and liberal

drift of Democrats, 63; and the modernization of Texas, 104, 119, 145n4; and the populist-modernist-traditionalist alliance, 158, 161–63
Moody, Dwight A., 65n5
Morris, Clovis Gwin, 57
Motorede. *See* Movement to Restore Decency
Movement to Restore Decency (Motorede), 131, 142
Murchison, Clint W., Jr., 107
Murchison, Clint W., Sr., 96, 106–107
Murrow, Edward R., 110
Muse, Vance, 6, 72; as Far Right lobbyist, 91, 123. *See also* Southern Committee to Uphold the Constitution (SCUC)
Mussolini, Benito, 21
Myrick, Walter Frank, 123

NAACP, 14, 18, 73
Nation, 4
National Association of Manufacturers, 72
National Association of Pro America, 126
National Association of the Ws, 143. *See also* Women Who Want to be Women (WWWW)
National Endowment for the Humanities, 4
National Federation of Republican Women (NFRW), 131, 132, 135
National Intelligence Test, Scale B, Form I, 22
National Labor Relations Act (1935), 5
National Review, 111, 166
National Rip-Saw, 44
Neff, Pat, 27; and voter suppression, 13
Nevels, Cynthia Skove, 18
New American Right, The (Bell), 104
New Deal, 10, 26; and accusations of communism and socialism, 68, 75, 81, 123, 128–29; and the agriculture farm bill, 69–70 (*see also* Agricultural Adjustment Administration); anti-New Deal organizations, 72, 81–84; in the context of the Texas Right, 5, 7, 10, 48, 145n4; "court packing plan," 77; and financial impact on Texas, 88, 93, 107, 162; and labor unrest, 77; opposition to, 57–59, 69–73, 80, 92, 111, 124–25, 129; and organized resistance to, 48, 61, 71, 93–94, 131; and partisan realignment, 155, 161; support for, 56, 69, 78, 93; and Texas Republican Party, 7n2; in violation of state's rights, 73
New York Times, 60
Newton, Louie, 62
Nickerson, Michelle, 149–50n94
Nixon v. Condon, 14
Nixon v. Herndon, 14
Nixon, Lawrence A., 14
Nixon, Richard M., 62, 168. *See also* Stone, Oliver *for fictional representation of*
Norris, J. Frank, 3, 42; and address to the Texas legislature, 62; and Allred, 61; and association with industrialists, 59–61; and the Baptist fundamentalists, 52, 58–59; and the Baptist Standard, 52, 64n4; at Baylor, 52, 64n2, 65n4; Christian fundamentalism of, 51, 55–56; and communism, 57, 62, 63 (*see also* communism); and Creager, 55; and the death of Chipps, 53, 59, 64; and Eisenhower endorsement, 62; and Entzminger, 60, 67n42; and family's poverty, 52, 64n1; at First Baptist (Fort Worth), 52, 55, 56, 59; and "folks between the forks of the creek," 52, 56, 65n7; and the *Fundamentalist,* 56–57; indicted for perjury, arson, and murder, 52, 53, 65n8; and Ku Klux Klan, 66n39 (*see also* Ku Klux Klan); at McKinney Avenue Baptist (Dallas), 52; and the New Deal, 56–58, 59, 61; as opportunist, 53, 56, 60–62; and opposition to Al Smith presidency, 53–57, 62; and political involvement, 56, 63; and

Norris, J. Frank (cont.)
the right-wing megachurch, 5, 63; and Scarborough, 65n9; and the separation of church and state, 54, 56, 63; and Southwestern Baptist Theological Seminary, 52, 65n9; and support of Hoover, 55, 56–57, 62; and Tarrant Baptist Association, 53, 65n9; at Temple Baptist (Detroit), 58–59, 60, 67n41; and the Texas Right, 61; and "Texas Tornado," 52, 65n6; and Truman, 61; and Vick, 60–61, 67nn41–42
Norris, Lillian Gaddy, 64n3
Norris, Mary, 52
Norris, Warner, 52
Northern Baptist Convention, 58, 59
Northern Liberty League, 73

O'Daniel, W. Lee "Pappy," 95; anti-union stance of, 88, 89, 90–92; and the Anti-Violence Act, 88–89; and control of college governing boards, 80, 81, 92; and the Far Right, 78–79; influence of, 80, 92, 161; and Norris, 61; opposition to, 90; personal history of, 79; paranoia of, 90; and the Texas Regular Movement, 83, 94
O'Donnell, Peter, 113
O'Hare, Frank P.: *National Rip-Saw,* 44
O'Hare, Kate Richard, 44
O'Hare, Tim, 27
Old Right, 166, 167
Oliver, Kendrick, 116n6
Order of American Patriots, 73
Order of American Women in Texas, 123
Order of Protestant Women in Texas and Oklahoma, 123
Oswald, Lee Harvey, 111, 112
Our World Today and Yesterday (textbook), 20–21
Overstreet, Bob, 134

Parker Chiropractic Research Foundation, 141
Parsons, Talcott, 3. See also *The Radical Right*
Paul, Ron, 167
PBS, 164
Pearson, Chad, 48
Perlstein, Meyer, 16
Perot, Ross, 164
Perry, Rick: Fed Up!, 2; and folksy populism, 161; and the Latino vote, 169; and the Republican Party, 1; and threat of Texas session, 115
Phillips, Michael, 5
Phillips-Fein, Kim, 9n9, 34
Politician, The (Welch), 112
poll taxes. *See under* voting rights
populism, 117n7; collapse of, 18; defined, 158; as Herrenvolk democracy, 158, 167, 168; as opposed to traditionalism and modernism, 159; paranoia of, 104; and populist image of conservatives, 56, 114, 138–39, 156; and the populist-modernist-traditionalist alliance, 161–63; and Populist Party, 5, 12; of the Scot-Irish "Borderers," 157; and race, 27; of the working-class and poor, 160
Populist Party, 5, 12
Porter, Jack, 96
poverty: and churches, 35, 37, 44, 45–46, 49n22; and immigrants, 17; of Norris, 52, 64n1; and race, 11, 15, 19, 26; and social welfare programs, 28; War on Poverty, 5
Pro-Blue indoctrination program, 110
Pro-Family Rally (in Houston), 144. *See also* Republican Party (national): "family values" agenda
progressive movement, 2, 159, 160–62; and "Californication" of Texas, 168–69; and contra movement, 77; and education, 23, 128; and populist-modernist-progressive alliance, 161; and the Roosevelt coalition, 155; shifting ideologies of, 13; and theories of conservatism, 156

prohibition, 10, 53, 54; and the Al Smith campaign, 53–54, 63; as a cause, 123; and Darden's run for office, 124; and the influence of preachers, 34–35, 37, 39–40, 48n8; and Neff's racial views, 13; and Norris, 54, 56, 63
Psychiatric Study of Public School Children, 22

Quin, C. K., 80, 90

race (racial): and African Americans, 10–14, 16, 17, 18 (*see also* segregation); assimilation, and "Americanizing," 15, 17, 158, 169–70; caste system based on color, 11–12, 17, 25, 39, 44; and class conflict, 11, 17–19, 23; and class marginalization, 11, 15, 18; demographics of Texas, 14–15, 22, 168–70; disenfranchisment based on, 27, 87, 158, 160; economic inequality, 10–12, 26; equality, 38, 46, 63, 76, 91, 121, 126; and identity, 10–11, 16, 47; inferiority, 11, 15, 20, 19, 26, 87; (*see also* eugenics; white supremacy) integration, 97, 105, 125, 128, 130, 169; and Jews, 16–18, 88 (*see also under* Judaism); and mental defectiveness, 20, 22, 27; prejudice, 3, 73, 75, 87, 91; and racism, 16, 26, 74, 78, 91, 105, 169; and status of Mexicans and Mexican Americans (Tejanos), 11, 13–17, 87, 158, 160 (*see also* immigrants); violence, 5, 10, 17–19, 81 (*see also* Ku Klux Klan); voting rights based on, 12–15, 17, 20 (*see also under* voting rights); and whiteness, 11, 14–17, 19 (*see also under* white supremacy)
Race and Class in Texas Politics (Davidson), 1
Radical Right, 77; origins of, 7n2, 83; and accusations of communist subversion, 68–70; and the radicalism of Dies, 78 (see also Dies, Martin, Jr.); as reactionary politics, 8n5; and regressive taxation, 89; and the Tea Party, 4 (see also Tea Party; Texas Tea Party); in Texas (defined), 4
Radical Right, The, 3; history of publication, 8n4; radicalism of, 102–103, 122; as response to Joe McCarthy, 8n4; as response to John Birch Society, 8n4; as response to Oklahoma City bombing, 8n4. *See also* Bell, Daniel; Hofstadter, Richard; Lipset, Seymour Martin; Parsons, Talcott
Rainey, Homer: gubernatorial bid of, 95; fired by the board of regents, 81, 92, 105
racism. *See* race (racial): and racism
Rand, Ayn, 166
Randolph, Frankie, 160
Raskob, John, 73
Rayburn, Sam, 60, 92
reactionary conservatives, 2–6, 8n5, 13; and attack on academic freedom, 80–81, 92; and civil rights, 116n7; and fear of communism, 96, 162; and government reform, 87; and the oil wealthy, 107, 162; and racism, 105; and white supremacy, 13 (*see also under* white supremacy)
Reagan Democrats, 2
Reagan, John H., 12, 27
Reagan, Ronald, 4, 6, 133, 168; and movement conservatism, 166–67; and success of the Republican Party in Texas, 114–15 (*see also* Texas Republican Party)
Reason (journal), 167
Reconstruction Finance Corporation, 161
Reconstruction, 1, 133; reforms of, 27; and segregation, 18
Record of America, (Adams, James Truslow and Charles Garrett Vannest), 21
Red Scare. *See* communism: and the Red Scare

religion, 131, 136; as litmus test for fitness for office, 53, 55, 95; and locus of authority, 36; and modernity, 160; and political beliefs, 140, 150n113; and political influence of the pulpit, 36–48, 60; and role in conservatism, 34–35, 47, 76; and school textbook controversy, 131; and separation of church and state, 54, 56, 63, 134; and "social gospel," 37, 60; and social status, 11, 17; and wealth, 37–42. *See also* socialism: in competition with Christianity
religious Right, 5, 34; the Lemmons template of, 45, 47, 48; the rise and fall of, 47. *See also* Lemmons, William F.; Norris, J. Frank; religion
Renfroe, Rose: as activist opponent of busing, 136–38; career of, 137; as housewife, 151n145; as politician, 138–39, 152n151
Reporter's Notebook, 4
Republican National Convention (Kansas City), 55
Republican National Committee, 55, 135
Republican Party (GOP) (national), 4, 53; "family values" agenda, 136, 144, 154n186; and right-wing extremism, 136; and the Goldwater nomination, 136. *See also* Texas Republican Party
Richardson, Sid, 90, 106–107, 162
Riesman, David, and Nathan Glazer: "The Intellectuals and the Discontented Classes," 3. See also *The Radical Right*
Right Nation, The, 4
Riley, William Bell, 59
River Oaks Country Club, 16
Road Ahead, The (Flynn), 107
Roberts Library, 65n11
Rockefeller, Nelson, 113
Roe v. Wade, 140
Roman Catholic Church, 54. *See also* Catholics (Catholicism)
Roosevelt, Eleanor, 57, 73, 110
Roosevelt, Franklin D., 5–6, 61, 83, 92, 106, 162; appointment of Hobby, 128 (*see also* Hobby, Oveta Culp); defense of New Deal programs, 68–69, 161 (*see also under* New Deal); and fireside chats, 68; the "Hundred Days" of, 69–70; and the Jeffersonian Democrats (*see* Jeffersonian Democrats: and opposition to FDR); opposition to, 57, 61, 81, 94, 99n11 (*see also* American Liberty League); and Republican progressives, 155, 160 (*see also* progressive movement); support of, 56–57, 61, 99n11; and the Texas Regulars (*see* Texas Regulars Movement); at Yalta, 107
Roosevelt, Theodore, 38
Rosenbergs (the), 105
Rossiter, Clinton, 161
Rowell, Chester, 24
Ruggles, William, 91

Sacco and Vanzetti, 54
Salon (online magazine), 119
Sanger family, 16
Santa Fe Railway, 72
Scarborough, Lee R., 65n9
Schlafly, Phyllis, 141, 142; Pro-Family Rally, 144
school busing. *See* desegregation: and busing
Schreiner, Scott, 99n11
Scofield, Cyrus, 25; *Scofield Reference Bible*, 165
SCUC. *See* Southern Committee to Uphold the Constitution (SCUC)
Seale, Jack, 112
Searchlight (newspaper), 55
secession: convention of 1861, 11; threats of, 2, 115
Sedco (company), 164
segregation (racial): of blacks, 18; in housing, 19; of Mexicans, 18; political support of, 73, 105; of public schools, 19, 26, 97, 130 (*see also* desegregation:

and busing); on public transit systems, 18; residential, 16; and support by marginalized whites, 17; and the Texas Far Right, 103–104, 107, 110, 125; as tool of the wealth/power, 18
Sentinels of the Republic (organization), 73
Sexual Information and Education Council of the United States (SIECUS), 130
Shields, T. T., 61
Shivercrats (1950), 2, 98
Shivers, Allan: board member of Facts Forum, 109, 161; election campaign of, 107, 129; and endorsement of Eisenhower, 96; homespun campaign style of, 161; as nominal Democrat, 98; and red scare campaign tactics, 97
Sid W. Richardson Foundation, 106
Slaughter, C. C., 38, 39
Sloan, Alfred P., 73
Smith v. Allwright, 14, 82, 93
Smith, Adam, 159
Smith, Alfred: and the American Liberty League, 71; Norris opposition to, 53–55, 62
Smith, Morgan A., 38–39
Smoot, Dan, 136; and *Dan Smoot Report,* 108; and domestic subversion, 108
Social Security, 111
socialism (socialist movement): and Christianity, 34, 37–39, 41–46; influence of, 156; and the populist movement, 12, 37 (*see also* populism); portrayal of political opponents as socialists, 51, 55, 57, 132; and racial equality, 38, 43, 46–47, 126 (*see also under* race [racial]: equality); and socialist agitation, 40; as subversion, 104, 109, 110; support of, 50n32; as undermining of capitalism, 71, 75, 124–25; and women, 46, 126; and woman suffrage, 120–21, 146n9. *See also* Socialist Party; Texas Socialist movement; Texas Socialist Party
Socialist Party, 44, 50n32. *See also* socialism; Texas Socialist Party
Southern Baptist Convention, 59; and Seventy-Five Million Campaign, 65n9. *See also* Baptist: Southern
Southern Baptist Theological Seminary (Louisville, KY), 52, 63
Southern Committee to Uphold the Constitution (SCUC), 3, 6, 73–74
Southern Conservative (newspaper), 125, 126, 127
Southwestern Baptist Theological Seminary, 52
Spanish-American War, 37
Spencer, Herbert, 45
Stalin, Joseph, 62
Standard, The. See *Baptist Standard*
Stark, Lutcher, 91, 92, 99n11
states' rights, 73, 121, 125; as a position of the Houston Minute Women, 126, 127. *See also* federal government
status anxiety theory, 3; reassessment of, 6, 157, 8n4; and roots of modern conservatism, 105, 156; and Texas, 8n4.
sterilization laws, 5, 23. *See also* eugenics
Stevenson, Adlai, 133
Stevenson, Coke, 75, 80, 90, 95; appointments of, 81, 92, 94–95; and control of higher education, 80
Stevenson, Suzanne, 126–27, 148n60
Stewart, Maco, 91
Stewart, Maco, Jr., 91, 94, 99n11
Stone, Oliver: *Nixon* (film), 101–102, 109; *JFK* (film), 101; 102, 103
Stop ERA (organization), 142
Stout, Harry S., 36
Strickland, D. F., 90, 91, 92, 94, 99n11
suffrage movements, 12. *See also* woman suffrage movement
Sumners, Hatton, 77, 89
Sunday, Billy, 58
Swann v. Charlotte-Mecklenburg Board of Education, 137

Taft, Robert A., 128, 166
Taft, William Howard, 45
Talmadge, Eugene, 73
Tammany Hall, 53–55
Tanner, John S., 64n2, 65n5
TAOWS. *See* Texas Association Opposed to Woman Suffrage (TAOWS)
Tarrant Baptist Association, 53, 65n9
Tasby v. Estes, 137
Taylor, William, 137–38
Tea Party, 3, 4, 7; grassroots movement of, 115; *See also* Texas Tea Party
Temple Baptist Church (Detroit), 58, 59–61, 67nn41–42
Temple (Congregation) Emanu-El (Dallas), 15, 16
Terman, L. M., 22
Terrell, George B., 70, 75, 85n3, 125
Texan Looks at Lyndon, A (Haley), 111
Texans for America, 111
Texans for ERA, 142
Texas Association Opposed to Woman Suffrage (TAOWS), 120–22. *See also* Texas Woman Suffrage Association (TWSA); woman suffrage movement
Texas Businessmen's Association, 121
Texas Cotton Association, 70
Texas Cotton Ginners Association, 70
Texas Democratic Party: and conflicts over the New Deal, 93–94, 125, 131 (*see also* New Deal); and conflicts over racial equality, 38, 43, 46–47, 125; defections from, 98, 105, 125, 161–70; divisions and factions within, 38, 83–84; and failure to maintain white supremacy, 55; and one-party rule/state, 93, 99n16, 102, 122, 128, 134, 160, 169; and party affiliation, 97–98, 110, 155–56; and the practice of holding two state conventions, 93–94; as reactionary conservatives, 2; weakening of, 56, 62. *See also* Jeffersonian Democrats
Texas Department of Public Safety, 79, 92
Texas economy, 10, 19, 35; based on primitive Christianity, 50n32; capitalist structure of, 45; early twentieth-century growth, 40, 44; and oil and gas industry, 162–64; and taxes on corporations, 95
Texas Far Right, 101–102; and the assassination of Kennedy, 112–13; associating communism to Roosevelt and the New Deal, 68–69; and civil rights movement, 116n7 (*see also* civil rights movement); constituent individuals of, 103–11 (*see also individuals by name);* and domestic subversion, 69, 78, 105, 109 (*see also* Dies, Martin, Jr.; McCarthy, Joe); extremism and paranoia of, 68–69, 74–76, 88, 104, 113, 115, 116n6; and the Jeffersonian Democrats, 74–76; legacy of, 113–15, 116n6; and marginalization of Tejanos, 158; and opposition to "big government," 70–71, 89, 103, 103, 105 (*see also* Cullen, Hugh Roy; Kirby, John Henry; Muse, Vance; O'Daniel, W. Lee "Pappy;" Southern Committee to Uphold the Constitution [SCUC]); organizations supportive of, 111–12 (*see also* John Birch Society); racism of, 87, 105; and social change, 87; and Texas Republican Party, 103, 113, 116n6 (*see also* Texas Republican Party)
Texas Farm Bureau, 142
Texas Federation of Business and Professional Women (TX-BPW), 140
Texas Federation of Republican Women (TFRW), 131, 135
Texas-for-Willkie clubs, 85n3. *See also* Willkie, Wendell
Texas Goldwater for President Committee, 135
Texas House of Representatives, 75, 80; Committee on Agriculture, 69; Committee on Constitutional Revision, 142; Concurrent Resolution 15, 25; and the O'Daniel anti-violence

bill, 88. *See also* Texas Senate; Texas State Legislature
Texas Instruments, 163
Texas Manufacturers' Association, 88, 95
Texas Mental Hygiene Society, 22, 23
Texas Monthly, 109, 138
Texas Observer, 1, 142; and John Birch Society, 152–53n165; and ERA, 152n165
Texas oil and gas industry. *See* Texas economy
Texas Rangers, 10
Texas Regulars Movement (1944), 2, 77; agenda, 82–83; and effect on the Texas Democratic Party, 84; financial contributors to, 82–83, 99n11, 125; and opposition to the New Deal, 81, 94, 125, 128; and opposition to taxes on corporations, 95; origin and demise of, 93–94, 125
Texas Regulars. *See* Texas Regulars Movement
Texas Republican Party: betrayal by, 4; and Christian Zionism, 165; contra paranoid extremism, 112; Democrats' tactics to crush, 12–14; in Denton County, 144; and the Far Right, 102–103, 113 (*see also* Texas Far Right); growth of, 107, 109, 110, 131; in Harris County, 134, 135; and image, 114–15; influences on, 107, 109; and John Tower, 7n2; Latino members of, 169; and the New Deal, 7n2; and objections to government support of minorities, 131; origins of, 7n2, 102, 103, 109; and partisan identity, 155; and the Radical Right, 7n2; and the Red Scare, 6, 96, 110; transformation of, 1, 2, 133–35; women's involvement in, 131–32, 135, 150n97. *See also* Dallas Women's Republican Clubs
Texas Right, 6, 78: agenda, 78, 82–83, 95–96; and anti-New Deal efforts, 69–71, 81, 83, 84 (*see also* New Deal); and attacks on academic freedom, 78, 80, 81, 83, 91–92; and biological causes of economic inequality, 10–19; and communism, 84 (*see also* communism); and cultural issues, 6, 62, 136; and the definition of whiteness, 19–26; and Democrats' support, 53; education of, 83–84; oil wealth support of, 4, 88, 162; origins of, 7–11; and party affiliation, 97–98, 133–34; and Republican Party electoral victories, 1; probusiness stance of, 2. *See also* Texas Far Right
Texas Senate, 120. *See also* Texas House of Representatives; Texas State Legislature
Texas Socialist movement, 37, 41. *See also* socialism
Texas Socialist Party, 5, 34, 50n32, *See also* Socialist Party
Texas State Board of Education, 131
Texas State Legislature, 122; and the right to draft women into the state militia, 130. *See also* Texas House of Representatives; Texas Senate
Texas Supreme Court, 19
Texas Tax Relief Committee, 73
Texas Tea Party, 2, 115; and the Texas Radical Right, 4, 7. *See also* Southern Committee to Uphold the Constitution
"Texas Tornado," 65n6
Texas traditionalist, 158–60; and federal government as enemy, 162; and interplay with populist, modernist, and progressive, 161; and oil and gas industry, 162–63
Texas Woman Suffrage Association (TWSA), 146n8. *See also* woman suffrage movement
textbooks in public school, 20–21; Gabler critiques of, 131; and influence of the right, 163; monitoring of, 143–44, 153n183; and Texans for America, 111

TFRW. *See* Texas Federation of Republican Women
Third Baptist Church (Owensboro), 65n5
Thomas, Helen Darden, 126–27
Throckmorton, J. W., 12
Thurmond, Strom, 95, 107
Tilotta, Becky, 141
Tobolowsky, Hermine, 140
Tower, John, 160, 169; and campaign for the US Senate, 110, 114, 133, 134, 135
Truett, George W., 63
Truman, Harry: and the Bricker Amendment, 149n80; and charges of communists in government, 96, 110; and oil-land legislation, 95; and the Texas Far Right, 107, 110; and fundamentalists, 61
Tullock, Sam, 5

unions (labor), 42, 137; and accusations of communism/socialism, 6, 16, 60, 78; and anti-labor sentiment, 72, 88–89, 124, 131, 161; labor unrest, 59–60, 71; and pro-labor sentiment, 41, 62, 160; and "right-to-work" laws, 91; and the Texas Regulars, 82, 94
United Auto Workers, 60
United Nations, 87, 107, 111, 133
University of Texas: and accusations of communist/socialist leanings, 76, 91; Board of Regents, 80, 81, 91–93, 99n11; funding of, 81, 163; psychology department of, 21, 27
U. S. A. (Dos Passos), 81, 92
US Bureau of the Census, 26, 29n16, 64n1
US Committee on Federal Relations, 25
US Conciliation Service, 89
US Constitution, 133; amendments to (*see* US Constitution—Amendments); and attempts to undermine, 51, 54–55, 74; and freedom of religion, 123; and lack of respect for, 43; and the open-shop proposal, 91; and prohibition, 37; and the role of federal government, 71, 77; and rule by the elite 21; secular status of, 36
US Constitution—Amendments: Bricker Amendment (treaty restrictions), 129, 149n80; Eighteenth (prohibition), 53; Equal Rights Amendment (*see under main entry* Equal Rights Amendment); Fifteenth (right to vote), 11, 12; Fourteenth (citizenship rights), 11, 13, 14; Thirteenth (abolishment of slavery), 11
US Department of Housing and Urban Development, 135
US Federal Reserve Board, 26
US House of Representatives: campaign of Alger, 132; campaign of Darden, 124; campaign of George H. W. Bush, 135; and creation of the Agricultural Adjustment Administration, 69, 85n3; Judiciary Committee, 77; Un-American Activities Committee (HUAC), 78, 97, 105
US Senate: campaign of George H. W. Bush, 113; campaign of McClendon, 108; campaigns of Tower, 110, 133, 134; election of O'Daniel, 80; Judiciary Committee, 77
US Supreme Court, 57, 77, 129; and conservative misgivings of, 143; and racial desegregation of schools, 136. *See also individual cases by name*

Vick, G. Beauchamp, 60–61, 67n41–42
Vietnam, 7, 102
Vigil, James Diego, 15
Villa, Francisco "Pancho," 40
Vinson, Willie, 81
Volanto, Keith, 5
voting rights: and poll taxes, 3, 5, 13; and racial identity, 10–14, 20, 27, 29n15; requirements to vote, 13, 21; voter identification laws, 3, 13; voter suppression, 12–13; "white

primary" laws, 3, 5, 13, 14. *See also* Voting Rights Act; woman suffrage movement
Voting Rights Act (1965), 116n7

Wadsworth, James, 71
Walker, Edwin A., 110–11; paranoia of, 110
Wallace, George, 4, 113, 139
War on Poverty, 5
War on Socialism, 3
War on Terror, 3
Warren Commission, 111
Washington, George, 21, 45
Washington, Jesse, 18
Watt, Eleanor, 127, 148n58
Wayne, John, 109
Weinert, H. H., 91, 94, 99n11
Weitinger, Faye, 127
Welch, Robert, 112; *The Politician,* 112
Wells, James B., 120
Wells, Pauline, 122, 143, 144; and race as theme against woman suffrage, 120–21 (*see also* woman suffrage movement)
West, James (Jim) M., 80, 91
West, Richard, 151n145
While You Slept (Flynn), 108
White Citizens Councils, 105
white supremacy: defended by terrorism, 12, 18; and disenfranchisement of poor whites, 11, 18–20, 27–28, 44; and the Klan, 73 (*see also* Ku Klux Klan); need to change attitudes toward, 47, 55; and the pulpit, 5, 38–39, 43–45, 55, 59; and racial inferiority, 19, 21–22 (*see also* race [racial]: equality); support/defense of, 13, 47, 55, 158; and the Texas Regulars' platform, 125; threatened by socialism, 43; undermined by Populism of the 1890s, 12; and wealth, power and whiteness, 11. *See also* eugenics
Wilkison, Kyle, 5
Willis, Doyle, 62
Willkie, Wendell, 84, 85n3
Wills, Bob, 79
Wilson, William B., 24
Wilson, Woodrow, 160
WKKK. *See* Women's Ku Klux Klan (WKKK)
Wright, Lawrence: *In the New World,* 118n28
woman suffrage movement, 123; and antisuffrage propaganda, 120–22; and communism/socialism, 120, 146n9; failures of in 1890s, 146n8; objections to from the pulpit, 46; and race, 120; and ratification of the federal constitutional amendment, 122; and similarities to the anti-ERA fight, 142, 143 (*see also* Equal Rights Amendment); and Texas Woman Suffrage Association, 145n8. *See also* voting rights
Women Activated to Rescind, 142
Women Who Want to be Women (WWWW), 141–43. *See also* National Association of the Ws
Women's Army Auxiliary Corps, 128
Women's Ku Klux Klan (WKKK), 123–24, 144. 147n31
Wood, W. A., 64n2
World's Christian Fundamentals Association, 52
WWWW. *See* Women Who Want to be Women (WWWW)

xenophobia, 158

Yancey, George, 169
Yarborough, Ralph W., 97, 108, 113, 129, 160
yellow-dog Democrat, 1, 114
Yerkes, R. M., 22
Young Americans for Freedom, 110
Young, Nancy Beck, 145n4
Ysleta Farm Bureau, 24

Other Titles in the Elma Dill Russell Spencer Series in the West and Southwest:

The Robertsons, the Sutherlands, and the Making of Texas, Anne H. Sutherland

Life Along the Border: A Landmark Tejana Thesis, Jovita González, Edited by María Eugenia Cotera

Lone Star Pasts: Memory and History in Texas, Edited by Gregg Cantrell and Elizabeth Hayes Turner

The Secret War for Texas, Stuart Reid

Colonial Natchitoches: A Creole Community on the Louisiana-Texas Frontier, H. Sophie Burton and F. Todd Smith

More Zeal than Discretion: The Westward Adventures of Walter P. Lane Jimmy L. Bryan Jr.

Yeomen, Sharecroppers, and Socialists: Plain Folk Protest in Texas, 1870–1914, Kyle G. Wilkison

On the Move: A Black Family's Western Saga, S. R. Martin Jr.

The Texas That Might Have Been: Sam Houston's Foes Write to Albert Sidney Johnston, Margaret Swett Henson, Edited by Donald E. Willett

Tejano Leadership in Mexican and Revolutionary Texas, Edited by Jesús F. de la Teja

How Did Davy Die? And Why Do We Care So Much? (Commemorative Edition), Dan Kilgore and James E. Crisp

The Texas Left: The Radical Roots of Lone Star Liberalism, Edited by David O'Donald Cullen and Kyle G. Wilkison

Drumbeats from Mescalero: Conversations with Apache Elders, Warriors, and Horseholders, H. Henrietta Stockel, with Marian D. Kelley

Turmoil on the Rio Grande: History of the Mesilla Valley, 1846–1865 William S. Kiser